DON'T LOOK AWAY
DANIELLE LAIDLEY

DON'T LOOK AWAY

DANIELLE LAIDLEY

with Konrad Marshall

HarperCollins*Publishers*

HarperCollins*Publishers*
Australia • Brazil • Canada • France • Germany • Holland • India
Italy • Japan • Mexico • New Zealand • Poland • Spain • Sweden
Switzerland • United Kingdom • United States of America

HarperCollins acknowledges the Traditional Custodians
of the land upon which we live and work, and pays respect
to Elders past and present.

First published in Australia in 2022
by HarperCollins*Publishers* Australia Pty Limited
Gadigal Country
Level 13, 201 Elizabeth Street, Sydney NSW 2000
ABN 36 009 913 517
harpercollins.com.au

A catalogue record for this book is available from the National Library of Australia

ISBN 978 1 4607 6254 7 (paperback)
ISBN 978 1 4607 1518 5 (ebook)
ISBN 978 1 4607 4476 5 (audiobook)

Cover design by George Saad
Back cover photo by Tina Smigielski
Project management by Andrea McNamara
Typeset in Berthold Baskerville by Kelli Lonergan
Printed and bound in Australia by McPherson's Printing Group

For my children
This story is for you, in the hope that one day
we will walk together again, side by side.
I love you – always have, always will.

This book deals with suicide and drug abuse. If you, or a person you know, is in need of crisis or suicide prevention support, call Lifeline on 13 11 14, or visit lifeline.org.au/gethelp

foreword
by craig silvey

I have an enduring memory of Danielle Laidley.

Midway through the 2006 AFL season, which had been a disappointing one for the North Melbourne Football Club, a verbal confrontation took place in the stands between Danielle, who was then head coach, and a furious spectator.

A few hours later, that same spectator took their own life.

At the time, beyond reflecting on the tragedy, I recall being dismayed by the willingness of the press to connect the two events, as though Danielle's outburst had been in any way causative.

Despite being absolved of blame by the spectator's family and the broader community, by all appearances it took an emotional toll on Danielle. She looked haunted addressing the media the following day. I was moved by the sincerity of her response, and the sorrow she expressed.

But what I remember most is what she had said to the spectator. It seemed at odds with the hostility of the exchange in the stands.

It was an invitation.

'Come down to the rooms,' she had said. 'Come and see how we're all hurting.'

To my interpretation, Danielle had extended the offer so the spectator could see that he wasn't alone. That they were all human, all fighting towards a common purpose, all sharing the same frustrations, all capable of fragility.

It was a respectful and compassionate gesture, and it put everyone on equal footing. In acknowledging the spectator's pain, Danielle was saying that she understood it, because she felt it too.

After a family member of mine intervened in the attempted suicide of a young trans person, I was inspired to better educate myself as to the challenges and pressures faced by trans and gender-diverse people in Australia. I was alarmed by the high incidences of depression and anxiety and self-harm, deeply concerned by the disproportionate exposure to violence, and heartbroken by the prevalent rates of attempted suicide.

It struck me as a crisis. And it still does.

I began writing a novel about a young trans character called Honeybee, who steps onto a quiet overpass in the middle of the night and looks down at a fatal abyss. It's a bleak beginning to a book, but I was seeking to answer an optimistic question: how might this person climb back over the rail and make their way towards a safer, more hopeful path?

Through my research and consultation with members of the community, I came to understand how the presence of support, love, acceptance, safety and allyship immeasurably improved outcomes for trans and gender-diverse people.

I wanted cisgender readers to be inspired by this. I hoped they might reflect on the extent to which our cisnormative social order has marginalised and undermined the progress of trans people, and how we all have a responsibility to correct that injustice.

But my principal ambition in writing *Honeybee* was to give trans and gender-diverse readers the opportunity to feel seen, and respected, and galvanised, and truly represented.

I'm proud to say that far beyond any prize or plaudit, the most profound reward of my writing life has been the opportunity to hear responses from trans and gender-diverse readers to whom *Honeybee* has given comfort and courage.

One of those very generous readers was Danielle Laidley, and I'll forever be grateful for her friendship.

Like many Australians, I have enormous admiration for Danielle Laidley. Throughout her many careers we have seen her leadership, her strength, her ferocious courage, her conviction, her generosity, her passion, her honesty.

But there have been aspects of her life that we haven't seen. Much of what has defined Danielle has been deeply private. Not just concealed from public view, but obscured from her own understanding too.

For previous generations of trans people, finding a language and a conceptual framework to process their feelings of dysphoria was often impossible. Outside queer, academic and progressive communities, meaningful discussions around gender identity did not exist. They certainly couldn't be heard in the back blocks of Balga or in our mainstream sporting culture.

And for many, contending with these issues in solitude often amplified the confusion and widened the disconnection and deepened the internalised shame. This is why the clarity of a clinical diagnosis, the euphoria of self-actualisation, and the introduction of acceptance and support can provide such relief.

It's also why books like this one are so vital and valuable.

Much of Danielle's memoir is about recontextualising her past, but it's also a reclamation of her narrative. After her truth as a trans woman was cruelly and disgracefully publicized without her consent, Danielle was again unable to control the perception of her own identity.

Until now.

These are her words. They are powerful, they are inspiring and, just like in 2006, they are an invitation.

Once again, Danielle is asking us to come and see. To come and see how she has hurt. To come and see how she has triumphed. To come and see how she has endured heartbreak and back-break, how she has self-medicated and how she has healed, how she has lost herself and found herself.

She's inviting trans and gender-diverse readers to come and see that they are not alone, that they need not feel afraid or ashamed. That they are loved. That they matter. That there is hope.

She's inviting cisgender readers to come and see a proud trans woman navigating the world with pride and purpose. To come and see the discrimination she has experienced, and how she has faced these obstacles with dignity and humility. To come and see how her story is emboldening and saving lives.

She's inviting us all to come and see things as she's seen them. To feel things as she's felt them. To live them as she's lived them – raw and confronting as it may often be.

Come and see. And don't look away.

this moment scares me

I live in Kilmurray Way, a hook-shaped street in the suburb of Balga, in the hardscrabble, sunburnt flatlands north of Perth. I'm six years old, and I don't know it yet but this is the first place I will remember in life.

Our block is huge, or seems that way to me. In the corner of the front yard is one of those massive pampas grass plants – a big ugly circular clump of long serrated leaves bowing outwards like sabres, with a few feathery flower things sprouting straight up out of the centre. There's a weeping willow, too, in the middle of the lawn. I like lying on the thick grass under its ropey yellow-green branches as they dangle and sway. The driveway is a thin layer of tar on the ground, and it gets sticky in the summer until it slowly melts away to the orange dirt and rock beneath. The back yard is bare, a plain expanse with a squat concrete shed and a hulking gum tree in one corner. I have to tilt my body back 45 degrees to see the eucalyptus canopy.

The brick house itself is nothing to look at. A lounge at the front feeding three bedrooms on one side and a kitchen on the other; a dunny out the back. I'm afraid to go for a wee in the middle of the night – scared a redback will have crawled in there and under the toilet seat from the pile of logs sitting next to the lav – the logs we feed into the wood heater, which gives us our hot water.

My memory of this age is patchy, and that's being generous. Happy vignettes are few and far between.

I want to see this time in my life clearly, but my recall is cloudy. I get a flash of Crawley Bay, a cove on the Swan River with a private yacht club and public jetties near Pelican Point, where we go to splash and swim and catch prawns for a cheap dinner. I see people setting up streamers on walls at the Wanneroo Football Club, for a cabaret night that ends in slurred arguments and fist fights.

Some things are vivid like that, but Kilmurray Way is a special kind of nothingness, filled with silence and something unsettled. I see the yellow seagrass tiles on top of the lino in the kitchen. I see wood-panelled walls in some rooms and funky paisley wallpaper in others. I can't see my bedroom. Or the bathroom. I cannot see my father or mother or little brother. I see clearly only the lounge room, and the lady with the red lipstick.

The lady with the red lipstick is surrounded by other ladies her age, young, or youngish. They sit in a circle by the fireplace, near the door onto the verandah. It's daytime, hot, and I don't know why these women are here. This lady at the centre of everything is attractive, blonde, and I can't tell if she has an accent or just speaks differently, but to me she seems cosmopolitan, chic, posh, though I don't yet know these words.

From inside a deep bag she takes out a range of nail polishes and holds them up to the light, displaying each colour for the ladies. She waits for approving murmurs as she shows them coral orange and burnt orange, then lime green and mossy green. I see the women sampling, admiring the new paint jobs they've just given their fingertips. I watch them laugh and titter and swap gossip, and I hear it all, because little piggies have big ears.

I watch it all from the corner of the room, silent and unseen, and while I don't know what any of this is exactly, I know it is exactly what I want.

I wait until near the end of the display, when all the buying is done, and my mum and her friends and the lady with the red lipstick are sitting around having nibbles and wine. I feel like a hungry rat now, waiting for a chance to sneak the cheese. The lipsticks and eye shadow and nail polish and blush and foundation cover our coffee table, so I find my way to the floor – still silent, still unseen – and sit for a moment, furtive but with a plan.

I inch closer, bum scooting softly across the carpet. Closer still. Close enough to touch. I swipe a bottle. Stick it in my pocket. Stand calmly. Walk down the hallway and – I'm not sure why – turn straight into my mother's room.

I try to copy what I remember from the demonstration out in the lounge. With my dominant left hand I draw the tiny brush from the bottle – like a sword from a stone – and delicately stroke the first fingernail on my right hand with paint. I do a toenail, too. Bright red. Rose red. Coca-Cola red. McDonald's red. Heinz red. Strawberry red. Santa red. A thick red layer, firming and shining before my eyes.

I blow on it, just like the woman did. I twist and turn the finger, twirling it like a conductor, and bend it at the knuckle to face me, just like the woman did. I tilt it into the light slowly, not quite sure what I'm admiring but admiring it all the same. I breathe deeply and I sigh.

Life often feels hostile to me, but not right now.

Right now I feel only calm. I feel warm. I smile.

I go to touch my handiwork, and the surface has stiffened. The paint has hardened like a ceramic shell. I pick at it for a moment, expecting it to flake and fall, but it's not coming off. I scratch it harder but it's fully set, like chrome over steel. This feels like something from a film, where someone is trapped behind glass and they punch it and hurl furniture at it but it won't break, and eventually they unholster their gun and impotently shoot rounds at the bulletproof surface. But I'm not a man behind bulletproof glass. I'm a boy in my mum's room, wearing stolen red nail polish, and so I panic, utterly and completely.

I bolt. Out the back. I'm on my knees now in the far corner of the yard, in the shade of that massive gum tree, rubbing my finger with water from a brass garden tap. The nail polish stays. I can almost see my reflection in it. I rub it with water and dirt next, but the gloss sheen is barely scuffed. I grab a fistful of sand and rocks instead, and rake the rough mix all up and down my finger, and it digs at the skin folded over the cuticle, which gets raw and begins to bleed. It bleeds bright red. Stop sign red. Fire alarm red. Blood-red blood weeps from my finger.

I'm not sure why this moment scares me so much. Is it because I've stolen? I know thieving is wrong, so I want to scrub away the evidence. But also … this fear isn't just about nicking something; it's about what I nicked. Little boys don't wear nail polish. I don't know much but I know that, and I know there will be questions if not consequences if I'm sprung. A confrontation will come, and I want to avoid that.

I run through the house and the women are gone; I bolt out the front door, over the verandah, under the willow tree and through the front yard. With a single flick I toss the nail polish bottle up into the pampas grass bush. Anyone who wants to find it will have to dive deep into the feathery centre, fighting through all those bowing, serrated fronds.

I run into the street, thinking and hoping I've managed to bury the evidence, the incident, where no one will look for it, not even me. I run and run and run, believing it's gone forever.

There's one final thing that scares me: the way I feel. I know nothing of gender dysphoria. I'm unfamiliar with the concept of internalised shame. I've never heard of transsexuals or drag queens or cross-dressing or sweet transvestites from Transylvania. But I know enough to understand that feeling the way I feel right now with nail polish on my hand – *calm, contented, happy* – is different, other, odd.

uncommon purpose

I was born in the St John of God Hospital in Subiaco, a good torpedo kick from the footy ground, in March 1967. Mum and Dad met when she was 14 and he was 17. That always sounded like a significant age gap to me, but perhaps it wasn't back then. People left school early.

Dad was a bodgie and Mum was a widgie, him with long hair and hers cropped into a bob. Based on the greaser subculture of the USA, they were all dark satin shorts and bobby socks. Both came from nice neighbourhoods by the beach, and they met at the local youth club one Thursday night. The place was called the Snake Pit – a walled-in hollow near the big Scarborough Hotel and the takeaway shack known as Peter's by the Sea. Parents would chat around the outside of the pit, while the kids jived and jiggled in the middle; beyond, the open-air dance floor gave way to a grassy slope and then to the beach.

It's a perfect spot, created over millennia as the dark sapphire waters of the Indian Ocean throw pristine white sand onto the far south-western edge of the continent. There are big warm swells in the morning, and after the sunset on hot days a chilly zephyr often dances in from the sea. They call it the Doctor, and as the sky darkens it blows and blows, letting you know it's cool enough to sleep, time to turn in.

David James Laidley was quiet, but known for his smile. Carmel Ann Giri, or 'Mad Carmel' as all the girls in her extended

Italian family called her, chain-smoked white Kent cigarettes and never minded the limelight. They courted for five years, and married young: Mum was 19; Dad, 22. The ceremony was held in the Immaculate Heart of Mary Church in Scarborough, the beachside suburb where they set up home.

Dad became a roofer, climbing onto the tops of the new houses springing up nearby in the expanding northern suburbs of Perth, in Woodvale and Wangara, Gnangara and Gwelup.

Mum was a bookkeeper, and her first posting was at the Foy & Gibson department store. Later she did accounts for Westin Cabinets. Sounds dull, but her personality was big enough to compensate.

I came along when Mum was 22 and Dad was 25, when they moved inland. It must have been odd for them, coming from Scarborough and moving to Balga. In Sydney it would be like leaving Double Bay for Cabramatta. In Melbourne, you'd be trading Albert Park for Broadmeadows. The little properties on the new streets in their neighbourhood were only a step above state housing. For $7000 you could get a house-and-land package. Write a cheque and sign up for life on the suburban frontier.

Aunty Val isn't really my aunty. She's just a friend of the family. I know this, but I feel good at her house. I get dropped off here sometimes, to spend the day. I like her husband, Les. He seems kindly. I like the five or six kids who always seem to be here, Val and Les's and others.

For lunch today Aunty Val makes me a Vegemite sandwich, cut into four triangles. She smears a heavy helping of butter on the soft white bread. She dips the same knife in the Vegemite jar, and with a thick brown blob on the point of the blade, she dabs it onto the layer of butter here and there, not spreading it but instead doling out thick, random, salty globs. I eat the sandwich greedily, never knowing quite which bite will offer the bland comfort of buttered bread, and which will explode in a flood of yeasty goodness. I love the anticipation. I'll make Vegemite sandwiches this exact way for the rest of my life.

I go out to play after lunch most days at Aunty Val's. She and Les live at the corner of Camberwell and Wanneroo roads, with an empty block of land next door. It has open water pipes and a deep drainage pit, the kind of place a new millennium parent would never let their kid play, but where kids of the early 1970s can roam freely.

In the heat of the afternoon we retreat indoors, or to the cubby house. It has toy guns and comic books and a big wooden chest filled with old clothes for dress-up games. Costumes for cowboys and Indians, cops and robbers, doctors and nurses. There are flannelette shirts and farmers' shorts, beaded necklaces and vinyl handbags, and one other item.

I see it the first time I open the chest – a long shiny dress with sequins. Black like the night. Like coal. Like a jaguar. Something inside me lights up whenever I see it.

On an adult woman, this dress would probably come down to mid-thigh. It's probably sexy, flirty. If the wind is gusting, it probably billows up a little, offering a shade of an outline of a hint of a glimpse of something all the boys want to see.

On me, at seven years old, it looks a little different. The hemline hits the ground. I probably look like Linus Van Pelt, Charlie Brown's best friend, dragging his little blanket. But I don't feel that way. I feel beautiful.

I want this dress. Every time we open the wooden chest I seek it out. I elbow my way to the front of the group of kids and begin to rummage with uncommon purpose. On the days I can't immediately see it – because it's jammed into a corner or drying on the washing line – I grow anxious and alarmed.

I've come to need the feeling I get when I slip that tiny black cocktail dress over my head.

It's the same feeling I got from the nail polish. Calm.

Night sky calm. Midnight calm. Eyes closed calm.

they can't catch me

Mum and Dad split up. I don't know why. I won't until much later. All I really know is that my little brother, Paul, and I are being sent to live with Nan, my dad's mother, and Pop, her second husband. Olive May and George Stewart. I love them both. I am happy to go.

Dinner at Nan and Pop's is at 5 o'clock. Pop sits down at the table at one minute to five, always with a cheeky gleam in his eye. I sit to his right and Paul, two years younger than me, sits to his left. We three men share a conspiratorial grin, waiting for whatever stew or roast is headed our way, always piping hot, always made from scratch. We hold our knives and forks in our fists and the moment the clock hits 5:01 we start banging that cutlery on the table in unison – *bang, bang, bang* – until Nan, laughing, piles the food onto our chipped china plates. Afterwards, we crane our necks towards the kitchen, wondering what treat she has in store. Cream puffs maybe? Sponge cakes? Puff pastry delights with icing sugar and custard, or rhubarb and ice cream in a bowl? We have supper later – that's a cup of tea and cake, or chocolate. Nan and Pop visit the retail store at the Life Savers lollies factory, so the cupboard is always brimming with sweets.

My nan is my hero. I feel safe with her. I feel loved. I feel as though there is always time for a hug. I stand with her in the kitchen sometimes and she sends me running outside to pick mint or passionfruit.

Paul is drawn more to Pop. Paul loves cartoons and toys, and playing by himself, making his own fun. Pop joins in his games sometimes, and sometimes Paul joins Pop in the garage, too, watching as the old man throws a hammer at little woodwork projects, or sharpens the lawnmower blade. The house has two huge lawns, which Pop mows proudly. In truth, he mows every lawn in the entire street.

We help Pop dig a well one day. It's 5 metres deep and bricked in above the ground. It becomes our fort, our castle. We help, too, when we're asked to pull the old red bricks from the driveway out front, so they can lay down a beautifully smooth stretch of concrete. We get paid 20 cents, and buy a bag full of mixed lollies to share.

Paul and I play with little plastic green army men together sometimes, but we don't really live together so much as exist side by side. Paul exists in Batman and Spider-Man and his drawings and imagination. I exist in sport.

Cricket is my first love. Nan follows me into the back yard every day for a whack of the willow. I say willow, but I really mean a flat piece of pine board. I watch her cut it into the shape of a cricket bat using only a handsaw. It's thin and light, and the handle is rough, but this is my Stuart Surridge, my Gray-Nicolls Scoop, my Kookaburra Pro, my pride and joy.

Nan bowls to me for hours. At least it feels like hours. Until I get tired, anyway. I don't ever remember bowling to her. That's not really fair, is it? I bowl when I play against other kids though. They notice that I'm ambidextrous, in a manner of speaking. For anything one-handed – like throwing, or bowling, or hitting a tennis ball, or bouncing the Sherrin – I'm left-handed. For anything requiring more than one limb, like handling a cricket bat, or guiding the footy onto a boot, I favour the right.

I go to the shops with Nan whenever I can, and she feeds my interests. I beg her to buy Omo washing powder because it has bios of Australian cricketers on the box. I think she favours Surf or Drive or Rinso, but she smiles and acquiesces. Chappell, Marsh, Redpath – I collect them all, and especially my idol, Dennis Lillee. He's a Western Australian. He has the same initials as me. And he's frighteningly quick. A killer. I love that about him.

I beg for footy cards, too, then throw away the hard sticks of powder-covered chewy. I'm interested in the names and faces on the front, and the blurry images on the back. I try to collect each grainy, pixelated piece of that puzzle, but I don't really come close. We can't afford that many packets.

My first footy is plastic, and brown, and has fake seams and stitching melded into the surface. In the back yard I play games between two teams, by myself. I'm both West Perth, Nan's team, and East Fremantle, my team. I kick that thing around barefoot until the skin on top of my feet is raw and bruised. It's the best pain ever. I don't get a real footy until years later, when I win best on ground in an under-11s grand final. That shiny red Burley becomes my prized possession.

Nan and Pop are the first people on the street to have a colour television, so everyone crowds around it for Sunday-night viewing. *Columbo. Kojak. The Benny Hill Show. The Dick Emery Show. Chips. M*A*S*H. My Favorite Martian.* I'm shuffled off into the spare room to watch the little black-and-white idiot box, because I want to watch *Countdown,* followed by *The Winners* – the latter beaming big league VFL footy into homes all over the west. Footy that makes me dream.

We see Dad sometimes. Occasionally I go down to East Fremantle with him on a Saturday for the footy. It takes forever in his work ute, but I don't mind. I sit up front with him, or if Paul comes we sit in the tray, tilting our faces to the breeze like dogs. We park on the lawn of a friend of Dad's, around the corner from the ground, leaving them a box of chocolates as payment in kind.

This might be suburban footy but it doesn't feel that way. A typical – viscerally parochial – crowd is 20,000. East Fremantle are blue and white, like North Melbourne, and so my WAFL and VFL allegiances are formed. My absolute hero is onballer and half-forward Graham Melrose. He's so tough and skilled.

I sit behind the goals at the northern end with my autograph book in hand. After the game, I sprint out and get as many signatures as I can. I gather Melrose's chicken-scratch mark more than a dozen times, but he eventually leaves East Freo for North, taking his beautiful drop kicks with him.

Footy has a hold of me, for sure. When I'm seven I play under-10s for the Westminster Balga Junior Football Club, the mighty Knights, wearing blue and gold – a yellow jumper with navy collar and cuffs. I run around aimlessly in a forward pocket. The coach, Mr Conduit, cares for me and my game, and sets boundaries, enforces discipline. He makes me run hard. I win most improved player and am quietly chuffed.

In my second year, the coach is Mr James, who will coach me for half-a-dozen years straight and who treats me like his son. His actual son, David, is my age. He gets leukemia, and he fights and fights until we are 12, then passes away. Two of his best friends, not yet teenagers, help carry the coffin out of a small Catholic church in Balcatta. You know those moments when a half smile slips over your lips, because you can't face the actual emotion you're feeling? That happens to me, right before I start crying.

Mr James coaches the following year, despite his pain, and he still makes me feel as though I am his son. It feels strange to step even part-time into that kind of role.

On field, I run through the middle of the ground and down into the half-forward line, and very quickly learn that I can win the football in ways others cannot. I also see that I can extract the ball and burst away. They can't catch me, none of them. I gather possessions at will. Twice I kick bags of nine goals.

Mr James teaches me to play an uncompromising brand and I develop a competitive fire. Winning helps. In one three-year stretch we lose maybe three games in total, en route to a premiership every year. That kind of winning becomes something I covet, something to protect, something to fight for. I chase hard. I tackle hard. I hit bodies hard.

I think maybe I like to hurt people.

glittering alien

Nan and Pop have a caravan. Almost every weekend we use it. We drive down to the Peninsula Caravan Park in Mandurah, where we hire canoes and go fishing from the bridge over the river. A sideshow carnival is always there, lights and tunes and treats. Mum comes down with us one time, and we go to the carnival together. She rides the octopus with me, and loses hold of her handbag. We spin in our seats in the fibreglass sucker at the end of our orbiting tentacle, and the contents of her purse fly through the air, and she laughs into the night as we rise and fall and turn, and I laugh, too.

Our favourite place for the caravan, however, is Horrocks Beach, just north of Geraldton. This is not a short trip. It takes around five hours to get there. Pop's family have a wheat and sheep farm inland from Horrocks, in a place called Binnu, where Aunty Maureen and Uncle Brian live, and that's always our first stop. My cousins Peter and Paul pinch some of Uncle Brian's ciggies one day, and we go down to the shearing sheds to smoke them. I don't want to try it, but they say they'll tell on me if I don't take a drag. It turns my gills green.

Heading west from the farm to the sea, up and over the cresting hills, we play a game to see who can spot the water first. I never manage to win. I only know I'm there when we roll into the shanty-town caravan park. The shacks are just fibro nailed together. There's no TV. Horrocks Beach is nothing more than a corner store with a petrol station, a boat ramp and a big jetty. It's heaven.

Every morning I'm up at dawn to cast a few lines and drop nets for crayfish. Out on the boat we go. The two-stroke engine belches perfumed smoke, powering the thin 18 footer with a cab at the front. We don't go out far to catch our quarry – maybe a few hundred metres at most. That's when we pull the cockies from the bag.

Farmers hate cockies. Not the beautiful black cockatoos, mind you, or those gorgeous red tails. The ones they hate are corellas – *Cacatua sanguinea* – those white bastards with a reddish tinge around the eye. They look like junkies and scream like drunkards, and you never met such grain thieves. And so my farmer relatives shoot the little buggers, then throw them into an old feed sack, and lug them out to the coast as bait. On the boat, you reach into that sack and pull out a few cockie carcasses, drop the stinking mess of blood and feathers and beaks into the net, and wait for the crayfish to get hungry.

I can't be bothered waiting for that, though, so I swim back to shore. By grade four I'm an athlete, and a 300-metre ocean swim is no great feat. Besides, I don't even like crayfish. Some kids howl when the crays hit the boiling water at dinnertime. They hear that high whine and think it's a scream, but I know it's just air escaping the shell. They have shit for brains anyway. They're bugs. And I hate the taste.

God it's fun at Horrocks. Sand so hot, water so cool, sky so big. There's nothing to do but cut loose. My cousins and I take a dodgy dune buggy out through the sand hills and down along the flat surface by the water. Sometimes we attach a rope to the back, and take turns holding it while sitting on an empty spud sack, flying along the water's edge until the driver turns sharply, whipping you around until you let go, then splash into the salty foam. It's a dangerous, giddy good time.

I have one other important ritual here, which comes at daybreak. In this bleached landscape you should probably wear a hat, but you should definitely wear sunscreen. Most people put zinc on their nose, or under their eyes. I'm a little different. I apply bronze zinc to my entire face. It starts one day with a dab, then a smear, and then another, and it feels so good I smear on a little more. I emerge from the caravan looking like a glittering alien child – a man from the moon. I am a sea of tranquillity.

People laugh at first but quickly get used to my habit. Nan begins to ask me before I head out for the day: *What about your zinc?*

I'm putting on makeup. I know this, just as I know it looks strange. But it takes me from *Where am I?* and *What am I?* to *This is it* and *This is you.*

Before we head back to Perth, I stand under the freshwater shower outside. I rinse my body and use a wet towel to wipe my face. The bronze layer has become so thick that it clings to me. It doesn't want to come off, and I don't want it to come off either, but I keep rubbing anyway, and clumps of it stick to the towel. I stand under the stream of cool water, rinsing and rubbing, until all of my makeup sloughs off my skin.

I feel annoyed now. Angry. This isn't a mask. This is me. *Why should I take it off?*

We ride east towards the farm, then south towards Perth, leaving Horrocks Beach behind, and I sit in the back seat watching the semi-arid desert and all its colours change and darken as the sun sets over the ocean and we roll into the city by night.

For my ninth birthday, I ask for a pair of clogs. I want moulded Dr Scholl's with a leather strap, to be specific. I've seen them in shop windows and I know they're girls' shoes – they're like a pair of pretty Mary Janes with a nice thick arch – but I don't care one bit. They give me a sense of me, and I wear them proudly to school.

I take the same stance with my hair. It's beyond shoulder length by now, and not a mullet either – just a whole head of long, flowing, shiny white-blonde locks. I hold on to that length rabidly. Nan gets me to the barber shop perhaps twice a year; I physically fight her all the way, kicking and screaming so much that most times she gives up.

I go to Takari Primary School, and I'm not afraid to be the way I am there. It's a curious thing. I learn much later the rule that people don't mind being different in life, so long as they can be different together – as goths or rockers or slackers or bogans – as members of one in-group or out-group or another. But I'm happy to be different alone. Maybe that's why people leave me alone. There's no teasing, no calling out my hairdo or my clogs. I play cricket and footy and marbles with everybody. You might even call me the cool kid.

Just after Christmas of 1976, I visit my cousins Vicky and Peter. They're older than me by a few years, and live one suburb over in Koondoola. Peter is big into music and sport, but also skating. I'm eager to show Peter the best present I got on 25 December. It's a new skateboard, royal blue with bright red speed wheels, and the word 'CONDOR' in lifted writing on its belly. Everyone loves it. I love it. We head to the hill near their house and race down it in pairs. It's called a dogfight, and the goal is simple – stay on the board and get to the bottom first. I'm not sure which neighbourhood kid I'm against. He's older than me but I have no fear, and so I win, and so I'm proud. Huffing with adrenaline, we walk home.

We find ourselves in the kitchen, and Vicky brings out some of her wardrobe. I don't know how she explains or broaches it, but she dresses Peter, and then me, in her clothes. She puts Peter in a flowery, horrible Hawaiian dress. She puts me in a light blue layered skirt, with a white button-up school shirt, arms rolled to the elbows.

The mood isn't serious or surreptitious. If we're crossing a Rubicon it's clearly in jest. The scene is all giggles and chaos. The chatter is *Have a look at you, ya sissy!* and *Oh my god, look at you, princess!* As the youngest, I pretend to be led by them, pretend I'm looking for direction, pretend I need to be convinced to take part. Underneath, I'm going exactly where I want.

We do makeup, too, and it's heavy-handed, costumey, exaggerated, but I don't care. Red lips, rouged cheeks, eyes like the tail of a peacock – bring it all on. We look like clowns and we laugh like them too. But again, I feel that same feeling I felt with the nail polish when I was six: calm.

It's a light kind of happiness, but there's a more sombre undercurrent, too. In flashes I wonder, *Shit, should I be enjoying this?* In other moments I know this is a rare chance, one that I cherish, so why am I mocking it? *Fuck I wish this didn't have to be a joke.*

Peter puts on one of his albums. I love his record collection and soon enough I'll be paying $5.99 for an LP and listening to Skyhooks and Sherbet and Dionne Warwick. I'll be blasting 'Baggy Trousers' and 'White Wedding' and 'Don't Pay the Ferryman'.

But right now, Peter drops the needle on some new vinyl by AC/DC, and he laughs, and so does Vicky, and so do I although I don't know why. I haven't heard this song before, and don't know the lyrics, so I don't get the joke right away. But then Peter points to the song title on the album cover – 'She's Got Balls' – Bon Scott begins booming and crooning, and I get it. I lap up every word because it's an awesome track, because it's hysterical in this moment, and because it's me. It's me.

everything turns to shit

Something is resolved in my life shortly before I turn ten. A court case is settled. It's the case that has kept me living with Nan and Pop for three years.

The custody battle between Mum and Dad is over, and Dad wins. This is not a good outcome.

There's a tempest within my mum, 'Mad Carmel', but a sadness inside my dad. The sadness is more dangerous, I think, and it goes back to his dad, James Crawford Laidley.

I don't remember my grandfather, but I'm told he was rarely home. He was a tent boxer in the royal shows, travelling Western Australia picking fights for a living. He was a heavy drinker and a nasty bloke, annoyed with his lot in life. When Nan came home each day from her job at the Coca-Cola bottling factory, which had taken over from the Golden West Aerated Water Company in Leederville, he would take his unhappiness out on her, and sometimes on my dad.

Dad rebelled a little, getting into mischief in his teens. Pinching cars, a few break-and-enters, but no jail time. He wasn't really a scrapper, although when kids made fun of the little drift to the left in one of Nan's eyes, he would savage them in a blind rage, out of love for her. He otherwise grew up quite quietly. He didn't drink even in his teens.

But in 1970, when I was three and Paul was one, Dad and Mum moved into that new house in Balga, at 85 Kilmurray Way, on the big block with the pampas grass and the weeping willow and the tall gum tree out back. And that was the year my grandfather took his own life.

Dad doesn't speak about it. If he's a closed shop about simple things like friendships, job prospects and hobbies, he's a locked and abandoned warehouse when it comes to the bigger issues of dreams, hopes and fears. He bottles it all up, and finds the bottle, too.

The Balga Inn is where he takes his poison. There are two sessions a day in the pubs of Western Australia in the early 1970s, and Dad is at the Balga Inn for both. He becomes a fighter there, too, like his father before him. And soon it goes from happening at the pub to happening at home. I'm told later that he was a great father. A great son. A great husband. But I never really get to see that man. I never know those traits. He's broken inside by the time we truly meet, and through my childhood eyes I see mostly a man intent on breaking the world around me. That's why Mum leaves.

When I'm six she picks me up early from school one Friday afternoon. Her lawyers have told her, *Go get the kids, now,* so she does, and beats Dad there by two minutes. We flee and stay in hiding for a few days, until he finds us. Mum gets custody initially but Dad fights that, and the pair of them spend a few years running one another down to any officer of the court who will listen.

Those years are the ones spent with Nan and Pop, and are filled with love but punctuated by all sorts of pain, often prompted by surprise visits from one or the other parent. Mum pleads with me to stand up in court and say that I want to stay with her – to tell the psychologist or the counsellor or the policemen about her. I look her in the eye and tell her I will – *I'll tell them, Mum* – but when the moment comes I can't do it.

I'm too scared. And then I'm ashamed for being too scared. Then I'm angry at myself because we end up being forced to leave Nan and Pop and move in with Dad and his new partner, Irene, and her kids, Tracey and Mark.

Life is different at Dad's. Messier than ever. You know the way children finger-paint on big sheets of butcher's paper? The dollops of colour start out so soft and bright, but before long the painting becomes a mess of purple and dark red and midnight blue and mouldy green as the acrylic goop gets swirled around, and soon after everything is just murky brown mud. That's my childhood. Primary colours, chaotically mixed, until everything turns to shit.

Things get worse quickly. Dad works for a roofing company called Westate Tiles, and he works hard, or that's what it looks and smells like when he comes home all dusty and sweaty. I go on a few jobs with him and squint up at this man, seemingly on top of the world, looking down at me on the ground below. But he's wounded badly in a fall one day, smashing into a beam as he plummets. It destroys his pelvis and forces him to wear a colostomy bag. It breaks whatever's left of his spirit.

What do Dad and Irene drink to get through the days and nights? When they can afford it, they drink beer. Swan Draft out of those big king browns, the longnecks. When they can't afford that we drive all the way up to Wanneroo, to the vineyards, to buy giant flagons of cheap red. Arguments are never far away.

Dad is meant to pick me up and take me to footy training most nights, but he's late every time. Every goddamn time. I get annoyed but also embarrassed. Because I know he's down the pub. Years later, if I want to see my dad I go to the pub.

The ride home from training isn't any better. Play poorly and he tells me I'm a pussy. Play well and I'm a show-off. *Poser,* he calls me. *Bighead.*

I win the best and fairest in junior footy every single year except for one, yet I never feel any confidence. I'm driven by what I know about life: insecurity and fear. When I hear someone say *My dad taught me that,* I get jealous.

rebel

Somehow all the fun things in my life end up tainted, coloured by consequences I can never see coming – punishments I never expect. It's been happening all my life.

Maybe I'm a rebel.

In my first week of grade two at Takari Primary School, I'm standing by the main building, and I notice how the beautiful grassy lawn slopes down one hill to the oval and another to the basketball courts. I run down them one after the other, a sense of delirious momentum dragging me faster and faster, until a teacher stops me in my tracks. It's against the rules. I'm supposed to use the cement stairs. My punishment is standing up outside the headmaster's office every playtime and lunchtime for two weeks.

Later, living with Dad and Irene, my stepbrother Mark and I get to know each other quite well. We're the same age. He's my solace in that household. We go into the delicatessen at the Balga Bazaar, high on that particular brand of wandering freedom you get when you're 11, and pinch some Certs – these little peppermint sweets. I think we've gotten away with it, until Dad comes home.

Get in the bedroom. Uh-oh.

Lie down on the bed. Pants down. Shit.

Crack!

The owner of the deli knew I'd pinched the Certs, and lagged on me to Dad, who naturally brought out the belt.

Crack! Crack! Crack! Crack! Crack!

I'm grounded, too. Not allowed to play in the second semi-final of my season in the under-11s. Pretty big penalty for a packet of fucking peppermints.

One time someone gets hold of Irene's smokes – Ardath is her brand – and this someone pokes 50 tiny little pinholes through the front of the packet. No one owns up, but I know it was my little brother, Paul. Maybe he's trying to get attention. I'm sure he feels left out, a little forgotten. I want to enjoy the sight of Irene trying to smoke those fags, none of them lighting or drawing properly because they've all been punctured, but I feel too sad for Paul, acting out just to be noticed. I'm not a good big brother.

At least we learn to play Dad and Irene to our advantage. On sweltering summer days when the sun is up and the land is baking, when you can sense the breeze blowing into the suburbs from the wrong direction – gathering heat across wheatbelt country – we sometimes pretend to fight with one another.

We time our fake skirmish so that the blue peaks just as Dad arrives home, knowing what he'll say: *Right, that's it, no cricket training!*

Sucked in. As if we want to get out there on a 40-degree day to practise slips catches anyway.

Moments like this are funny, but life is generally a bit shit. It's about to get a lot shit.

i'm a shadow

I notice the red welts first. I don't understand where they've come from or why I have them, but my 12-year-old frame is covered in the little buggers. I'm tired, too, all the time. Then I start to get really sick. Aching limbs. Dizziness. I can barely get out of bed.

Dad takes me to the doctor, who says there's nothing wrong with me. Another says the same, and Dad is not-so-quietly pissed off. I'm costing him money. The third doctor figures out why I'm suddenly a shadow of the kid I was before. It's glandular fever.

I have no idea what glandular fever is, and yet it is about to keep me out of life for a year. On scorching summer days I listen to Paul and Mark and Tracey and their friends running around the yard, playing with the sprinkler and hose and occasionally water balloons. I stay inside feeling like the Elephant Man, sweating and crying, the line between perspiration and emotion blurred and uncertain.

My room contains a single bed with a blue-green doona, a crescent-shaped lamp, and a bunk bed on the other side for Paul and Mark. They show no mercy, relentlessly taking the piss out of me. One of the doctors says that eggs are supposed to be good for me, might help me mend, and they use that against me. If I'm feeling a bit weak: *Want some eggs, love?* If I'm testy and impatient: *Chin up, deary – maybe some eggs would help?*

They aren't always mean, of course. We have a radio in our

room. It's the size of a microwave and we always have it running when we go to bed. In these moments, I feel connected to other people as Paul and Mark and I all drift off together, listening to the same tunes. On weekends it's even better because Casey Kasem plays our favourites on the American Top 40.

I can't play football but I go sit in the car parked on the boundary line fence and watch others play. That's my winter. In summer I miss cricket season, too, after a half-hearted attempt to rejoin my team. I play three games, and go out for four ducks. That hurts most of all. I love cricket. I love everything about it.

I've had a big book about cricket since I was very young. I don't remember the title but it's green, and teaches bowling in a technical way. Off spin, leg spin, inswingers, outswingers. As a left-hander, it's hard to translate the images from the page, but I make do. I'm strategic, figuring out from an early age how to trap batsmen with my deliveries. In one match, I dismiss seven of them for one run.

When it comes to batting, I do anything I can to put the bowler off his line and length. I block and parry, and they bowl faster and faster, and I block and parry some more, until they get angrier and angrier, then I use their wayward rage to smack them around the oval.

I even love fielding, and the way you become part of a team that can intimidate and frighten an opponent. I don't mean sledging them – I mean walking in with the bowler, I mean staying on your toes, I mean keeping your eyes on their eyes, making them think. I love the way a collective can contribute to this mounting pressure felt by an individual.

Mr Lucas is my coach. He's a lovely family man whose son plays on the team. He always has everyone back to his place after a match. He has a pool and a barbecue with a big wide hot plate for cooking dozens of pork sausages.

After one winning final in under-13s we go back to Mr Lucas's, and I line up holding a piece of white bread, ready for one of those sizzling, popping snags. The bloke flipping them smiles and says, *Nah nah, yours is over there, Laidley.* I turn, and there on the table is a plate of cold, uncooked sausages. I don't understand. *We've gotta feed you raw meat for the grand final next weekend,* he says, and people laugh.

Despite my year off with glandular fever I've apparently developed a reputation as a competitive animal, a beast who feeds on raw meat. I don't especially mind, but it does perplex me at times. I don't feel good enough for any acclaim, in footy or in cricket. I still feel like an imposter. *Poser. Bighead*

it's a furnace

I hate Storrington Crescent. It's one of the many places we end up as kids, a crappy little house with a sparse garden. I'm 12 and can feel myself drifting from this family. But I try to make the best of it. That's what we do as humans, don't we? Adapt to survive and thrive?

That's what Dad is trying to do. He's back at work after his accident, not in the sun and the open air on rooftops but inside the ceilings themselves, laying pink batt insulation. I help him once a week or so. Sometimes I miss school to clamber up into manholes with him all day.

You cloak yourself head to toe in protective gear before lugging the rolled-up batts into the roof cavity. It's a furnace in there, and when you slice open the plastic wrapping with a Stanley knife, the batts expand. Somehow, despite the gear you've got on, you always emerge with sharp fibres nestled into your softest skin, bringing up this rash that burns on the inside of your forearms. Finish a week of work like that and you need a good rest. Dad does this for a long time. He must be exhausted.

It's Sunday night. Bedtime is 8:30pm for us kids – after *Dallas* or *The Dukes of Hazzard* or *Chico and the Man*. Basically we have to be in bed before *Number 96* comes on, so we won't hear all the titillating sex talk or see all those gorgeous tits. I'm a mess of raging prepubescent hormones. Mark and Paul and Tracey head off to bed, and I'm ambling behind them until Dad stops me. *Stay here,* he says.

What's this? I wonder.

This will be bad, I think, *probably the worst.*

But what exactly is the worst?

Whatever it is, there's a preamble and a pre-apology, but both are short and clipped and I don't remember them at all because of the gravity of the punchline.

I can't afford you, Dad says. *You're gonna have to go.*

I have to leave this house – this family, in a way – and find some other place to live, apparently. I have to find some other people to eke out an existence with.

I don't hear anything else. There might be detailed reasons or considered explanations for why Dad can no longer pay to keep me under the roofer's roof. Maybe there are circumstances mitigating or driving this moment – things beyond Dad's control – but I'm deaf to all that. I hear nothing.

Later in life I'll see something similar from the other side. I don't know what I look like as a wave of incomprehension washes over me on a Sunday night at bedtime, but I know the look on a player's face when you tell them they're dropped from the team or delisted from the club. As soon as you say those words, they don't hear anything else.

I leave, and I don't speak to my dad again for five years, until I'm 17, in year 12, when I get picked to play in the seniors in the West Australian Football League. I go to the pub to tell him. Just as I know he'll be there, I also know the exact seat he'll occupy, at the corner where the big mahogany bar top bends. I walk up behind him and he's talking to some bloke.

Yep, he's playing footy for West Perth, Dad says. *This weekend.*

He's talking about me, and bragging. It knocks me for six. He's spent my whole life telling me I'm a pussy then a showboat. *Poser. Bighead.*

Then he kicked me out of his fucking house.

He doesn't get to trade on my name, I think. *He doesn't get to brag on this moment of mine.*

I'm not angry, but in that second something is severed between us. Something I can't come back from. Facing the back of his head, in the front bar of the Malthouse Tavern, I make a sad, silent decision.

You cut me out of your life, I think. *I'll fucking cut you outta mine.*

unfathomable divide

I go to Mum. She's my only option. It's good to be living back with her, but she doesn't escape blame for the hurt I'm feeling. Dad can't cop all of this. My dysfunctional adolescence is a group effort. It takes a village. She left, after all. And I don't mean she left Dad – she also left me and Paul behind.

I'm 11 when she tells me she's moving to Sydney. We're on the way back to Dad and Irene's after a weekend with her. She gives me a long hug and a wet kiss when she drops us off, but what does that matter? She's going to live with her new beau, Leif – *like Leif Garrett* – on the other side of this incomprehensibly wide country. I feel utterly abandoned. She only goes to New South Wales for four months, it turns out, but at the time all I know is that she's headed across the Nullarbor, an unfathomable divide.

At least the big goodbye drop-off passes without incident. Previous drop-offs after visitation weekends with Mum didn't end so well. I used to like those visits. I remember getting teary when late Sunday afternoon drew close, knowing I was about to be returned to Dad and Irene. I remember physical dust-ups on the lawn – the pair of them screaming and scratching and clawing at each other. I remember standing on the grass next to the verandah, my hands shaking with anger as they fought, then taking a running jump at the bastards, to break them up. Poor Paul stood to the side, his face damp with unending tears.

In Sydney, Mum and Leif marry, and they buy a huge caravan – a 36-footer with two bedrooms, a shower, toilet, kitchen and dining space – and drive it fair across the country. They settle in Kingsway Caravan Park, 20 kilometres north of Perth, while building themselves a house nearby. After Dad kicks me out, that caravan park becomes home.

Fortunately, the years I spend there are the best of my childhood. There are kids *everywhere.* There's a park nearby, for cricket and footy. There's Lake Goollelal, for fishing. There are dusty lots where kids ride speedy little dirt bikes. I don't have one but I do have a sweet 10-speed road racer.

My bike is grey with a dark brown leather seat, and curved handlebars. Mum pops it in the back of her car and drives me to school in the morning, then I ride home, leaning into my grip, flattening my back and going like the clappers. Pick up a tailwind or a good downslope and I'd swear I'm flying, white-blonde hair behind me like the tail of comet. What's a helmet?

I'm home alone a lot, too, which opens up my world. Sure, I've experienced separation and divorce, seen drunkenness and violence, felt confusion and rejection, but now I'm secure – *sort of* – and I have time and space to explore. I use it immediately.

My room is the size of a closet, with just enough space for a bed and a cupboard, desk and mirror. But it's mine, all mine, and there's little chance of anyone walking in on me in here. I am safe to daydream, gazing at myself in that mirror, imagining pert breasts – mine – nestling in a pretty bra.

I make a conscious choice to experiment. What should I try? If my life were a movie, it would be time for a montage, set to music, like that bit in *Pretty Woman* where Julia Roberts goes on a shopping spree in Beverly Hills and tries on all the outfits in all of the stores. Only my montage would be filled with false starts and fuck-ups.

Mum has these hot rollers she puts in every morning. I try them, and burn my hair. But even if I look in the mirror and see a lilting curl or a nice wave, I panic and get immediately in the shower, forcing the hot and cold water to rinse away any visible expression of who I want to be.

I try her hair gel, too, scooping the claggy clear jelly onto my fingers and running it through my mop. I feel the hair harden but my resolve is soft, so I rinse it all out in the shower as well.

I try Mum's makeup and get self-taught lessons in what *not* to do. The eyeliner stings. The lipstick smears. But I have no online tutorials, no YouTube, not even any books. You can't imagine what it's like to learn this shit in the autumn of 1982.

I have to be careful about my research. In the end the safest option turns out to be the most creepy. I find myself looking at women all the time, studying their makeup, and staring I'm sure. They probably think I'm sneaking a look at their cleavage.

The scrutiny helps me figure things out. Like the way you can use a dark liner around the edges of the lips, setting a boundary, before filling it in with red, colouring inside the lines. I look hard enough and realise that, depending on complexion, a little blush on the cheekbones can change the shape of an entire face.

This is all happening after school. I race through the wind on my 10-speed to maximise my time at home alone.

Friends ring up: *Are you coming out?*

Nah, I say. *Homework.*

Such a bullshit excuse.

I do panic occasionally, afraid someone will walk into the caravan and see me, look at me, point at me and yell, *You. Dirty. Disgusting. Pervert.*

a little help

I'm 14 when I play my first full footy season after illness. My comeback game is at Des Penman Reserve in Nollamara.

A guy named Barry Miller is my coach. He's a funny man. Big glasses and skinny legs. Always in blue footy shorts, never wears shoes. He has slicked-back hair and a little curl at the front, like Con the Fruiterer from *The Comedy Company*. And he walks with his chest out, puffed up like a pigeon.

By the end of the first quarter, I know I've returned physically but not mentally. I'm on a forward flank and playing like a busted arse. I know my girlfriend is here watching me, because I can see her mum's red Torana over the fence. By half-time I want to dig a hole on the wing and bury myself there.

This is when funny-lookin', four-eyed, skinny-legged, pigeon-chested, slick-haired Barry Miller comes running out to me. He runs two thirds of the field to get to me before anyone else. I'm expecting a spray. I deserve one. Instead he puts his arm around me.

How're you going?
No good.
What can I do?
Nothing.
Okay, son.

And even though there's nothing he can do, he keeps that arm around me, walking by my side in lockstep towards the

35

pavilion. I'm 40 kilos soaking wet, and he's crushing me with that big right arm. He's not letting go.

He hugs me all the way to the rooms, a slow 150-metre walk. People play this game to kill, to compete, to express their creative self, to find some sort of aesthetic beauty in this world, but some also play – and coach – to connect and to share, to support and to love. Some people find footy just to help those who need a little help.

Enjoy yourself, he says. *You're a good player. And you can help us win.*

road warrior

One day after school I'm messing around in my little covert beauty school, trying something frosted and glittery. I wash it off before going out, but not well enough apparently. I have a girlfriend now, and she's a checkout chick at the supermarket. I go there most days for my Nanna Flo – Florence Jordan, my mum's mum – to buy her cucumbers, milk and Coke. That's basically what she lives on. Cucumbers cut up with a sprinkle of salt. A brandy with milk. A Coke in the afternoon sun. At the register, my girlfriend spots the glitter on my face and calls me on it: *You've got makeup on.*

I deny it. She nods. But there's a conspiratorial look in her eye. She doesn't believe me, and she doesn't really care either. That makes sense. We're so tight. We live 250 metres away from one another, and there's a pizza place equidistant from us both, 125 metres from either home. We go there for a medium ham and pineapple often, and we see my mates from school, and she asks me if I wouldn't rather be with them. *Nah, I'll see them tomorrow.*

One Sunday afternoon, my girlfriend and I are bored and we get into her things. She tries on a dress and I tell her it's ghastly, but she wears it anyway. It's time for her makeup and I ask: *Can I do it for you?*

I give it my best, and we are all laughs and smiles – jovial and casual. Covering these moments by joking throughout is still

37

the only way I can share them with anyone. When I finish, she looks at me with a smile. *Righto, up you get. Your turn!*

She gives me her best makeover. I look beautiful by her expert hand. I want to ask questions but I watch her reflection at work instead, trying to take it in, trying to treat it like my first tutorial.

She does big eyes on me, severe and yet so restrained.

She applies bronze shadow to my cheeks, but not too much.

She slicks back my hair, lifting it up into this high wave, like the surf at Cottesloe or the fins on a Cadillac.

I look futuristic. I look badarse. I'm Tina Turner in *Mad Max*. I'm a luminous copper fox. I'm a road warrior.

one magnet to another

It's March of 1983, I'm 16 years old, and in year 11 at school. To get home in the afternoon I sometimes catch the school bus through the streets of Balga. It drops everyone off one by one, until I'm the last kid left. The end of the line is Wanneroo Road near Warwick Road. That's where I need to get on my second bus of the day, the 350, for one final 7-kilometre stretch north to the caravan park in Kingsway.

I'm sitting at the bus stop now, wearing a white T-shirt, jeans and a pair of Adidas Romes – white with three royal-blue stripes – when I look across the street and see a woman waiting at the opposite stop, for the 350 south into Perth.

It's a wide road. I'm probably 30 metres away from her, yet transfixed. I'm drawn to her. Why, at first I can't say. There's something different about her. Something statuesque. Her physique stands out. I look closer. She must be in her mid-twenties. Flowery top. Matching skirt. Dark brown hair, rich and flowing with sweeping curls. A deep burgundy satin scarf.

Something clicks in me and my eyes widen. I don't have the vocabulary for it, but what I'm seeing – for the time – is a transgender woman. I guess I was drawn to her for a reason, not like a moth to a flame but one magnet to another.

I look south now, down the road, and notice my bus is coming. I can see it from a long way off, but I keep staring back across the road at the woman at the bus stop. The bus advances and then stops. I look at her. It advances and stops again. I look at her again. A decision is coming and I make it. I cross the road, and let the bus headed for home blow past me without stopping.

I reach her bus shelter and don't say anything. I don't make eye contact. I sit behind her, too embarrassed to make my presence at all felt. I don't want to sit and stare from the side, disturbing or scaring this woman. I want to regard her quietly.

Her bus arrives and I watch her get on. The doors are closing when I leap up and on at the last minute. She sits near the front, on the left, big sunglasses framing her cheekbones. I walk past her and sit two rows back on the right. There's no one else on board. If she's headed for the city, there's another 15 kilometres left to go, time to steal glances at her short, painted nails. Time to watch her remove her scarf, revealing the shadow of an Adam's apple. I feel myself reaching out to say something, but it's all in my head. In reality my mouth won't open and my body doesn't move an inch.

The bus stops near the Perth Entertainment Centre and she gets off. I follow her onto the pavement. The hydraulic doors hiss shut and the bus drives away, and off she goes, walking up over a concrete ramp and down onto Wellington Street.

I watch her disappear from view and wonder why I didn't follow, why I couldn't say anything, and what I would have said anyway.

I sit in the bus terminal reliving the whole trip, questioning what I didn't do and should have done, chastising myself for my fear. I stay there for an hour – *she might come back* – before finally giving up, crossing the street and waiting for my bus home. The 350 north arrives soon, ready to speed me back into my life.

fuck your rules

I might be better at cricket than footy. At the end of 1983, just after Christmas, I get picked in the under-16s state cricket team, and we travel to Sydney to play in a national round robin tournament. At state level I'm a left-arm first-change bowler, but I bat at number seven. When I'm batting, the bowlers always seem to know that middle and leg is my weakness. I'm best on the back foot, up in the air. I can be acrobatic there – a merciless and calm striker. But bowl it at me low and leg side? I'm nothing. I know this when we play against New South Wales and I get to see the Waugh brothers up close. They're so great off their pads, just whipping it away. I see Steve and I see Mark, and I know I'll never quite do what they do.

This is my first real visit to a big city, and I'm 16. We're staying at the University of Sydney, where the tournament is being played. We're told to stay there, too, in our dorm rooms. We're specifically told *DO NOT go to Kings Cross*, but we're Jack the Lads from Perth, the star swingers and strikers in the state, so fuck your rules. We do exactly that.

I feel cool walking the mean streets of the Cross with a beer in hand. I feel like I've arrived.

We get away with that but not with something far more trivial. Near the last day of the trip we're hanging out with the Queensland team at night, having beers. The coaches of both states walk into the halls of residence and we try to hide our drinks. I put a cricket cap over mine. They read us the riot act anyway. *You will NEVER represent Western Australia again in your life!*

Fuck you, I think. *I'm not interested in that anyway.*

I've let people know that, but they've been trying to change my mind. People from my local cricket club. People from the Western Australian Cricket Association. *You've gotta play,* they say. *This is where your life is going to go.* But I can already feel it isn't. It's too hard to succeed in this sport. Too hard to be in that best 11 to play for Australia, and there's no T20 yet, no Indian Premier League, no sense that you can make a life for yourself playing the gentleman's game. You can only win at cricket if you're the pointy end of the spear – not some kid who looks like a whippet and has a weakness down leg side.

I choose footy. I have to. I'm only 16 and I've just won best first-year player in the under-19s for West Perth, where Tom James is my coach. I'll be a regular senior footballer soon enough. This is the path. But I also never stop wondering, *Have I made the right call here?*

The summer of 1984 arrives and I'm training with the men. And they're brutes.

The coach is Dennis Cometti, who will one day be the best commentator in the game, but right now he's a demanding coach who's spotted a weakness in me. I'm far too slight.

I need to hit the weights but I hate them. It's not the exertion I hate – it's the product. I don't want to get big. I don't want muscles. They want me to bulk up – I want to slim down. They have me on a diet filled with carbs and protein. They sit me under a bench press and demand shorter sets with heavier reps. What's the word they use now? Swole? They want me to look swole through the lats and pecs and triceps.

I see the effect it's having, too. Mirrors don't lie. Little by little, I'm getting ripped.

The typical reaction to this in a young teenage male is self-adoration and narcissism. I can see others bathing in their own reflection as they get shredded – fasting occasionally in order to shed body fat, so that every little muscle pops just right. Their six packs become eight packs, and below that the inguinal fold appears – that v-shaped line that leads the rippled ladder of abdominal muscles down to your cock. *Dick abs*, they call them.

I want none of that. I never will.

I quietly lift lighter weights than I should, and do far more reps that I should, toning my muscles rather than pumping them up. I get stronger without getting bigger.

Cometti sends the playing group on 20-kilometre runs sometimes. These are not fun. You arrive at training in the heat of December, and he sends you on a half marathon. The bottom of Kings Park. The old brewery by Matilda Bay. Nedlands. St Georges Terrace towards Subiaco. The University of Western Australia in Crawley. Mounts Bay Road.

You get giddy in the sun and your head begins to spin, but I eat up the pavement. I'm a whippet. I'm a rabbit. All I can think of is the water weight I'm losing with every kilometre.

I run and I sweat, and the pain mingles with the satisfaction of slimming down.

We'll do this all again next week.

the pixels make the picture

I turn 17 in March, get my driver's licence in April, and Mum buys me a car. It's a Ford Falcon, tan with a white roof, long bonnet and a bench seat in the front. It looks boxy. It looks like freedom.

I start shopping, building my wardrobe. A miniskirt is the first thing I want, and I get one: blue and black, chequered. I buy it at Target in Balga, a 10-minute drive from the caravan park. I expand into blouses and leggings and underwear, sometimes from Kmart.

Why yes, thank you, I could use some help, I say to the nice ladies in the shop. *I'm after something for my girlfriend. She's about the same size as me.*

I begin to crave these shopping trips. And this is when my life becomes tangibly compartmentalised for the first time. I no longer only have thoughts to hide – I have very real physical evidence to conceal.

I keep all my new clothes in my car boot. One night at footy training my mate Darren Bewick, a little star who later plays for Essendon and coaches with me at North Melbourne, sees me open it to fetch some footy gear, and of course that's the day I've left a goddamn blue flowing evening gown with a plunging neckline lying flat across the pile of crap in my boot.

It's my girlfriend's, I blurt out. Only later do the questions start rolling around in my head. *Did I say that too abruptly? Should I have said anything? Did that seem suspicious? Does he know?*

Sometimes I wonder what would happen if one person saw all of the revelatory moments in my life so far, before I've even turned 18 and become an adult. What would they see? Would everything be clear to them?

Nail polish from the blonde lady in the red dress. The shiny black frock in the cubby house at Aunty Val's. The dress-up game with Vicky and Peter. Dr Scholl's clogs. The long hair I refused to cut. The zinc cream at Horrocks. Makeovers with my girlfriend.

Individual acts, performed in isolation, mean no one person in my life can make out anything with any clarity. But collectively, every little scene is there. And if you're me – living it all – the mosaic is crystal clear. The pixels make the picture.

I buy fishnet stay-up stockings. I buy a dark-blue halter top. I buy shoes later, and they're actually the simplest thing to buy. Apparently I'm a women's size 10 in any shop.

I'm building an ensemble but to do what? Go out? Go where? With who? And when?

I drive home with my purchases, in my Ford Falcon, feeling an illicit little thrill, and a deep urge to try on my new things at home in private.

But most of the time Mum's there, and I have to wait until the next day after school, or the day after that, or the fucking day after that when I can finally be myself.

I stuff my new treasures into a plastic bag and twist the looping arms together. I scrunch up the bag and shove it down the end of that car boot, next to the tyre iron and the jack and the jumper cables. And I wait.

feral

My season builds slowly. I work my way up, starting with three Colts games then 10 reserves games, and a six-week thigh injury in between. I finish strongly, playing three senior matches.

In the first, we play against Claremont and I line up on a wing against Allen 'Shorty' Daniels. He is in devastating form, about to be picked up by Footscray to play in the VFL the following year, but right now he looks me up and down and sneers, *So they're playing fucking school kids on me are they?* I laugh timidly and get on with my game. I don't have enough runs on the board yet to be cheeky back.

I do enough to keep my spot, and play the following week against South Fremantle at Leederville Oval. My opponent is one Neil Elvis 'Nicky' Winmar – the first of more than a dozen times we will line up on one another. He is not yet soured by the racism he will encounter while playing for St Kilda in the VFL, the hounding that will prompt him in 1993 to lift his jumper and point defiantly to his skin, a moment that becomes so iconic it will one day be immortalised in a statue here in Perth. He is instead immediately friendly. *How are you, cuz?* he says. *Whatchu been up to?* We play out what feels like a nil-all draw between us, running around fighting for the same wing, me grinding and feral and fast, him dancing and gathering with balance and light.

The last game of the season we go to Bassendean to play against Swan Districts. And I play on Keith Narkle, the doyen of Indigenous players in Western Australia. I've watched him for so many years when his side was so ordinary, and now they are so strong and this is his reward. The Swans win the flag in 1982, 1983 and this year, 1984, too. Playing against him is a huge honour, and he shows me not exactly deference but respect, and I love the way that feels inside. I love that my coach has faith in me to play on such men. I'll never again wonder if I should have chosen cricket.

I'm 17, playing on Daniels and Winmar and Narkle, and something inside of me feels free. I feel unbound. I have some recklessness to enjoy – some youth to indulge. Halfway through year 12, Mum applies for a job at a local bank on my behalf, and I get it, lined up for the following year. I will be paid to play footy, and walk around the corner from the ground into an easy job. Now I can't be bothered studying or even going to school.

If the swell is up, I drive down to the school car park in the morning with my massive single fin mini malibu board on roof racks, and recruit a few fellas to wag school with me. The waves off Trigg Beach one day rip the fin off my big beautiful board, so I buy a 6 foot 3 tri-fin Cordingley surfboard, and that becomes my stick. I'm at the beach maybe five days out of every seven.

I often go with a group but I like being alone out there, too. I think it's because I'm a basher, crashing against the world my whole short life, so I'm at home out in the rolling foam, duck diving and being dumped, howling at the curls the ocean sends my way, exhausted each day by what Mother Nature serves up. And afterwards, the tired calm of waterlogged exhaustion is bliss. Surfing balances me.

We buy cartons of beer and guzzle them down in the dunes. We use fake IDs to get into the Malthouse Tavern on Friday afternoons for the titty shows. The barmaids are topless and one of them walks around with an empty beer jug every hour or so, and we drop one-dollar and two-dollar notes inside, and when it's full she does a dance, a striptease, bending over so we can see everything, and we roar and grin because we're blokes, and blokes are the fucking worst sometimes.

We burn through heaps of weed, using my little gold bong with the silver bell at the base, where you pop those fat sticky buds, unmixed, no tobacco. We light up in my car, turning it into a hot box. If you don't get stoned ripping a cone or two, you can simply sit back and enjoy the contact high. Second-hand smoke from first-rate dope.

A family friend tells me one day where a crop is growing. I get the address and drive there with a few friends. We peer over the fence and see the plants, all about a metre high. We rip them from the ground, stuffing them into black plastic garbage bags and squishing the whole haul into the deep boot of my car. We're high for months.

It has to end though, and in early 1985 it does. I'm at pre-season training in January and I fly for a mark; the session has only just begun, so I should be fresh and eager but I'm tired and distracted because I'm sinking beers all day and sinking deeper into my weed all night, and I miss the ball completely. The heavy Burley comes at me like a bullet, goes right through my hands and smacks me square on the nose. My head is rattled, my nose is bloodied and my pride is stung.

I know I've got a decision to make, and I make it. I drive to the house where my mates are hanging out and somehow they don't judge me, or mock me. They just listen and nod, as I tell them the way it has to be. *I can't do this anymore, and I won't see you anymore,* I say. *I need to give this thing my utmost attention. I need to focus on footy.*

It pays off. Only a few weeks later, feeling clearer and more driven, I get sat down after training one night. We have a new coach. John Wynne. He's been deciding things, too.

I've made a decision, he says, *on keeping you or another guy. And I've decided to keep you.*

Footy was almost over before it started.

kill or be killed

John doesn't coach in a way I've seen before. He gives people autonomy. He doesn't seem to care if I value running more than I do lifting. He doesn't bother with fire-and-brimstone histrionics. He gets us to play tennis as part of pre-season preparation, and offers no explanation why. He looks at the game differently, I guess, and he most certainly looks at my game differently.

I've always been a forward or an onballer or a winger. I've been that quick player who finds the ball easily and surges it forward into scoring range, into dangerous territory. He no longer wants that from me. He wants me to be a backman. To defend. And to counterattack from defence. He does this not because he misunderstands my abilities but because he knows them well. He saw the reserves coach give me a clip one night, while doing 200-metre sprints.

We would always do ten 200s in a row, and towards the end during the last few sprints I would always pull away and start winning. The reserves coach knew I was able to do that because I was holding back on runs 1 and 2 and 3 and 4 and 5 and 6 and 7, and he told me in the clearest, harshest way that *that way* of doing things was weak as piss. That it was the way of the pussy. A cunt move.

You need to stop hedging and scheming, he says, *and start driving hard.* I need to blow the other guys off the park in the first run, the second run, the third run and every run after that, until I blow up trying, until the engine overloads and a geyser of hot vomit shoots up my throat and projectiles onto the oval. Drink a little water – *Suck it down and suck it up, son* – and go again.

I begin to realise that, for me, this is the way. At this level, and any level above, I don't have the skills or tricks or talent to survive otherwise. My living will be made by my aggression. I've always been competitive, not used to losing, expecting to win, and now this mindset has a name. *Kill or be killed.* That's my mantra, from here on out.

How does it look on the field? I run all day. I run them ragged. I run until my feet bleed. Until they fall down. I take to my new position as a half-back flank and I play it with daring. I go for the mark instead of the spoil. I run past teammates and call for the ball, screaming out their name, demanding possession. I win the ball first, instead of waiting and corralling and tackling. *If I have the ball,* I reason, *then they don't.* The best defence is a good offence.

I start getting 25 touches a game, then 30, then 35. Every AFL side has that kind of defender in the new millennium, but in the 1980s, none of them do. Until me. I bring attitude to my role. Spite and snarl. I grow a mouth and become a bona fide back-talking smartarse. I show no respect to older players. In fact I clip them more, because I know the disrespect will anger them more coming from a young upstart.

I feel disliked. I feel muscular. I feel bulletproof.

I feel further away from my true self than I've ever been.

i look away

Sunday sessions are a big deal in Perth in the 1980s. The pubs open up for set stretches in the afternoon and evening, and the punters pour in from all corners. Hotels across the city try to make their offering as enticing as possible, with drinks specials and bands. All the big acts cruise through these parts, too, from the Painters and Dockers to INXS, and guys and girls sing along and dance while wearing double plugger thongs and Golden Breed board shorts.

The good times don't last, of course. The Shenton Park Hotel becomes a retirement home. The Coronado in Claremont turns into a medical centre. The Mosman Park Hotel is converted into apartments. My party spot is the Fitzgerald Hotel in Northbridge. They say nothing good happens at night in Northbridge, and they would be right. Still, the Fitzgerald lands Hunters & Collectors, and The Triffids, and Paul Kelly, and so I go there from 7 to 10pm every Sunday, and I watch and listen from inside their sprawling beer garden, with what feels like the rest of the city.

Truth be told, I'm thoroughly cooked by the time I arrive. After most home games on a Saturday, a group of us end up in the centre circle of the oval, standing in the darkness and smoking fat joints, reminiscing about our exploits on the same grass hours earlier. We go out all night until late Sunday morning, then crash, then get up for that Sunday session at Fitzgeralds.

One night I leave the pub briefly, heading out back to my car to have a few bong hits. I go back inside to where the West Perth boys are gathered, down the back, like royalty, waiting for all the people to come pay tribute. A little drunk and distracted, I case the floor of the pub and that's when they walk in – a group of transgender girls. *Oh my fucking god*, I think. *Look at them. Amazing.*

I can barely breathe. I'm transfixed, and soon my teammates lock onto where I'm looking. They laugh. They point. Not at me though. They just think I've spotted a good target.

Look at these fucking blokes, they go.

How's about these fucken poofters, they cackle.

Why the fuck are they lettin' fucken faggots in here? they roar.

I'm supposed to chime in, I think, or at least laugh. For all my smart-arsed attitude, I'm still a young player in the team – group dynamics dictate that I should defer to my elders. I'm supposed to love what they love. Hate what they hate. View with cowardly suspicion what they view with cowardly suspicion.

But instead I do nothing. I don't lead their chorus nor do I follow. I look away. I recede into the wall. I excuse myself and head to the bathroom, then leave altogether. I buy a kebab to settle the toxic swirl in my guts, or maybe I just have the munchies.

I see the girls on the way out and the strangest part is that I don't know whether I want to talk to them or be them, but I know either way that I hate my friends for wanting to slay them, and I hate myself for not being able to ignore the pricks and approach these girls – to say hello and ask them a question or three. I've become a minor star in the biggest game in town, the ultimate insider. But I'm on the outside of the circle I really want to join.

we are the kings

For all the violence and toxic masculinity and hedonism of this life as a league player, I also have a day job. I work at the R&I Bank – Rural and Industries Bank of Western Australia – the precursor to Bankwest.

I count bills manually over the counter. I compute checking. I help balance accounts. I'm becoming a teller and my day-to-day pride is clearing my till. The whole branch has to balance off before everyone can leave for the day, and when that doesn't happen you need to trace that one mistake through every transaction until the books can be reconciled. It is precisely as numbingly boring as it sounds. But I'm good at it. If you balance your till you've had a 'slicker'. *I had a slicker today*, you'd say. *I've had four slickers this week.*

In the middle of 1986 I'm working one of my shifts there when the phone rings. It's for me. No doubt it's my best mate, Sean King, with some new dipshit variation on his oldest prank call. *Hello, Dean – it's Barry Cable here. We want you to come play for North Melbourne.*

Idiot.

Someone hands me the receiver. *Hello, Dean? It's Ron Alexander here.*

Right. It's Ron Alexander, the Simpson medallist, the former Fitzroy ruckman and current captain-coach star of East Fremantle. Sure. Whatever.

But it *is* Ron Alexander. And Ron Alexander is currently coaching the representative state side for Western Australia, and he wants me to play for him in an upcoming game against South Australia. He wants me to represent the Sandgropers against the Croweaters.

I am suspended for two weeks and haven't played but he says he needs me – *fucking needs me* – to join them in playing against Andrew Jarman, Mark Naley, Michael Aish and Tony Hall.

We fly over to Football Park in Adelaide and we fucking *whack* them on a cold and dewy night. I'm still a kid and still not doing my weights, so I wear a long-sleeved jumper to cover up my thin arms, but I play a really great game.

Ron keeps me in the side to play the final game of this Australian Championship series, the old version of State of Origin football. It's a combined WAFL team, one that would go on to form the nucleus of the first West Coast Eagles squad. We play against Victoria at Subiaco in front of 39,863 fans.

Once again I'm surrounded by great names – Dwayne Lamb and Peter Wilson and Phil Narkle and Brad Hardie. And we take it up to them – this team of Terry Daniher and Justin Madden and Greg Williams and Dale Weightman and Paul Roos and Mark Thompson and Trevor Poole.

It becomes quite possibly the greatest state game ever played. There are seven lead changes in the final quarter, and we win by three points. Andrew Macnish takes the hanger of the year. Brian Peake, our captain, kicks seven goals. Brad Hardie is best on ground. I swap jumpers after the siren with Dermott Brereton.

We are the kings of this town – the princes of Perth – with invitations to every party and people waving us beyond every velvet rope into every backroom. Free meals and free drinks. No queues and no questions. It's an interesting city in which to be a star.

There are whispers at this time, in 1986, about the emergence of a new team in the VFL. A team from Western Australia. It's been on the cards for a while.

East Perth tried to join the VFL in 1980. Their application was rejected but it sparked a debate. Investigations into the long-term viability of a club based in Perth are commissioned by the premier.

A 64-page report, co-authored by Richard Colless in 1986, finds that a national VFL competition is inevitable, and, in spite of some opposition from struggling Victorian clubs, the green light is given. An independent WAFL board is appointed. Colless becomes the inaugural chairman of Indian Pacific Limited, the publicly-listed company that owns this new club. He quotes Machiavelli when reflecting on the local opposition to this new venture.

There is nothing more difficult to plan, more doubtful of success, nor more dangerous to manage than the creation of a new system. For the initiator has the enmity of all who would benefit from the preservation of the old system and merely lukewarm defenders in those who would gain by the new one.

That's the context, but I'm not yet sure what any of this means for me. Clubs have now seen me playing for Western Australia on the big stage, and they're calling, and that's a heady thing, to suddenly have Essendon and Collingwood and Carlton touching base.

The powers that be have 160 days to set up a new team from Perth to play in the 1987 VFL pre-season competition. There is talk of millions of dollars. Hearsay and innuendo fly about town.

A former player and coach, George Michalczyk, is tasked with putting the list together. He goes about it carefully and people begin to learn the names of the players who will shape this new team, the A to Z of it all, from (John) Annear to (Mark) Zanotti.

Not everyone wants to sign. The VFL clubs are adept at seeding doubt, too, convincing many players that this new team will never become a reality.

Peter Wilson – a star at East Fremantle – signs instead with Richmond. The 1986 Sandover medallist – Mark Bairstow – goes to Geelong. Winmar to the Saints and Bewick to the Bombers. Others resist huge offers to come home. Brad Hardie stays at Footscray. Gary Buckenara remains at Hawthorn.

But the new team is nonetheless strong. Ross Glendinning returns from North Melbourne to be captain. Young stars from the state team – like Phil Narkle and Chris Mainwaring – sign up. The club also beats various VFL suitors to their preferred young talent from Perth, outbidding Footscray for Chris Lewis, and Collingwood for John Worsfold.

I want to stay in Perth, too, so when I'm eventually asked, I choose to join this new endeavour. But I don't yet know how I'm going to deal with the scrutiny and attention it will bring.

How am I going to manage this other part of me, the part of me that buys makeup and dresses and stuffs them in a plastic bag in the boot? It's still there. It's going nowhere. Will those two worlds coexist or collide?

I'm 19 years old when told I'm going to become a West Coast Eagle, and my life is about to change, in more ways than one. My girlfriend is pregnant.

a chance to right some wrongs

I met Joanne at the pub one night. I was meant to go to the presentation night for my old junior club, to hand out trophies to the kids who were where I was a few years earlier. But I wasn't feeling great about myself, for no particular reason, and went to the Balga Inn with friends instead. I got ID'd and couldn't get in, so I jumped in my car and headed to the Floreat Hotel, where I knew the West Perth players would be, where I knew I could go inside and drink.

Joanne was there. I knew her from school. She was 18 months ahead of me. Slim and blonde. Attractive and interested. She wanted to know why I skipped the presentation and the speeches and awards. I don't remember how I answered exactly, but I found myself talking easily, comfortably, all night. We left from there, and it grew from there.

We've been together for more than a year when we find out she's pregnant. We move in together. Our place is in Harborne Street, Wembley, reasonably close to Subiaco Oval – on the bottom floor of a three-storey red brick block of flats. I'm earning $150 a week at the bank, and getting $80 a game playing for West Perth, and we struggle to make ends meet. We drink Cottee's red cordial and eat Heinz baked beans. We can afford one bottle of Coke a week, a big 2-litre job that always seems to go flat within three days. I ask the club for help and they offer to kick in an extra $80 a week for rent.

I am immediately overjoyed to be having a child. Not every 19-year-old feels this way, but for me it's a chance to right wrongs – to provide that which was never provided to me. So I go to work. I go to footy training. And I go home.

Joanne gets bigger and bigger as the day draws closer and closer. She gives up her part-time job as a typesetter for magazines and newspapers and stays home. When I can, I massage her feet, swollen with fluid.

On 29 September 1986, we're an hour north of Perth, looking at strata title blocks in Seabird, a caravan park, with her mum and dad. Then Joanne looks at me. *This is it.*

We drive to our flat for clothes, then I take Joanne to hospital. The nurse tells me to go home, that they'll call when there's something to report. I'm the man, so I stay at home while the business of birth is left to the women. That's how things are, and I don't know any better. But as the hours pass by I know I can't wait alone any longer, so at midnight I speed around the corner to the Osborne Park Hospital, where I find Joanne breathing into a brown paper bag, limiting the oxygen she inhales with each panicked breath.

I stay by her side and massage her side, too. She is grouchy with me, but right now I want her to be grouchy with me – I want her to vent what she's feeling.

Just give me the fucking bag! she yells.

Yes, dear, I reply.

Rub here – bloody here! Bloody now! she demands.

Yes, dear, I reply.

Our baby girl comes into the world at 4:45am on 30 September. In our haste, on the birth certificate we mark the day as 29 September. That's her legal birthday now and always will be, but we'll always celebrate on her true birthday, the 30th. It becomes an in-joke for the family.

We have a name picked out for her. Samantha Joanne. Sammy Jo. But we look into her little eyes and see that she's not a Sammy Jo. She's a Brooke. Brooke Talia, 8 pounds 11, a big girl. And all I want to do is give her everything I didn't have.

We leave the hospital with her the next day. We have no baby seat – just a white wicker basket with lace netting over the top. It's her baby carrier and crib all in one. We fasten it to the car seat by looping a belt through its handles. Things were different then.

We have no nursery. Joanne shares my worries about life – a fatalistic approach to the world – and refused to allow any baby gifts into the house, any nappies, any decorations, anything at all until the baby was born healthy and brought back to our home. Only then could she be sure – could she believe it was real and that nothing bad would happen.

Brooke is my whole world now, my perfect poppet, with hair like Punky Brewster and an appetite for food and attention and sleep, always giggling gaily and pooping prodigiously. The following fortnight is a beautiful blur of sleep and swaddling and cloth nappies, and then I have to leave.

I have to travel 1628 kilometres north to Port Hedland, on secondment to another branch of the R&I Bank. My bosses see no problem in sending a 19-year-old new father halfway across the country two weeks after the birth of his first child, stationing him in 'Boystown', the roughest port city in Australia. Things were different then.

it's gonna be alright

Up north, I miss my girls. And I miss out on something, too: the launch of the West Coast Eagles. It's a $50,000 spectacular held at the Merlin Hotel on Thursday 30 October, in which the inaugural 32 players are unveiled, along with the team name and colours and logo, in front of a crowd of maybe 400 captains of industry and big swinging dicks.

I'm stuck in a bank office in a town full of rum pigs, boys cashed up from working on train lines and mines, who spend their money on Bundy and beer and boats and bikes, on choppers and strippers.

I can't wait to get back and start living my new life. Playing for West Perth I was paid $10 per Colts game, $25 per reserves game and $80 per seniors game. Now, as a West Coast Eagle, I am on a contract worth $120,000 over three years.

It's a big thing, being picked by a league club. George Michalczyk, the man who is putting together the new squad, signs me in the car park of Leederville Oval. I flick through the legal document on the boot of his car, and suddenly I feel as though my life is on some kind of solid ground. *It's gonna be alright*, I think. *It's gonna be alright*. On the drive home from that meeting it feels as though the tyres aren't even touching the road.

Much later in life I get to see it from the other side, as the coach giving scared young boys a chance. Some kids get selected by clubs and know the AFL will be theirs to dominate, but others have to wait and hope. In 2006, I watch the under-18 national championships, sitting in the John Elliott Stand at Princes Park in Carlton. The South Australian team clears out its entire forward 50, giving all that space to one Indigenous kid, and he puts on a show. Lindsay Thomas dazzles and baffles. *I'm drafting this kid*, I think, *no matter what.*

I learn later that he is from Port Lincoln but travelled to Port Adelaide to play for the Magpies when he was only a kid. I learn that a few of his friends died in a car accident, and while that floored Lindsay, he also resolved to stay and nurture his career. That shows me his desire.

We take Lachlan Hansen with our first pick. We take Gavin Urquhart next, and he struggles gamely. With pick 41, I have to fight with our recruiters, because I want Lindsay but they want a tall, dark-haired kid who grew up playing basketball, Todd Goldstein. We get Lindsay with pick 53, and after calling out his name at the draft I ring him up to talk, and I hear him and his wife Hannah, both in tears. A year later, he comes to visit me and he's quiet and crying a little.

I bought a house today, he says. *I'm the first person in my family to buy a house. Ever.*

Giving someone a chance feels as good as getting your own chance. I love his story. I love my story. I love that football has such stories to tell.

this uniform

I'm not the youngest player in the first pre-season of the West Coast Eagles, but it feels that way. I have a job and a partner and a flat, and a kid of my own – but in truth I'm still a kid, pretending to be an adult. And I'm joining a squad of stars.

I grew up barracking for North Melbourne, so I stand in absolute dwarfed awe of Ross Glendinning, our captain.

Rob Wiley is a WA icon who won eight best and fairests with Perth before and after his stint at Richmond. I remember he didn't play in the recent State of Origin series, but came out to celebrate anyway, and we noticed he wasn't drinking. We asked why and he said it was because he wanted to play the following week. In that era, that was different. He is professionalism personified.

Laurie Keene and I have already spent three years beating the shit out of one another, and should have a tough time building a relationship, but he has just had a baby girl, Jasmine, and so we bond over 3am feeds and shitty nappies. Laurie is 6 foot 8, but can move and stoop and rip a pass across his body on the left foot.

Steve Malaxos played in the great Claremont sides as a small forward alongside Ken Hunter and the Krakouers, and although it didn't work out for him at Hawthorn, he tells me grisly war stories about what it was like to play in the brutal VFL. I hang off every word.

Chris Mainwaring is a runner and a rogue – I never saw anyone play so hard and train so hard through injury and pain. But you would need to ask the directors of the club about the places they found him in the early hours of the morning on the weekend. God rest his soul.

Chris Lewis is here. Our families knew each other growing up, when he was playing for Mirrabooka and evidently born for stardom. Parents of opposing teams used to complain about Chris, convinced he must have been playing out of his age group. I saw that in reverse, up close. I played on Chris during his first game for Claremont, when I was 18 and he was only 16, and he pulled my pants down. I couldn't catch him. In that first season at the Eagles he's loyal and fierce and funny, but it takes him time to work out the rigours of training, and what's required.

Phil Narkle has been brought to the club to show the way and set the standards. Out of earshot – so as not to embarrass him – the veterans tell all the rookies: *Watch what Phil does.*

Michael Brennan puts opponents to sleep and becomes the kind of player whose magnet is the first one picked each weekend. Dwayne Lamb is a running machine, built like a wombat. Peter Davidson is a tall winger with the longest stride and the loveliest kick. Andrew Macnish is elusive, uncanny and the highest of flyers.

Paul Peos goes by the nickname 'Pudu', which he got on an East Perth footy trip to Malaysia. He had climbed a coconut tree, and the police warned that if he didn't come down he would be off to Pudu Prison. He played in the 1985 side that won the Teal Cup for Western Australia for the first time, with 'the young messiahs' – Peter Sumich and Chris Waterman and John Worsfold.

John is quiet and unassuming, but already has an aura around him, an early strength, a quiet confidence. He is the subtle antagonist. Karl Langdon is the epitome of white line fever, running around like a chook with its head cut off, but for John, silence is power.

I look around during circle work and I'm overwhelmed by the entire premise of this side. *How am I going to get a game in this fucking team?*

We train first on the leafy grounds of Aquinas College, an upper echelon school down on the Swan River. It's hot. And tough. In drills you run from cone to cone, and if you stop short before a cone – if you dare slow into a jog instead of continuing that sprint – the coaches roar: *We're all going again!*

We do a triathlon one day, and a midfielder named John Annear gets a flat tyre on the bike leg. He shows us what to do. He picks up his bike and holds it above his head, and runs the rest of the cycling leg while carrying the thing aloft. He is a machine, and he makes you feel as though you need to be one, too.

But the relationships we're trying to build are not yet there. Are we friends? Not really, not yet. There is a lingering hangover from the old league, from our playing days in the WAFL. The year prior there was a massive and spiteful WAFL grand final, and a good chunk of our team were playing on opposing sides. Keene, Lamb and Macnish suited up for Subiaco, while Brennan, Lockyer and Mainwaring lined up for East Fremantle. The WAFL is a competition that has thrived for more than 100 years, in which rivalries are deep seated and bitter, and people have long memories.

There are personality clashes, too. People like to believe that all players on a football side love one another – as if they're all united, all striving towards a common goal. But there are clever guys and dumb pricks. There are happy blokes and sour shitheads. There's competition for spots, and jealousy over wages, and people you just don't particularly like. I don't particularly like Darren Bennett. He's a full forward who can kick the ball a million miles, and he fucking knows it. *Poser. Bighead.*

Before our first game in the VFL, against Richmond in Perth, the back page of the paper has a headline: 'War without weapons'. And that's what the public imagines we are – a band of brothers willing to fight and die together. We're not that, but we're ready to rumble anyway.

We run out onto the oval past the Town and Country Eaglettes, pretty young things dancing in sparkling stretch satin, and as we step onto Subiaco we feel as we always do there when playing against a team from the east. We are 10 feet tall. We will not be fucked with. The Tigers are not dismissed but we are going to win. It's decided. Simple as that.

I kick a goal at the grandstand end, and I play well enough to get votes in the best and fairest. I feel good in this uniform, wearing the colours of my boyhood team, playing now as a man.

jigsaw dream world

This thing inside of me that I let out once in a while – it used to be fun. It used to feel like natural exploration – justified curiosity – but that begins to change now. Now I have too much at stake, and fear enters the picture.

The plastic bag in the boot of my car won't do as a hiding place anymore – not for an array of blouses and skirts and shoes and makeup. I can't have that kind of bomb lying around in open view, ready to blow up my life at any moment. I hide it in the shed, underneath boxes and rags and garden tools.

I sneak moments to explore myself, to dress and look the way I feel inside, but they are fleeting and few and far between, and I feel guilty taking them at all. I feel like a thief, pinching time from my career and my family. I feel selfish. Can you feel selfish when you don't really know your true self?

I go to training one day and a property manager looks at me. He tilts his head askance. *What's that on your lips?* he asks. *What's wrong with them? They look … pink.*

I freeze. I swear 10 seconds pass while I summon my answer, while my mind scrambles and circles and tries to land on something that will save me. It's like a game of musical chairs. The music has stopped and I'm not expecting the silence, and I sprint wildly around the circle looking for a chair, please, *fuck*, I need a chair, any chair!

Adrenaline kicks in and the answer comes, and with it sweet relief.

I've just eaten an icy pole. Strawberry, I say. *Fuck it's hot out here today, eh?*

As the first season begins, the trappings of adulthood take shape in my life. I buy a block of land in Marangaroo and have a house built there. I go to visit an insurance agent – a guy from AMP – and set up our superannuation. I walk across the road afterwards and a thought occurs, so I share it with Joanne. *We've got a house, we've got a child, we've got investments – we'd better get married.* Some proposal, but she says yes, then and there.

I spend a fortnight of bank pay and one month's worth of my Eagles retainer on an engagement ring. We have an engagement party on the same day as the christening for Brooke. We go to a church in Nollamara first, and baby Brooke is dressed in frilly white lace, like a beaming bright flower. I wear a horrible grey knitted jumper and a long mullet, curly at the sides, and we gather next in the back yard of Joanne's parents for a barbecue. All her extended family is there, dozens of them, but there's little of mine. My mum. Nanna Flo. I realise how thin and tattered is the fabric of the Laidley clan.

I want to say that it feels as though another piece of this jigsaw dream world I'm trying to build has fallen into place, but I'm struggling more than ever. I feel that other thing, that other me – *the real me* – pulling at this compromised version of me.

I've always thought of those urges and feelings and proclivities as living inside me, deep down, buried within. But they're bundled now, and bigger, and they're trying to pull away. I visualise my other self now as something I carry with me. I don't know why, but in the image in my mind, I carry this other self on my right side, just above my hip.

This other self sits there throbbing, a lump on my waist, trying to get out, wanting air and light and love, like a conjoined twin I couldn't quite absorb, who's still alive and whose heartbeat is growing stronger. There is another person walking alongside me at all times now. I can throw an arm around her, and hold her, this little vulnerable version of me. And sometimes I do.

Sometimes she's soothed and happy and contented, or at least placated. But most of the time she's struggling, trying to break free and lashing out when she can't.

whack, whack, whack

I start getting suspended. The footy field feels like the perfect place to let the anger out. The fights can be nasty because the people you're fighting are athletes and full of pride, but professional players also don't like getting reported. Players know the crowd is watching and that the television cameras are recording. They know if they miss games they'll miss match payments, and have to win back their place in the side.

A footy fight isn't a street fight anyway. There are rules to obey. Niceties to observe. Pick a quarrel out here and it quickly becomes a pantomime melee, and your mates charge in and it becomes a silly rolling scrum, and the niggling punches and headlocks and elbows you inflict are largely consequence free. The football field – if you're willing to miss a few matches for your crimes – is the ideal place to spend any menace you've been saving. And so that's what I do. I've been doing it for a while, actually – holding on to my anger and letting it go on the ground.

In 1986, just ahead of the State of Origin game, I'm playing for West Perth against our arch rivals, East Perth, and I chase a player down. When I'm angry I tackle in a very specific way. I catch the player and grab them using my right arm, and once they're held, I swing my dominant left arm into them – a whack to the gut, a smack to the head, fist on kidneys, knuckles on ribs. This day my hand is cocked and firing on repeat – *whack, whack, whack* – and

I'm not even sure who I'm hitting or what he's done to deserve it. Beat me in a contest maybe? He probably did nothing.

I play against Swan Districts one day, and I notice Shane Renfree on the team sheet. I don't like Shane Renfree. I forget why. It doesn't even matter. But for some stupid reason he matters to me. *You'll get yours, sunshine.*

I barely remember the passage of play, but it's impossible to miss the newspaper the next day. There I am on the back page, on top of him. My knees are on his shoulders and his arms are pinned. He's defenceless and I'm belting the living shit out of him, unloading everything I have. The shot they choose is of my fist in his eye socket. I get four weeks on the sidelines.

I do a lot of fitness work these days, with Laurie Flanders, the guy who trained Maurice Rioli through his Golden Gloves bouts. I box on off nights as an extra training session. I box before games to warm myself up. I can go 12 rounds now, which feels like a feather in my cap, but it's not. Friends and family come to me. *You've always played on the edge*, they say, *but you're tipping over. It's no good for your footy and it's no good for you.*

This is true in the new team, too, playing for the Eagles. We play against Carlton on a Friday night at the WACA, and I line up on a big unit called Paul Meldrum. The ball comes into their forward line and Meldrum rises to take the mark. I come screaming in from a distance, throwing a roundhouse that fucking hard, and knocking him right across the temple. He takes the mark anyway, doesn't even turn around, just trots off to take his shot from 35 metres out. He has claret streaming down his face, but offers no reaction at all. I look down at my hand, and my left thumb is hanging 2 inches lower than it should. It's dislocated, removed from the socket, and the long bone itself is broken. I stare down at that busted hand, and up at him, and down at the hand again, and I am livid.

It happens again and again and again: against Footscray with a fist to the guts of Matt Hannebery at the Western Oval – *Number 15, you've been reported!* – against Sydney with an elbow to the head of Leon Higgins at the SCG – *Number 15, I'm reporting you!* – against Geelong with four punches in a row to Andrew Bews on the boundary line of the WACA – *Number 15, you're in the book this time!*

dancing until dawn

Joanne and I get married after the season ends and it's a strange few weeks. I go to the 21st birthday of an old friend from school a week beforehand, and there's a blue, a big one, and I crack the window of a car with my hand. The glass shatters and slices my finger – my ring finger – and it swells up and refuses to heal. Joanne will have to force my wedding band on over this cut next Saturday.

We have a bucks party but it's quiet, no strippers, and the night before the wedding my groomsmen all stay with me. Just the boys. Joanne and the girls are at her mums.

The wedding is held on 7 November 1987, at the Anglican church in Yokine, in front of 110 people. A few of my teammates are there. Keene, Lamb and Macnish. John Gastev, Steve Sadowski and Les Fong.

My mum comes and my brother, too. But not my dad. That's the way things go now. My daughter is a toddler, dancing at my feet, and when she gets married decades later, I am the only person from my family there.

I'm nervous inside the church. I think I probably look it, too. I'm wearing a black tuxedo with a white shirt and an upturned collar. The bridesmaids wear lilac, and Joanne's dress – made by her mum – is gorgeous. No meringue, she is a vision of slender fitted silk, with a long thin veil that trails down her back.

I'm emotional throughout the whole ceremony, and not because of what I hide inside. None of that is relevant to this moment. I am in love and this day is a pinnacle for me – a chance to build the home I always wanted. *Yes*, I say. *I do.*

The reception is held at Alan Bond's recently completed Observation City hotel in Scarborough. We do speeches and a buffet dinner of hot dishes is served from bain-maries. We're upstairs less than 45 minutes and then we're downstairs in the nightclub, dancing until dawn to 'Locomotion' and 'La Bamba', 'Livin' on a Prayer' and 'Funkytown', 'Nothing's Gonna Stop Us Now' and 'Boom Boom (Let's Go Back To My Room)'.

We honeymoon in Bali and on the first day there we hit the swim-up bar in the grotto, and drink all afternoon on the stools in the pool. I get absolutely poleaxed. We get ready to go out for dinner to celebrate the beginning of our life together, but I fall asleep in the bath.

this is us

Ron Alexander is no longer the coach of the West Coast Eagles in 1988. He gets toppled by his board, which comes as a surprise. Usually 11 wins and 11 losses and an eighth place finish would be enough, particularly for a new team. But Perth lacks patience.

When news breaks of his sacking there's something of a minor player mutiny. Ross Glendinning is the most vocal. The man lured back west to be captain stands down from that position in protest. But it matters little. We have a new coach. John Todd. He's coming. Ron was brought to the club to draw the new group together, and those seeds are just beginning to sprout, but Todd has a fierce finals record in this state. Perhaps the powers that be see him as the next step, the person most likely to deliver immediate success.

Todd brings his own players with him, too. The Eagles had the absolute pick of the litter only one year earlier – a handcrafted mix of youth and maturity, steel and flair. Todd doesn't care. He immediately recruits six players he's coached at Swan Districts – Kevin Caton, Joe Cormack, Brent Hutton, Don Langsford, Murray Rance and Troy Ugle.

To him: six familiar, loyal faces. To the rest of us: six favoured faces to compete against.

The legendary Todd is an interesting man to work under. He reads from the book of fire and brimstone, and looks like he belongs on the cover of that book. He has quite a bad limp, courtesy of a knee injury as a teenager. His fingers are horrible, too – bent and swollen and gnarled at the knuckles.

Yet I find him more affable than anything – willing to try new things. In the early days at the club, for instance, we struggle to play well in Melbourne. We can never get our flight schedule right, and the losses are blamed on touching down at Tullamarine Airport too late or too early.

But Todd believes something else is happening. He believes we're just not used to playing on waterlogged Victorian mudheaps. And so we begin training temporarily on the grounds of Guildford Grammar, a beautiful high school campus on the banks of the meandering Swan, where the clay surface becomes a sodden, sticky quagmire when the rain falls. We train there to mimic the appalling conditions out east, but for too long, and our tired legs are stuffed by Saturday.

Before an early game at Subiaco Oval, Todd makes us sit down in a circle, cross-legged, like kindergarten kids. He's got a flagon of plonk, and passes it around without explanation. Taking a heavy swig one by one, our mouths stink of drink mere moments before we run onto the field to play.

Todd tries another tactic – landing in Victoria at 11pm the night before the game. We catch a bus to a hotel on Royal Parade and he orders us to get changed, get our runners on, and head off for a jog through Royal Park. It's pitch black and past midnight when he blows his whistle for attention. *We're gonna do a handball drill,* he says. *Three points at that end. Crisscross lane work. Off you go.*

We look around at one another. No one has a footy. Troy Ugle screams out, *Oh, there it is!* and he runs off into the darkness then back again, pretending to cradle a football in his palm. Troy is black, and his white teeth seem to light up in the night as he grins. He gives off a fake handball and we're away. We do this pantomime training drill for 15 minutes, screaming and calling, laughing and guffawing.

But I learn quickly not to mistake this maverick edge for softness. Todd's training sessions are long – we do one exercise, a standard kicking drill, for 45 minutes. He's never far away from an old-school punishment – one hundred 100-metre sprints for a bad performance is standard operating procedure. And he likes to mimic the crucible of the game itself whenever possible – he has one murderous exercise where he kicks the ball high in the air to a group of three, while setting another group of three to storm at them as they hover unprotected beneath the falling Sherrin. If you're in the first group, you better not show him a short step. If you're in the second group, you better not show mercy.

On those nights training is quiet. No one speaks. The only sound is the muffled slap of skin on skin.

Player turnover causes tumult within a team. No one feels set or rested or relaxed. But we start talking about solidarity and sticking together in spite of it all. One guy stands out: Phil Scott from Subiaco.

Our first game in 1988 is against Geelong at Kardinia Park. I'm not named in the side. I watch from home in Perth as Phil kicks a goal and then raises a fist in the air and holds it there like an exclamation mark. He holds it high for what might only be 10 seconds, but he stretches the moment. It feels defiant and unifying – like the Black Power salute. It resonates with the group, and even with me, 3381 kilometres away.

It feels like he's saying to the squad and directly to me, *This is us.*

in and out of myself

Sometimes I think I'm good at this hiding who I am stuff. Other times I know I'm not.

Like the time my old girlfriend finds my wardrobe. *What's this?* I'd been helping Nanna Flo clean out her house, so it's easy enough to pretend the dresses are just a few more unwanted items, cast-offs from an old woman, a gift for the Samaritans.

Or the time I'm at home in Marangaroo, taking a moment to be myself, and I walk out to my car dressed as myself – *How could I be so fucking reckless?* – and I see the car of a football mate coming up the street. I bolt inside and he knocks on the door. *I know you're in there, mate!* he yells. *I just saw a girl coming in from your car.*

He keeps knocking, and I'm gulping down terror, choking on fear. He leaves though, eventually, but never quite lets it go. Many times in the future, he brings it up unprompted. *What happened that day? Who were you with?*

But the worst is what happens to Joanne. We've built a home that we love, and we're making the family we always wanted. She drives my car to the shops one day and finds discarded tissues with makeup smeared all over them.

She challenges me – as she should – about having an affair. I suppose, in some way, I am.

She asks me who it is. She demands an answer and deserves one.

Should I blame one of my teammates – say they used my car and I don't know who the tissues belong to?

Or should I make up a one-night stand – a fling with a footy groupie that means nothing to me?

What lie will feel better than telling the truth?

I own up to cheating.

I'm so sick of being afraid.

As the stress builds, I feel the muscles above my shoulders contract, and they tighten and twist into what they call a wry neck, into agonising torticollis. I'm in hospital all night and can barely move the next morning. But we have a game to play – round 7 against St Kilda – and I play anyway.

I rebound the ball out of the defensive space as well as I can, away from the arms of Tony Lockett. I'm exhausted at half-time and the club doctor gives me a can of Coke – *Scull this, now* – for the sugar hit. I go out feeling a little better but crash and burn all the same. I finish on the bench and Todd calls me there from the coaches' box. *You've had a monstrous 36 hours, mate*, he says. *Have a rest.*

This is only my second season of league football, and already it feels too much. Or too little. Too heavy. I'm too young and too close to the fringe. In and out of the side. In and out of love with football. In and out of myself.

I leave for the airport, for the final game of the season against Footscray, and I find out my car has been stolen from home. The police want to search for it and I accidentally give them the wrong registration. We win the game. We're going to play in the finals. I should be elated but instead I'm sitting in the change rooms at Whitten Oval, wondering about my car, wondering what else can go wrong.

The following week we play in front of 43,000 people – the lowest finals attendance in a long time – in an elimination final against Melbourne at Waverley. It's Ross Glendinning's last game, and he kicks five goals, and people will remember that.

We're two points up in the final minutes when Murray Wrensted runs towards goal and bounces and misses his shot, and now we're in front by three points. People will remember that, too.

The ball is kicked out from full-back, deep into the middle, and then it gets kicked forward to a pack at the teeth of the Melbourne goals, and it spills to Garry Lyon, who snaps the winner for the Demons. We lose by three points. People will definitely remember that.

What no one seems to remember – but I know – is that when that ball was kicked to the teeth of the Melbourne goals, it didn't have to end up with Garry Lyon. A West Coast defender launched at that pack, and he spoiled the ball. He spoiled it directly to the front of the contest. Directly to where he shouldn't have. To where he'd been taught his whole life *not* to spoil the ball.

That Eagle is me. I'll always remember that, even if no one else does.

I retreat into my cave immediately. I talk to no one on the plane ride home. I grab a window seat and feign sleep with my face against the cold glass. I dream of a season of cresting and crashing waves, of swallowing water and gasping for air, of being a parent and partner and player. Of balancing and failing. And falling.

I am 21 years old.

men are weird

We win the first round of the pre-season competition in February 1989, knocking off St Kilda in the Panasonic Cup at Waverley. A win away from Perth demands we go out. We go to Chasers nightclub in Prahran, and lose ourselves in glasses of cheap Scotch and Coke.

It's a Wednesday night so the club is far from full. There are dark corners where you can even hear yourself speak, and that's what a handful of us do – chat and carouse, and make new friends. We find our circle merging with another – a group of trans girls who've wandered over from queer headquarters in Commercial Road, and are out for a bit of fun.

It's late at night, or rather early morning, when we stumble out onto Chapel Street to hail cabs. One Silver Top follows the next, speeding us in the direction of St Kilda East, to the home of one of the girls we've just met, to keep on partying.

We sit there – six players and four transitioning women – and drink more, talk more. I fight to stifle a laugh many times as I'm sure the other boys don't have any idea what's going on.

Men are weird, you see, and although they often save their strangest private predilections for when they are alone with a woman, they also do strange things in the company of their teammates. One of them alone might feel uncomfortable here, but they fall easily into a tribal dynamic. Tonight, in this drunk and delirious room, we're just a bunch of teammates who found somewhere to kick on after a win.

For me, though, this is the first time in my life my two worlds have overlapped. It feels surreal and I want more of it.

I talk to a couple of the girls all night. I accept these girls for who they are – a group of young girls, out midweek – and I have a million questions. They're all presented under the banner of simple curiosity but there's no way known I don't seem a bit desperate.

How do you buy bras? Who knows? How do you choose who to let know? How did you tell your family? When was the first time that you thought that maybe you were a little different? How has it been understanding yourself – going from being unhappy and depressive and anxious to out and proud?

This night is my biggest education so far. My only education so far. There's no internet. Not really any books. There's no lexicon or language for what I am or who I am. No resources. These girls are my only resource.

It's late now and we have to be back at the hotel by breakfast. I leave their house feeling full, smiling at the vanilla sky of the morning. As we wait for the taxi back to Carlton to arrive, there's one thing that we all acknowledge with absolute conviction. We all know that spending time with these girls is not a good look to anyone who wasn't there.

Right, we agree. *This does not go anywhere.*

treading water

The 1989 season begins poorly. We lose the semi-final of the pre-season cup to Melbourne, who had beaten us only six months earlier in an elimination final. This is not a good sign.

I'm not playing but instead sitting injured in the coaches' box. It's odd to see Todd work in this space. He's different in here. He's a barracker, almost a fan. *Attaway, boy!* He's positive about every little thing we do. *Good onya, Johnny!*

Then he leaves the box and goes down to the field for his address during breaks. He goes to those same players pointing and barking, all orders and admonitions. Maybe it's just that he sees the loss coming, and can't stomach the notion. Maybe he's afraid of where this season will go from here. He's right to be worried.

In round 1 we play at our WACA fortress but lose to Essendon. Todd's switching up the side, bringing in those Swan Districts boys of his, but also blooding young rookies, the spearhead Peter Sumich and midfielder Don Pyke. Craig Turley plays his first game, too. These players will be crucial cogs in the West Coast side for many years, but right now they're green. We get beaten by a more experienced team.

We keep losing in that manner, too. The next week we're beaten at Geelong 26 goals to 11, and again it comes down to experience. Todd has jettisoned the veterans, a mistake compounded by the fact that those veterans – Mark Zanotti,

Alex Ishchenko and John Gastev – are popular club men. Todd begins losing even the players he's brought into the club. We play a game at Princes Park and he storms into the huddle at quarter time, walking past a handful of players to find Turley, who he punches at close quarters, throwing a rising fist that catches the bottom of the wingman's chin.

He tries in vain to turn things around. We lose to the Swans in Sydney one day and our bus is probably going to be late to the airport, so Todd has the bus driver pull over. *Right*, he says. *We played like a bunch of drunks today. We're late, and gonna miss the plane. We can head to the airport and get the next flight, or we can stay, and get out on the piss.*

He's hoping we'll choose the latter, opting to drown our sorrows and perhaps come together as a team in foreign territory. But we're tired, beaten, and we've heard 'Good old Sydney' ring out 20 times – once for every goal they kicked – and it's Sunday night.

Nah, the boys say. *Gotta get home. Gotta work tomorrow.*

We lose 11 of the first 13 games. Hawthorn beats us 141 to 50. Essendon beats us 160 to 18. That one is the coach killer. Todd loses his job.

I have a few injuries, a few dips in form and another hefty suspension. I've been a VFL player for three seasons yet year on year I've played only 10 games, 11 games and 10 games. No full seasons. No settled position. No continuity. No happiness. I'm an underachiever, cheating on my dream. Time is ticking. What's going on with me anyway?

My suspension means I miss a month of match payments, and it's not well timed. In August I had quit my job at the bank, found a shopfront in Balga and opened up Dean Laidley Sportz.

The business starts slowly, as all new businesses do. But I've put a second mortgage on our home, and money quickly becomes tight. Interest rates are hovering at around 15 per cent. 'The recession Australia had to have' is just around the corner.

I sell footy boots and cricket bats, aerobics gear and bathers and goggles. T-ball is big in Western Australia, so I sell plenty of T-ball stands and baseball gloves. The 'Life. Be in it' federal fitness campaign started 15 years ago, and 'Let's Get Physical' was a smash hit back in 1981, but I still sell running shorts to a lot of Norms and leggings to a lot of Olivias.

All the same, I'm not sure I've done the right thing. I'm not in a shopping centre but rather a strip mall. I don't really have widespread name recognition, and more worryingly, I don't have much foot traffic either. It's not that the store instantly ruins me. It's not that I'm forced to close. It doesn't crash and burn so much as smoulder and smoke, threatening to catch fire in a big way but never really doing so.

It's basically an added responsibility. A new worry. A new drain on my finances and attention. I have to keep watching that store, tending to that smoke, hoping it'll spark, not quite understanding that it never will – that it will in fact eat away at my bank balance and my time for almost a decade, until I finally let it go. It's a poor decision in a string of poor decisions.

I know I'm not drowning but I'm also not swimming. I'm treading water and tiring myself out.

belief

There's no social media in 1989. Not even cable television. And so the traditional 24-hour news cycle for the current affairs of the day has not yet ramped up to its dizzying millennium blur. But if there is one area of Australian life that hints at our ravenous appetite for information and innuendo, it's football. And football in the fishbowl of Perth even more so.

The rumour circulating almost immediately after John Todd departs the West Coast Eagles is one name, whispered again and again and again, to the point that it's no surprise when Mick Malthouse simply wanders into our aquatic training centre one afternoon.

Malthouse, of course, had played the game for St Kilda and then Richmond, retired at 30 and stepped immediately into senior coaching at 31, leading Footscray for five years. Now he's here, bringing with him a reputation for being uncompromising. *I'll fuck off anyone who puts themselves before the team*, he tells us, and we believe him, because we've heard all about his falling out with Brad Hardie, a Brownlow medallist who refused to curtail his free-running play in favour of the defensive discipline of the coach. Hardie left, Malthouse stayed. Malthouse won, because Malthouse always wins.

I'm splashing around in the lanes recovering from a session when Mick wanders over to the edge of the pool. When he wants you to hear him, Mick points right at you. That's what he does now. He aims an index finger at my chest: *I love the way you play.*

Pre-season training usually starts around Melbourne Cup time. Perth is three hours behind Melbourne, of course, meaning our spring racing functions start at 9am. This year a few of the boys ask if they can skip Tuesday-morning weights, and we get our first sermon. Mick doesn't whack us for asking the question, but he explores what might happen if we go down that path – where we'll end up as a side if we allow that kind of lazy exception to the rule. He will not have it, least of all when it comes to weights.

Weights are important to him. There are rumours developing about the Eagles, about steroids – about players getting on the juice. We have a knack for taking young boys and building them up into supermen. They take the field and their biceps and triceps bulge. Their calves and quads are defined. Maybe it's the sun over here, an optical illusion, the result of our tans and the way the sweat seems to glisten on each bronzed body. More likely it's that we get big quickly because we place value on size. John Worsfold is an early and ardent believer, and he brings others with him. Players like Guy McKenna start out wispy and breakable then quickly build shoulders and backs and cores and hips that can be used as weapons – frames that can demolish other people.

Mick gets into it, too. He's only just turned 37 and has a barrel chest and a set of guns. He pumps iron as hard and as long as the players, because player see, player do. It might be the only part of what he does that doesn't rub off on me. *You've gotta put on weight*, he tells me. *Gotta put it on, mate.*

Fuck that. Sopping wet, I might tip the scale at 71 kilos, maximum. I'm never much heavier than a jockey and I like it that way. I won't let Mick change that about me. I'll do something else instead. Work on my kicking maybe.

He has a philosophy of stretching your abilities, and doing something more than the set program. Doing 'enough' is never really enough. Footy clubs are good at drilling that mindset into you. They usually call it doing 'extras'. Mick calls them 'specials'.

Mainy, what special are you working on? Strength. *Right, off ya go.*

Bluey, what special are you doing? Kicking. *Yep, off ya go.*

There is nothing optional about these bits of self-assigned homework. You do them or else. And if you miss one of the regular sessions – the actual core training – bloody well look out.

Mick knows the message he wants to send. *This is what it will take to win a grand final. These are the sacrifices.*

And what you begin seeing from here on is the formation of a methodical team, clinical about group success. At training you see players rising, pushing one another out of the way, demanding better of one another, making sure they're part of it. Mick inherits the makings of a great side, too. Worsfold, McKenna, Lewis, Turley, Mainwaring, Sumich and Pyke are all young. Glen Jakovich is coming. Dean Kemp, too. Brett Heady. Peter Matera. Ashley McIntosh.

I haven't lost my talent but I'm on the precipice of being passed by these pricks. I need to make 1990 count.

I eat up the track. My fitness grows and my confidence, too. We win five of our first seven games and I'm on fire. I gather 19 touches in one game, then 27 in the next game, then 24, then 30. I'm finding the footy, gliding over the ground and grinding opponents into the dirt. I'm coming of age, on track for my best year yet.

It's all Mick. I feel as though I can finally play in the VFL the way that I did in the WAFL. He gives me belief and entrusts me with knowledge. He breaks down the game and the players I'm playing against, giving me a new perspective or strategy every week. *We can beat them,* he says. *And you can beat him. Here's how.*

I share an ethos with my coach – no quarter given and none asked – and this makes football so simple. My ideas and his ideas sit so well together. I like this feeling.

Kill or be killed.

I love the way you play.

poleaxed

It's Friday night in Melbourne, 11 May 1990, and because the old southern grandstand of the MCG is being demolished to make way for the new Great Southern Stand, we get changed in the dank old Richmond rooms.

I put my uniform on – proud royal blue and light, bright yellow – and chat idly with Steve Malaxos. He was our inaugural best and fairest winner and is now our captain. A year or so ago he tore the posterior cruciate ligament in his knee, and missed a good chunk of the season. I've had little injuries here and there but nothing like that, so I wonder how the knee's going. *It's good, mate*, he says. *Pretty pleased with it.* Then we run out together to play the Demons in front of 32,269 people.

It's a tough game but I'm running strongly. When the ball is kicked down the wing near the remains of the old grandstand, the absence of a crowd on that side of the stadium is a little eerie. It's quiet as the ball soars over my head. I track it in flight over my shoulder. It hits a pack and I run front and centre to scoop up the crumbs.

I feel a light tackle on my hips. It's Melbourne midfielder Glenn Lovett, grasping and clutching at me from an arm's length distance. I'll be able to shake him off. But another player – one with a shock of blonde hair – cuts me off. Stephen Tingay comes out of nowhere and tackles me from the side. Together, the pair of them have me pinned.

That's not a big problem, except that the studs of my left boot are sticking to the surface of the MCG, and my left leg is locked dead straight. It won't budge, so as the tackle unfolds the full force of Tingay's body falls directly upon my leg, and the joint buckles.

The knee collapses inwards. The lower leg folds outwards. It's broken at a right angle.

I thought I had a high tolerance for pain, but it turns out I don't. I want to scream. A few seconds pass and I can hear a voice. *Get up!* Standing above me is John Worsfold. *Fucking get up!* He says it half-a-dozen times but that won't change anything. *I can't get up, Woosha. I can't fucking move.*

My team is on top of the ladder. I'm in the form of my life. And now. And now …

They lift me onto a stretcher, and the pain is sharp and throbbing, both a sting and an ache. In the rooms I begin to feel queasy. The doctor pulls and pushes and prods, and I can see fear in his eyes. It occurs to me that I might never play again.

After half-time they take the ice off the joint, tell me to shower, and help me up off the bench. I lift my left leg so I can slide my shorts off, and my lower leg wobbles and dangles, like it's barely attached. I have no control over any part of my calf or shin or ankle or foot.

I feel a deep creeping panic as I look down at my lower limb, while it swings and sways, back and forth, pendulous, like a metronome, like a rusty gate on a broken hinge. I throw up all over the change room floor.

I've been to Mount Hospital once before. Two years ago I played against Essendon on a warm autumn day at Windy Hill. The crowd was so close at those old suburban grounds you could feel their angry breath on your cheek. We were going really well, too. I remember running off half-back and charging towards a loose bouncing ball. Coming the other way was ruckman Paul Salmon, who stood 206 centimetres and weighed 112 kilograms.

It was one of those times in footy when it's 'your turn'. Coaches have a thousand different directions for this moment – *play your role, do your job, hold your line* – and that's what I did. I charged at the ball knowing a much bigger man was charging at it, too. I turned to protect myself and his knee collected the bottom of my spine, cracking three vertebrae: L3, L4 and L5. Back in Perth I spent the next four weeks in a 3-metre by 3-metre medical pool, lolling on an inflatable ring, my backside through the centre, because it's the only way I could exist without feeling pain.

Now I'm back in this place, talking to Dr Tim Keenan. He's chirpy, I'm not.

Wasn't that a bloody great weekend a few weeks ago? he asks. *Great day.*

I remember now. He's a mad Claremont fan, and earlier that month I was up in the social club with him, watching a WAFL game and we got poleaxed together. Now here he is again, and I'm poleaxed in an altogether different way.

This is the worst knee I've ever seen, he says, by way of introduction. *This is worse than any knee I've seen in a CAR CRASH, and I've been operating for 25 years.*

For fuck's sake. When a patient asks for the straight dope, they don't always want the straight dope. But that's what I get. Now his analysis becomes surgical.

Look, you've torn your anterior cruciate ligament, he says. *You've ripped your medial ligament off the bone – we might not even be able to find it. The ligament at the back of your knee – the posterior cruciate ligament – has been shredded. The lateral collateral ligament is snapped. This is going to be a long road. A long road.*

a particular kind of loneliness

Buzz, hissssss ... Buzz, hissssss ...

Before I can open my eyes, that's what I hear.

I've been under – having surgery to repair this mangled knee – and I was warned in advance by the doctor that he was trying something new. Namely, tightening the grafts more than ever before in a reconstruction. He thinks it's the only way the knee will hold.

The downside is that the joint will be stiff initially, and will need immediate movement, which is why my left leg is now Velcro-strapped into a fibreglass casing, which is attached to a set of hydraulic pistons, which flex the repaired knee. Bend, straighten, bend, straighten. *Buzz, hiss, buzz, hiss.*

I know I can't train and that I won't be playing for a while, but it's still hard to get home and do nothing. I sit in front of the television watching the 1990 World Cup, taking in every soccer match every night, the heroics and the failures, West Germany over Argentina, Italy against England. I see more than most do of the 52 games in that tournament.

I move myself around on crutches and tell people I'll be back by finals, not yet realising I won't be back for two years. The club is great. They say all the right things. *You're the first West Coast Eagle to do a knee, but you won't be the last,* they say. *We'll support you.* Blah blah blah.

You have empathy from everyone but you want it from no one in this situation. A particular kind of loneliness settles in. The umbilical cord is cut. You're not part of the mothership anymore. You're not on the training track or the field. I pass the time by following Mick around at training. I stand silently, trying to learn whatever I can. I begin to understand the game differently from before.

Subiaco Oval is a long oval – 180 metres end to end – but also a very skinny oval – 122 metres across. Mick wants to use the space available efficiently, using angles to pass the ball by foot, going off the straight line, finding creativity in geometry. He marks dots all over the ground. One dot for where a forward needs to stand to launch his leads. Another dot for the place a defender needs to stand to best guard ground at stoppage. He talks me through it all – how to use the safety of the boundary line often, and the open corridor sparingly. He marries regimentation with flair. It's freedom within a framework. Structured spontaneity.

I begin to see how a single coaching manoeuvre can stop the cogs of a match from turning, and how a little oil on one moving part can send the gears of the game whirring and spinning again. I know these revelations are changing the way I see football, and will perhaps change my career path. But it's hard. It's very hard.

I start running after 12 weeks. The barest shuffle. I can't bend or extend, or really even lift my thigh. Bluey McKenna has started a side job as a sports reporter on Channel 10. He's heard that I'm seeing a physiotherapist and making progress, and wants to come and film a segment on my recovery, running in the park near Dean Laidley Sportz. I see it on the news that night and I'm horrified. My knee has no flexion at all. I'm limping. I'm crippled.

I see the surgeon again and get a new course of treatment. I get put under local anaesthetic so he and his assistant can climb up onto a medical examination table and press and bend my knee manually. The two men use all their muscle and body weight to force the joint into the shape they want, attempting to break up the gnarly scar tissue that's hampering my range of movement. The surgeon calls it 'crunching' my knee. They do this procedure three times. It's painful every time.

When they're not doing that, I see a physiotherapist in his office, and he straps me into a new machine. I start with a bent leg and try to straighten it myself, and the machine resists me. Then I start with a straight leg and try to bend on my own, and the machine resists me. I drive in and bind myself to this contraption for two hours every day. And at night I have homework – a rudimentary version of the machine involving me lying on my back with weights attached to my ankles.

I miss out on the Eagles playing finals in 1990, and spend all of 1991 in and out of rehabilitation. I play tennis, because the biometrics of the sport require me to move backwards and forwards, and side to side. It requires dynamic movements and short lateral adjustments. I begin to find some sense of fluency on my feet. My proprioception returns.

I get myself fit enough to play in the WAFL, for West Perth against Claremont at the WACA, but other players are running past me, literally and metaphorically. I've been a grumpy bastard getting over this shit, and now, as the second half begins, I just feel sad. I go to mark a ball and a pack of eight players falls on top of me, fracturing my vertebrae again. My spine is brutalised. I'll miss another month.

I go to training on Wednesday night and can barely get my bottom lip up off the grass. I don't want to look up. What is there to see anyway? I go to see Mick, chat with the coach, tick that box before going home. We're in a briefing room with a huge wall-to-wall whiteboard.

He knows I'm struggling. *Look at the whiteboard.*

I look, but it's blank, wiped clean of whatever tactical diagram it once presented. *Huh?*

He tells me to look again, so I do, but it's clean. I feel like everything in the world is conspiring against me now. *You're mad, you bastard,* I say. *What are you trying to do to me now?*

Mick smiles, and speaks softly. *Look in the left-hand corner, down the bottom.*

This whiteboard is perhaps 4 metres wide and 1.5 metres high, and there on the very bottom edge is a tiny bit of writing, maybe 1 centimetre high. This is what Mick wants me to find.

See your initials down there?

Yep, DL.

Well, what's written straight after it?

2. DL2.

Dean Laidley. Two games. That's all I wanted from you, Mick says. *Play two games in the WAFL, and I was going to play you in the seniors.*

My coach had pencilled in my comeback. My injury fucked it up, but he was going to play me. I feel gratitude pour out of me. The football club re-signs me soon after as well, for the 1992 season, knowing I probably won't play for them again until then.

I don't quite have my speed back, or my power, and the penetration on my kick is weak, but I have the faith of the coach. He was gonna play me. *I love the way you play.*

family first

Maybe things aren't so bad. Maybe I should think about someone else for a change.

On 1 July, Joanne and I go to the doctor. She's heavily pregnant and struggling with it, and I haven't been paying attention to that. I can feel her looking at me, pleading for this pregnancy to be over.

The doctor wants us to wait another week, but I won't have it. Maybe I'm angry on Joanne's behalf, or maybe I'm just sick of listening to medical professionals. Either way, I unload. *We are coming back here at 9 o'clock tomorrow morning*, I hiss, *and YOU are taking that baby out then.*

Perhaps having that date with destiny relaxes Joanne. It relaxes me. Her water breaks early the next morning. On 2 July 1991, our son is born. We name him Kane. He's a long skinny thing, red and peeling. Absolutely cooked, well overdue.

I'm able to give him my attention, too, especially in those weeks immediately after the birth. I've been such a poor parent, partner, son, brother and teammate of late. Oddly enough, my injury now allows me to maintain a better work–life balance, putting family first, football second and myself third.

I have a final knee operation when Kane is six weeks old. Exploratory surgery in late August. That's when they see it – the ligament catching on the bone, the cause of all that tension and pain.

It's an issue with a quick fix. They shave 1 millimetre off the bone and all of a sudden the ligament glides smoothly, the knee moves freely. The swelling comes down and I can run and jump. I can pivot and turn. I can balance and stretch.

I can finally shift my focus away from what's happened to my body, and back to what's happening in my mind.

i'm the matchstick and the flame

The girl inside me is angry. She knows what's up, and realises the lights have been turned down. She doesn't like the darkness, and who can blame her? She wants what any person wants – a chance to be themself – and I haven't been able to give her that for months on end.

There was no time. No space. No air. Things bubbled and brewed and who knows, maybe I took that time with injury so badly because I neglected this other part of me. It makes sense. If you place your very identity in limbo – cast it into indefinite purgatory – is it any wonder everything else falls apart?

But now, on a Friday morning in the spring of 1991, I'm finally able to calm that anger, and soothe that soreness. I fetch a chair and bring it into the corridor of our house in Marangaroo – the central hallway that links the lounge room and the kids' rooms and the master bedroom. I place the chair below a manhole in the ceiling, which is smudged a little with my dusty fingerprints. I push the wooden plate up into the roof, and reach an arm inside. I find a black plastic bag, inside of which are my skirts and tops and shoes and makeup. The manhole is my hidey-hole.

I have a few precious hours to myself today, and I'm planning to use them well. I'm going to try on a few things, and then a few more things. I'm going to apply a little lip gloss and then a little lipstick, and see which one I like best. I'm going to go even further, in fact, and finally indulge a desire that's gone unmet for years now. I'm going to do something I've only dared to dream.

I find the outfit I like most, the makeup that looks just right, blow a kiss into the mirror and walk out of my front door. I walk down the pathway to my car, open the door, get inside, turn the key and drive off down the street. It is the first time I've been in public as myself.

I'm going to the Subiaco markets. I decided this days earlier, I'm not sure why. Regardless, I'm headed there on a mission, to walk among the people of Perth as they buy their fruit and vegetables, and eat their lunch off plastic trays in the food court, but I'm petrified just driving down Wanneroo Road.

I cruise into the city, trying to turn away from every pedestrian, then I veer off onto Main Street, head all the way down over Scarborough Beach Road, then past my old flat on Harborne Street up towards Wembley, with Lake Monger on the left. I go through the traffic lights near the little primary school and reach a stop sign. This is when I feel most vulnerable, when I throw all my willpower at the passing traffic to clear – *Hurry up! Hurry up! Hurry up!* – in case someone pulls up beside me.

I look up at the car sitting next to mine, and there in the driver's seat, waiting to turn, is one of the directors of the West Perth Football Club. This is a man who knows me, and knows me well. He would know my car, too – a Commodore, red the colour of a Sherrin, with a few West Coast Eagles stickers on the rear window. Is he there 20 seconds, or 20 years? I'm not sure. He doesn't spot me, but from this moment on when driving dressed as me, I will never pull up directly alongside another car. I make it a rule to stagger the place I stop, to offset my car against the next one by half a length – like the teeth of a zipper, or a row of bricks.

It's amazing how much you inhabit your body in such moments. Fear creeps coolly across my skin. My mouth feels parched, so I gulp again and again and feel as though I'm choking on each dry swallow. My belly drops as if my guts are empty.

I might be a wreck on the inside but I'm fabulous on the outside. My hair is up and full, blow-dried with mousse. I wear Blues Brothers black sunglasses. Blush and foundation and eye shadow and eyeliner, applied as best I can. I'm wearing a long maroon flowing skirt, with matching sleeveless top, and red high heels. I'm the matchstick and the flame.

I search for a parking space. This one looks too far away. This one looks too close. This one looks perfect – except for all the people nearby. I try Haydn Bunton Drive and Hay Street and Rokeby Road, where the hairdressers and upmarket cafes and restaurants are bustling, and I finally roll to a stop in a car park on Roberts Road.

As I step out of the car, I learn another lesson. I learn to park on asphalt or concrete, instead of what I've parked on here – a bumpy mix of rock and scoria and old rough topping. My heels sink into the dry, crushed rubble and I stumble. All I want to be is a fucking person – a woman in the goddamn world – but to get there apparently I'll have to hobble across an empty yard trying not to fall.

I walk into the market, finally, and I'd like to say there are moments I enjoy completely, where I don't feel afraid, but fear envelops every step. My entry through the door is so frightened and fast that I T-bone a poor woman, knocking her over completely. I apologise and recoil, imagining all the eyes turning my way, which causes me to scurry even more quickly, and that causes me to worry more intensely about scurrying so quickly, and whether I'm going to topple over again.

I do one lap of the market – past the food stalls and the art and craft stands and the T-shirt shops and the record tents and the old ladies who've crocheted their toilet-roll holders and the people selling fairy floss and toffee apples – and I get out of that dizzying space as fast as I fucking can. It's a success and a failure. A thrill and a defeat. An awkward first step but a step all the same.

The word transgender doesn't exist for me. I've heard about cross-dressing as a sexual fantasy, as a way to get your rocks off, a turn-on, a kink, a delicious twist. But this is not a fetish. This is about feeling calm, and comfortable, and self-aware. It's about feeling right. Unfortunately I just feel afraid and the fear is visceral. I have the most overwhelming urge to get home, now.

What are you doing?

Why are you this way?

Do you want to get fucking caught?

At home I get changed, get washed and get settled. I pack my clothing and makeup away in my hidey-hole. I get the Ajax spray from the laundry and wipe the dusty fingerprints from the ceiling. I curse my craziness and shake my head at my recklessness. I sigh and reflect and go to bed.

But I wake up with the memory of yesterday, and I enjoy that memory. It feels good to have it. It felt good to be me. I want my next excursion. In 12 hours I've gone from *Never again* to *When can I do that again?* The push and the pull are at war now. The fight inside is growing.

always a space

I'm in a good space, coming into the back end of the season. But I suspect it won't last.

West Coast are flying, and hovering in the back of my mind is a constant worry. *Success is coming for this group, and you're gonna miss it.*

Sure enough, the Eagles finish the year as minor premiers, on top of the ladder, and they knock over Geelong in the preliminary final, earning a place in the 1991 Grand Final against Hawthorn.

The whole squad goes over to Melbourne. Players like me, who aren't in the side or even a chance to be selected in the side, stay in separate accommodation to the senior team. We stay in self-contained units at the Carlton end of Exhibition Street, five guys to a flat. A group of the unwanteds go out to dinner in Chinatown. It's me and Paul Peos and Don Holmes and Phil Narkle and others. We sit down to dinner and Laurie Keene asks the group a question – *What's the best thing that's happened to you this year?* – and we go around the table slowly answering. When it's my turn there's only one thing to say. *Boys, it's now September, and I had a son in July, and his name is Kane James Laidley, and he's everything to me.*

The guys nearly fall off their chairs. They didn't know. My teammates have no idea I have a newborn son. That's how far removed I've become – how withdrawn from the group.

They're mortified by this, as if it's their fault, but it's a reflection only on me and the remove I create between myself and others. There's always a space I keep people from entering, and without knowing it this secret valley has grown into a canyon.

Football is a big deal in Victoria. The grand final is a big deal in Melbourne.

The fans turn out for each ritual on the finals calendar, but the Eagles thumb their noses at one of the most sacred – the motorcade through the city streets on grand final eve. They're a no-show, and in this city that qualifies as a scandal.

The justification is sound. Mick wants his side's preparation to be the same as for any match, flying in on the afternoon prior, with a captain's run training session before the game the next day. But in practice this means that the Hawthorn players all ride through the city streets in the back of convertibles while the Eagles players are mid-air. From the corner of Swanston and Collins streets I stand watching as the empty Eagles cars drive past. Maybe it's just theatre – the upstart interstater attempting a raid on a Victorian prize – but it doesn't sit well with the public.

I wake up on grand final day and I'm not part of it. Having wanted to play on the last day in September my whole life, I don't quite know how to describe the feeling. It's like waking up on Christmas to no presents. Going to an anniversary dinner after a fight. Celebrating a birthday with a terminal illness.

It's spring in Melbourne but the wind is brisk, and it feels even more so out at Waverley Park, where the season decider is being held while the MCG is rebuilt. It's a good day for footy folklore and trivia. Daryl Braithwaite sings the national anthem. Rob de Castella laughs with the rest of the country as Angry Anderson performs from inside a car that looks like the Batmobile. I don't find anything that funny on the day.

The players who miss out on grand finals often mouth platitudes about the team. If they admit anything of what they're feeling, they hide their real emotion in pride. *This day is bittersweet*, they say, *because while I'm not out there playing, I'm so happy for my teammates to have this chance. No grudges*, they add. *I'm just stoked for the boys.*

But it's bullshit. Complete bullshit. A part of me – and not a small part either – hopes we lose today. Because if we lose, I won't be missing out. If we lose, I'll be a better chance of getting a spot in the side next year. If we lose, I won't have to look back on this day forever with lingering regret.

These thoughts are powerful but they're also fleeting. Shame is what chases them away. You get bitter for a while and the bitterness feels righteous, but then you catch yourself and you get a little disgusted with yourself. *Hang on*, you think. *We've been in this together. We've worked our arses off. I can't wish bad luck upon them – not just so I can get my lick or my look next year.*

Hawthorn win convincingly, 139 to 86, and I feel awful. I feel awful because I think of Craig Turley who struggled out there today. I think of Michael Brennan, a rock in defence, who found himself trailing the imperious Jason Dunstall on lead after lead, until the legendary spearhead kicked one, two, three, four, five, six goals, on the grandest stage. I think of Peter Wilson, playing with a jaw that was broken only a week prior, and how he was mauled by the Hawks only days after I visited him in hospital and handed him a bucket into which he could spit and spew blood.

I think of Theodore Roosevelt's famous 'Man in the Arena' address. It's actually part of a speech titled 'Citizenship in a Republic', which was delivered at the Sorbonne in Paris in 1910. Professional athletes love it, and any wonder …

It is not the critic who counts; not the man who points out how the strong man stumbles, or where the doer of deeds could have done them better. The credit belongs to the man who is actually in the arena, whose face is marred by dust and sweat and blood; who strives valiantly; who errs, who comes short again and again, because there is no effort without error and shortcoming; but who does actually strive to do the deeds; who knows great enthusiasms, the great devotions; who spends himself in a worthy cause; who at the best knows in the end the triumph of high achievement, and who at the worst, if he fails, at least fails while daring greatly, so that his place shall never be with those cold and timid souls who neither know victory nor defeat.

Am I a cold and timid soul now? The fans, the industry, the media – they don't know what these guys are going through. But I have more than an inkling. I know. And I should know better than to wish defeat on them, even in the barest passing thought.

hit, hit, hit, hit

Squats are my friend and my enemy next pre-season. My friend because they return me to the athlete I once was, and my enemy because they burn my fucking thighs and I hate them. I do lots of dead lifts, too. Solo sprints. Change-of-direction running. Fartlek running. I build back my fitness base with time trials. Two kilometres, 3 kilometres, 4 kilometres. I do the Eagles program with my teammates by day, then go to a public green space and do my own striding by night.

Cabrini Park on Marangaroo Drive is my spot. It's lush, but the oval has an artificial wicket in the centre, the kind of surface they pour sand over in winter, so that footy players won't fall on it and wrench their knee or burn off their skin. The park is well lit by night. I'm the only one there. I barely see my surrounds anyway. All I can see is the premiership cup. That's what I'm doing this for now. I'm not training to get back – I'm training to get better.

I've had an interview with Mick, who still has faith in me, but who noticed the same thing I did about my last season – my kick has lost distance. My ball drop isn't what it was either, and needs recalibrating. Missing targets is a career killer – at least it is when your coach builds mantras around possession football. *We fight that hard to get it,* he reasons, *why give it up?*

I'm a small defender now, with no designs on the midfield or half-forward. Time to put away childish things. I know my role. My role is to shut down and run off the quicker forwards in the competition, whether Phil Krakouer or Graham Wright or Nicky Winmar or Matthew Liptak or Chris Naish.

There are other Eagles who can play that role, and a few of them are playing it exceptionally well. I'm against Worsfold (the skipper), McKenna (the best half-back flank in the game) and Pyke (who brings the defence of a tagger and the attack of a centreman). They're savvy players, who will all go on to become senior coaches.

The only spot I can see to take is the seventh defender, maybe from a guy like Chris 'Muddy' Waterman, a swingman who has settled into his spot and won't be easy to dislodge either. But if I can do it – if I can find my way onto the field – I can hold on to that spot. The analogy I use is of the Australian cricket team: It's harder to get in than to get out.

I need the coaches to trust me and so I tick every box, and do every special on offer. I've been training while the boys were winding down from their grand final, meaning I'm in front in most drills, winning contested work, running through to every cone. I'm desperate again. Ravenous and rabid. *Kill or be killed.*

Before Christmas that's seen as a positive. People love it. Because there's nothing physically competitive yet. All they see is my work ethic and desire and confidence, and it costs them nothing – no dented pride or bruised abdomens. But in the new year when spots are on the line, the talk turns a little more plaintive. *Ease up, mate, for fuck's sake.*

The Australia Day long weekend is a turning point. Mick has designed a drill where you move the ball around a crisscross pentagram star, with a brutal five-versus-five at each point. I build myself up for this stinking hot Monday-afternoon session. The drill doesn't start until after weights and running and conditioning and ball work, and in the 90-second scrimmages of play you often find yourself isolated against another player.

Your legs are jelly, your lungs are acid, and you want water but not too much in case it makes you hurl. I find myself in a footrace against Chris Lewis, our 1990 club champion, who has only just begun to take the competition by storm. Who will get to the ball first? This is it. This is the best practice I could ask for.

I'm a hare but he's a cat. What does Mick always say? *Don't worry about the guys who've got pace – just hit, hit, hit, hit, and you'll slow them down, you'll wear them out, you'll blow them up.* And that's what I do.

We run parallel and I start leaning into him, taking control of the line to the ball, pushing him away, knocking him off course. They have a saying in NASCAR – *Rubbin' is racin'*, and that's how I race. I push off him at the last minute, scoop up the footy and deliver it to the next group. No one says anything, but I know I'm back.

I play 14 games in 1992. Round 12 is one of them. We play against North Melbourne. Wayne Carey punches Glen Jakovich in the arm and gets suspended. Matty Larkin kicks a spinning freak goal, contender for best of the year. And I have 23 touches, enough to pique the interest of the Kangaroos powerbrokers.

The following week against Collingwood is my 49th game and I get a corked calf, ahead of my 50th game against the Hawks. I want this milestone so much. Mick warns me though, *I know it's been hard to get to 50, but their oval is shithouse, it'll be heavy going, and I don't want you playing if it's going to affect you.*

One of my worst traits is impatience, and so I play. And the oval is shithouse, and it's heavy going, and the corky affects me. I get benched and then I get dropped, and then I can't get back into the side. All of which makes the approach from North Melbourne perfectly timed.

They call me at the shop. I don't have a manager, so they just dial the main number of Dean Laidley Sportz. They call on an average day when I'm setting up the till or doing a stocktake or unpacking new deliveries. Air Jordans come in on Tuesdays. Reebok Pumps on Thursdays.

The football manager Greg Miller is the one who rings. *Would you entertain the idea of coming to Victoria and playing for North Melbourne?*

They're a young side, he explains, in need of guidance and a sure hand. They have talent – Carey, Stevens, Archer, Schwass – but they're all young. They need a mentor and a leader. They need some steel and resolve. They need toughness and experience. Would I be interested in anything like that?

Yes, I say, *I would be interested.*

Yes, I say, *I have always been interested in playing in Victoria.*

Yes, I say, *I did indeed grow up barracking for the Kangas.*

Yes, I say, *it probably is now or never.*

Their coach, Wayne Schimmelbusch, comes to Perth next, and takes Joanne and me to dinner. It's strange to be embedded in one tribe while whispering sweet nothings to another. By the end of the year, 10 clubs have sounded me out. I'm feeling the love because it's coming from all directions, except from the Eagles, where I still can't break through. They're into another grand final, too.

The end of the season is here and I'm exactly where Mick thought I was at the start of the season – in their top 25, but not quite in their top 20. I train hard in the approach to that grand final, all the way up to the last session of the year, the day before the match.

They give us the guernseys we're going to play in – mine will only be used if a handful of teammates are hit by lightning, or come down with the flu, of course – and I take it off after that session and drop it on the floor. I know it's the last time I will ever wear an Eagles jumper.

catching up with the girls

They win the flag, of course, and when the siren goes I just walk back up the hill through Yarra Park to the Hilton Hotel. I go to the function, because I have to. I've worked my arse off for 12 months and then some, and here we are, the whole club celebrating, all of them overwhelmed by the moment, while I'm overwhelmed by dejection and jealousy.

I begin fuelling up. The boys are on beer. I'm on bourbon and Coke. I think it's the sugar I like. I have a habit, which includes a 600 ml bottle of Masters iced coffee every morning, and 3 litres of Coke throughout the day. Mixing the latter with booze keeps my nights rolling.

The people around me are having so much fun. They're laughing, and I laugh with them darkly. They're grinning, and I grin with them through gritted teeth.

When the time is right, I pull a scrap of paper with an address written on it from my pocket, walk out the front onto Wellington Parade, hail a cab and sit back as it speeds me down Punt Road then onto Commercial Road. I'm catching up with the girls tonight.

I've been speaking to my trans friends now and then since we met that night after the Panasonic Cup, since we found each other at Chasers and went back to their house in St Kilda East. I talk to them on the phone – there's no email in 1992 – and we chat openly about footy and family and what it feels like to be your feminine self. They are the only people in the world I can do this with, and they're responsive even when I go on and on and on about this fucking sport I play, this industry I work in and the things within that system that weigh me down.

They are my counsel, not my hook-up. I've stumbled across them but I'm still naive and confused about what I am. I find a term written in a book – *autogynephilia* – which means becoming aroused by imagining yourself as a woman, but that's not me. Arousal has nothing to do with this. What this is about for me is peace. The things I find in books aren't helpful at all, but the girls are. When I talk with them it's like I'm letting go of the struggle for a little while.

I arrive at the address they've given me expecting a home, but it's a club in Prahran. Three Faces. I hit the footpath after midnight and there's no line. The security guard recognises me. *Sure you want to come in here?*

It's quiet on the street but going off inside. Good loud music and the place is buzzing. I'm on my tippy toes trying to take it in and get my bearings. I'm not used to this landscape. A young guy wanders up to me. *What are you doing here?*

I'm looking for a couple of girls.

He laughs in my face. *Yeah, that's what they all say.*

Another guy approaches and asks the same question in a different way. He's not just bemused by my presence, but almost seems concerned for me. *Hey, are you sure you know where you are?*

That's when I take it all in. The rainbow flags out front. The boys and men as far as I can see. I'm in a gay bar. A gay club. In the gay precinct of Melbourne. I spot the girls and retreat to a little sanctuary with them, out of sight in a darkened corner, and settle in for the night.

I am uncomfortably comfortable. With being in a place like this, and people recognising me. With the music throbbing, and getting a smack on the arse while walking to the loo. With the lights pulsing, and my own pulse racing.

The girls can see it might be too much too soon, and so they become my gatekeepers. Anyone with a question for me about football can turn right around and fuck off back to the other side of the room. We sit and laugh and talk. They ask me questions, too. *Are you attracted to men?*

I'm not. As my trans identity grows inside, my attraction to women extends a little to transgender women, but cis males? I don't find that form interesting or attractive at all. The girls respect that. When Three Faces is your average Saturday night, I guess you understand the spectrum of human existence a little better than the average punter.

They ask me about my life outside footy, and they make no assumptions. A trans person probably feels imprisoned by their partner, right? They've gotta feel boxed in by their kids, yeah? Nah. I love my wife. I adore my children. The girls understand these seeming contradictions and complications. They empathise and sympathise and smile.

I catch the red-eye flight home the next morning, headed for the sky above the Nullarbor at 6am, and sleep the whole way there. All I can think about when I land in Perth is going back east, seeing the girls again, asking more questions and having more fun. I get into my car and leave the airport, down the long driveway that is now lined with wild and delirious Eagles fans, cheering and waving, welcoming us back, celebrating a victory I had nothing to do with. I'm 25, and I know I'm done with this town. I'm leaving.

exit

*W*hat? Mick yells. *Why the fuck do you want to do that?*

It's my exit interview – that end-of-season chat every player has with his coach, about how the year has gone and how the next one might play out – and Mick doesn't understand why I would consider leaving, given I'm contracted for next season, and given he has ideas for my development.

Let's face it, Mick, I'm behind Woosha and Bluey, I tell him. *Whatever talent I've got, I don't want to waste it. With your blessing, if we can get something to work, I'd appreciate a trade.*

He wants to know who I've spoken with, and I tell him the 10 clubs who've come calling. He runs down that list, one by one, zeroing in on some aspect of their existence he thinks I should consider a deal-breaker.

They'll be a hard side to crack.

Really? You wouldn't want to go to those guys, would you?

Hmm, they've got no money.

They're shit.

You really want to live over there?

I tell him about North Melbourne and Sydney, the contenders who want me most, and he spins on a dime, turning genial and wistful. *You know, I changed clubs,* he says. *One week I was playing for St Kilda, and the next week I was playing with the Tigers. It was the best thing that ever happened to me. I get where you're coming from. If we can get the right balance in trade, I'll do that for you.*

I'm not the only one to depart, of course. This happens to every premiership team. The peripheral players who just miss out on glory usually look for an opportunity elsewhere. I'm just the first disappointed Eagle to seek a fresh start. Scott Watters missed out, too, and asks for a trade to Sydney. Paul Peos watched from the sidelines with us, and he heads to Brisbane.

Ross Glendinning wants me to stay. He calls me up and visits me at the shop. He warns me specifically about North Melbourne, where he once played. *Don't go. Whatever you do, don't go to North. They're on the brink of financial collapse. It's not where your future lies.*

But I don't care what Rosco says. I'm going, because I'm not going to sit here and waste any more time. I was once a talented teenager. Now I'm a mid-career veteran, hanging on to the fringe.

West Coast agree to trade me to the Kangaroos for pick 8 in the national draft. The guy handling the paperwork is Mick Moylan, and he tells me I need to come into the club and sign on the dotted line. He seems in a hurry, and it angers me. Maybe it's in my mind but all I can hear from the Eagles now is a hint of hurry on. *Get going, get a move on, and don't let the door hit you on your arse on the way out.* I begin to see football as the full-time business it's quickly becoming. I'm a commodity and pick 8 is a commodity. The Eagles are a company and North is a company. The AFL is a corporation and the game is a product.

I walk out the door of the club I helped form with a pair of football boots, a bottle of premiership claret and a framed team photo. I pull out of the car park of Subiaco Oval at lunchtime on a weekday in October, and I hear Susannah Carr on the radio: *West Coast Eagles great flies the coop: Hear it tonight on Seven News.*

West Coast Eagles *great*? No, I'm not. I'm just some player who couldn't get a game when it counted. I've been allowed to leave, to walk away with no great fight to keep me. In this trade – this exchange of goods – I'm apparently as valuable as a kid who has never played a senior game. This move is of my own making, but I begin to cry anyway.

skin in the game

Do you believe in omens? I visit Victoria in late 1992, during the Spring Racing Carnival. Joanne comes with me, and Kane, who is nearly 18 months old.

A club guy who handles recruiting, development and welfare takes us to Errol Street, the main shopping strip in North Melbourne, for a bite to eat at the bakery – just a quick sandwich and a moment to orient ourselves before a tour of the club. He's driving the CEO's car – a huge purple Ford Fairlane. We've brought Kane's car seat with us, but I tell Joanne not to worry about installing it – I'll just hold him for the 300-metre drive around the corner.

We're moving now, on Arden Street, and we stop at the intersection of Macaulay Road, near the pool. We're all chatting, excited by this move and by new things. Our driver begins to turn right but the arrow is red. I can see it – why can't he? *Why are we turning? Hasn't he spotted that oncoming car? What the fuck is happening?*

I'm sitting in the back seat behind the driver, and it happens so quickly I have no time to react or warn him. Instead I simply watch this car come at us, almost in slow motion, and I hold Kane tightly, and lift him up, bringing my arms around him while bracing for impact. I hear the screech of rubber on road, and the smash of metal and metal, and shattering glass.

Kane is fine, albeit screaming, but the whiplash from the collision causes my head to thump the interior of the car. I have a concussion that'll force me to lie low in the first week of off-season training, when all I want to do is impress.

It could be worse of course. Luckily no one is hurt. The CEO's car, however, is a write-off. The T-bone collision has crumpled the entire rear passenger side. The car seat sits there, smashed in half, caved in by chance, empty by happenstance. We've been in Melbourne less than an hour.

I walk into Arden Street for the first time. I'm in a small office block with a tiny reception area, off which there's a room for the marketing manager and the membership manager, the CFO and the CEO. *Is this it?* Forget West Coast – West Perth's facilities are probably better than this.

The tour continues down a narrow passageway with thick navy blue carpet and pictures of administrators lining the walls – a veritable wall of history – and then we're into the football department with its massage tables and workout mats and weights.

The walls are tainted with the perfume of stale cigarette smoke from the cricketers who share the premises in summer. The showers and toilets are horrible, old and dripping, with that sour ammonia stink of old piss you really only get in a men's dunny.

The football manager, Greg Miller, can see my mind turning. Can he hear Rosco pleading in my head, too? *Don't go. Whatever you do, don't go to North.* Either way, he offers me my first lesson about the culture of the North Melbourne Football Club. *We may not have the best physical resources*, he says, *but our real asset is our people.*

He then explains the Shinboner spirit of the club, the way the abattoirs in Kensington and the butcher shops along

Macaulay Road kept the area employed, and the way these meat merchants used to hang shinbones off the railings out the front of their establishments after breaking down beasts for sale. The players who worked there walked down the street every day, past all that blood and marrow, on the way to training and playing, and that grit and exposed flesh built a feeling here. A sense of raw sacrifice – of skin in the game.

West Coast doesn't have that history. We were making our own there, building it on guys like Chris Mainwaring (work hard and play hard), Phil Scott (a fist held high in solidarity), and John Worsfold (cool ruthlessness). The Eagles are forging an ethos, but the Kangaroos are living theirs.

Finally we get to the lockers. I'm staring at each storage slot on the edge of the change room, some of them marked with the names of premiership players, or those who reached the 100 games milestone. Dench and Cable, Krakouer and Blight. Keith Greig and Doug Wade. Nolan and Kekovich and Briedis. And Graham Melrose, my childhood idol. They're all up there, too, on the honour boards hanging high on the walls. Legends in gold lettering, embossed on dark varnished wood. I tell Miller – although I'm telling myself as much as anyone else – *I want to be up there.*

It's a quiet group, this team of young Kangaroos.

Wayne Carey is only 21, and although there's an aura to the boy – a kind of bogan braggadocio – he's not yet swaggering the way he one day will. The playing group idolises him so he doesn't need to amp anything up. In a way he's like the Pied Piper – they follow him because of the things he does, which no one else can. What also strikes me is how good he is at getting groups of people together, connecting players with staff, volunteers with fans, CEOs with bootstudders. He's more disarming than you might imagine.

I see Anthony Stevens often at the front of our running sessions. *Who the fuck is this guy,* I wonder, *who can run and run and run?* He's shy, and determined, and has no idea how important he'll be to me in the coming years, particularly 25 years from now, when the footy stuff is all over.

Mick Martyn is a monstrous figure whose natural habitat is the gym. He sets himself for bench presses and the bar bends. When draftees join training and they're introduced, the coach pulls Mick out the front of the group and asks him what their names are. He can't name a single one. I might be 25 but I'm also a skinny kid from Perth. I'm just glad he knows my name.

I drive Adrian McAdam to every training session that pre-season while he recovers from stress fractures in his foot. Joining us from the Northern Territory Football League, he kicks 7 goals on debut, 10 goals a week later, and 6 goals the week after that. No one has ever kicked 23 goals in their first three games.

Ben Buckley is the most well read, the one who'll go on to be a director at Nike, a general manager at Electronic Arts, then GM of the AFL, then CEO of Football Federation Australia. He's the smartest guy in all those rooms.

Alastair Clarkson is just a schoolteacher and nuggetty half-forward flank, bobbing along with his football but never standing out. He's quick and sharp, but you don't sense he will become the greatest coach of the modern era.

Glenn Archer is reserved but already plays like a general. Wayne Schwass is chilled out and a bit outside the square. Anthony Rock is a buzzing mosquito, chipping everyone with shit jokes.

John Blakey is like me, a new mature face, and he wins a pre-season footrace – 12 laps of a triangle marked out on the oval.

Afterwards we do a fitness circuit, not with dumbbells but with bricks, and as the pavers dig into my palms I show the boys how to endure pain.

Greg Miller says the standard is raised from the day we walk into Arden Street. That could be seen as an indictment of the group who are already there. They could easily take it that way and be resentful. But they don't.

one of those tales

I don't dislike many people, but I don't like Judy Francis. She's the 'house mother' for the Kangaroos – cooking and cleaning for a handful of the young players living together, probably living out of home for the first time. She makes pasta and soup and salad for training nights, too. She doesn't sound sinister in the slightest, but she does something before I even arrive at North Melbourne that damages me and taints my reputation forever.

She's heard – through one person or another – about my night at Three Faces. Not all the details – probably none of the real details, actually – but she knows that I was there, in a gay club, and that I stayed all night. This isn't information she decides to keep, or confront me with, but rather she treats it as a tidbit to be shared with others. Many others. She knows exactly what she's doing and I become one of those tales people tell.

Have you heard about Dean Laidley?

Yep, gay.

I know, right?

Yeah, right there in Commercial Road, partying with a bunch of queens.

In clubland, such stories spread like a bushfire in a southerly wind. How do I know this whisper is out there? Someone tells Joanne. We're at a barbecue when another player's wife starts up a conversation with the vicious icebreaker *Do you know your husband's gay?*

Joanne keeps this to herself at first.

I arrive home one night after the first interstate game I play for the club, and she walks right past me in a stormy way. I wonder what the fuck I've done. My stomach sinks when she tells me but I convince her I'm not gay – which is easy because I'm not – and we smooth things out between us. But the trust has taken a battering. And I'm livid.

Only many years later will I learn that the playing group has heard all of these rumours – that this story becomes the root of a weed that spreads within the club and into other clubs and throughout the entire industry – and that my teammates did not mind.

Wayne Carey – the ultimate alpha – is the most magnanimous of all. *We didn't care*, the King tells me over breakfast one morning in 2020. *We knew you could play football, and we wanted you in our football team.*

Judy Francis dies more than a decade later, when I'm coaching the Kangaroos. She's very sick and I go to the hospital to visit, because I'm the senior coach and that's what you do. I'm there by myself, and have to put out of my mind the carnage she caused. I'm there as a figurehead, to visit a person who has given her all to the club, and to pay my respects.

I sit for 20 minutes, rolling it all around in my mind, trying to think only of what she gave.

I say a quiet goodbye, and leave.

don't go

The pre-season of 1993 is a summer of warnings.

It starts with training at Trinity Grammar in the leafy east of Melbourne, with running and more running. I hate it yet I know I need to do it; it's the direct line to my best play, so I don't complain – but others do. Then we go into ball work and the skills are horrible. Coming from a side steeped in precision passing and surgical kick selection, I begin to wonder what I've walked into here. I begin to hear Ross Glendinning, yet again. *Don't go.*

We go on a footy camp to Puckapunyal Military Area, an Australian Army training base outside of Seymour, north of the city. We stay in tents in the bush and are woken at 4:30am by machinegun fire. Bleary eyed and groggy, we limp straight into a 20-kilometre run. A tall drink of water named Corey McKernan is in pain, and vomiting, but Schimma wants his players primed, and sends McKernan on the run anyway. His appendix bursts halfway. He loses 20 kilos and half a year of football.

At our final dinner in the mess hall we're allowed a couple of beers each, but by the time we finish it's still only 8pm and sweltering, after a 39-degree day with torrential rainfall. This is the same weekend Guns N' Roses play an infamous concert at Calder Park Raceway, where punters battle dehydration and transport woes and overpriced water bottles. I think they have it better than us.

The whole squad goes wandering around the army base looking for more booze, the coach monitoring this mission from a distance. Slowly the players drop out of the search until it's just the ratbags left, and they find a house where a family are living, and invite themselves in to drink for the evening. This is a training camp – not a Saturday night after a game. It's meant to be about resilience and endurance and discipline – elite behaviours, and only for a few days. I hear Rosco again. *Don't go.*

We're supposed to play against Adelaide at Waverley in our first pre-season game, but the turf isn't ready, and we're told we'll have to play at Football Park in Adelaide instead. With the Eagles I got used to travelling the width of the country every second week, so it makes no difference to me, but my new teammates see it differently, sooking about a 40-minute flight to South Australia. We jump on a kite to the City of Churches; the plane is a little late, but we get there in time for my first game in the colours. Adelaide beat us 27 goals to 5, and Rosco is now a fucking earworm on repeat. *Don't go. Don't go. Don't go.*

I've been recruited to this club in large part by their coach, Wayne Schimmelbusch, who played 306 games for the club and was named in its team of the century. Schimma has wooed me, backed my talent, promised me a role running off the half-back line and down the wings and occasionally through the middle. He's a god to me, and I'm only just getting past that as this season begins, as I see how he operates.

I've seen Ron Alexander, and John Todd, but mostly I have Mick Malthouse as my point of comparison, and what stands out with the latter is the way he deals with individuals. Chris Mainwaring could be lying on the floor almost asleep until five minutes before the game, and get changed barely in time to run up the race, while Karl Langdon would be frothing at the mouth an hour before the bounce. But Mick knew who needed a chat and who needed to be left alone. He used to say that consistency is overrated, because what works for one player won't for another. Individuality is where the magic lies, so he would react to individual needs in the warm-up.

Watching Schimma stalk the change rooms at Football Park, I wait to see that connection with each of the guys, Mark Roberts or Brett Allison or Craig Sholl, but it never happens. He jogs around the rooms, bouncing the ball to himself, keeping on his toes, almost as if he's preparing to play.

Maybe Schimma's view of leadership is that it comes from your deeds on the ground, but when you're coaching it has to be more than that. You have to impart your knowledge and direction, and you can't do it by shuffling past your players on game day, footy in hand. We lose by 147 points, and so we know what's coming. It's announced to the group ahead of Monday-night training. Schimma's been sacked.

Names are thrown around for a replacement. Dermott 'The Kid' Brereton. 'Rocket' Rodney Eade. But the name that keeps coming up is Pagan. Denis Pagan. I ask the boys about him. *Who is he exactly?*

He's just won a flag with the Essendon reserves but used to coach the North Melbourne under-19s. Quite a few of my new teammates came through that junior pathway program, as members of the old recruiting zone. Jose Romero. Anthony Rock. Ross Smith. Peter German. Brett Allison. They're all products of the Essendon District Football League, and they all know Denis well.

Oh fucken hell, they say.

He's a fucking nightmare, they declare.

Demanding, they note.

Exhausting, they agree.

His appointment happens quickly – that week in fact – and we play under him against Geelong at Tatura, a regional Victorian oval outside of Bendigo. I'm out with a broken rib but make the journey anyway. I drive up there with Peter German and he plays 'Radar Love' by Golden Earring on this boom box stereo sitting on the back seat of his car.

Fucken Denis, he mutters to himself. *Fucken Pago.*

I begin to realise that I'm starting from scratch now. I'm not a prized recruit to this new coach. I'm just one more name on a long list of players looking to impress a new boss – a boss trying to make statements about strength, given what's happening at the club. Our captain, Matty Larkin, has stepped down. We've lost our major sponsor in Qantas. By all reports it's only hours before the joint gets locked up and we all walk away without a job. The Kangas are in dire straits. I hear a faint echo again. *Don't go ...*

little goat tracks

Pagan's first meeting with us is his pre-game address, and he wants us all there, huddled into the country clubrooms, whether we're playing or not. He's very clear about how we're going to play. Fundamentally, his plan is to win contested ball, get the Sherrin inside 50 quickly, and score quickly. It's about aggression and efficiency. 'Possessions per goal' is his most prized statistic. Seventeen possessions per goal is ideal. *Two kicks to one handball. No short stuff. Don't fuck around with it. Long to the contest. Crumb. Go again.* Simple formula. Old fashioned. We lose the practice match by only a few goals, but it's a heartening performance against a team that were almost premiers six months ago.

I play the next practice game in Bendigo, against the Bulldogs. Halfway through the second quarter I'm on the bench. *Fuck … this is not going to plan at all.* I talk to Denis about it during the week and he gives me a swift clip. *You were sitting off your man too much. Trying to read the play too much. You could get away with that at West Coast, because the pressure from your teammates was stronger. You can't get away with it here.*

Fair enough.

Denis points next to a small elastic brace around the front of my left knee. I've worn it since I tore that joint to pieces. The surgeons cut my ligament graft from the patella, and this brace nudges up against it, making me feel a little more secure every time I run out to play. *You're never wearing that again*, Denis says. But I need it. *No you don't. You don't need it. It's a security blanket. You look like Jack Dyer. Get it fucking off.*

At training he hammers his game plan into us, until the routes we run become muscle memory – little goat tracks in our minds. We do the same exercises night after night, until I can almost see the divot lines we've been running into the turf.

He drills us in the same way during meetings, stopping mid-thought for a terrifying pop quiz about his game plan. Players get called to the front to answer impromptu tactical brainteasers. Some of the guys begin volunteering to do so, in fact, so they won't be called on during those final few questions about the obscure stuff no one can remember. Better to get the easy question right than the hard one wrong.

And something about all of this works. After 10 games of the 1993 season, we're 9 and 1 and sitting in first place. We have a new sponsor – New Zealand Insurance. We have a new captain – Wayne Carey. We go from a basket case to the top of the ladder.

We play West Coast in Perth and Denis pulls me aside. *I've seen a lot of players go back against their old team and get caught up in the moment, lose their way. Don't lose your way.*

I make a pact with myself that I won't talk to anyone out there. I'll face the Eagles in silence.

I play on Brett Heady and put him to sleep. I've lost some length in my kick, so when I mark the ball 51 metres out from goal, I reckon I'm no chance. It sails through. It's my only goal for the season. We win by six points, defeating the reigning premier – my old team – in their own little kingdom.

Winning is fun – so is kicking huge scores. 166 against Brisbane. 125 against St Kilda. 128 against Melbourne. 159 against Richmond. TWO HUNDRED AND TWENTY NINE against Sydney. 141 against the Bulldogs. 121 over

Adelaide. 134 over Carlton. 126 over Collingwood. 146 against Brisbane again (312 for the year). 160 against Sydney again (389 for the year). 123 against the Dogs again (264 for the year).

I have time on my hands. As part of my contract, North Melbourne is meant to get me a job – footy isn't full-time yet. But a job doesn't eventuate in the first year so I'm home a lot.

We live in a rented two-storey four-bedroom townhouse in Avondale Heights, next to East Keilor. At $350 a week it's expensive, but also paid for as part of my contract. I'm 10 kilometres from the city, an easy shot into town or the markets or the club. We join a babysitters' club, and meet the neighbours. I take my young family sightseeing, and we visit the Melbourne Zoo, eat fish and chips in Williamstown, ride the Scenic Railway at Luna Park and watch the penguin parade at Phillip Island.

Most days, I drop Brooke at school and head to the club to do weights. Then I'm back home with Kane and we spend a lot of time having cappuccinos and donuts at Highpoint Shopping Centre, that gleaming monument to commerce. I pick Brooke up from school and then head back into the club for training.

The football fixture inevitably means I miss birthdays and some important social occasions but those absences don't feel huge because I am part of my kids' everyday lives. I am embedded in the detail of family life.

Things get tougher as the season progresses. We get beaten by a point by Fitzroy – the bottom side – at Princes Park, and I get my first taste of the Denis I was warned about. He goes around the rooms after each match, evaluating each player. Not just a handful – every single player. It's been positive throughout the year so far, because we were winning. Now it's different.

He finds moments to make it personal, sometimes singling out a player and being needlessly cutting.

Adam Simpson and Glenn Freeborn and Matty Capuano cop it worst of all, almost every week. When we leave the rooms, the boys have to pick these guys up off the floor. If training is the homework and sport is the test, Pagan is that arsehole teacher who loves his red pen, who revels in letting you know why you failed.

Oh, and just in case he somehow misses you in that circle after the match, he writes down his judgement of every player, and leaves them all up on a board back at the club every Monday, for everyone to read. Attached to his paragraph summation is a rating from poor to below average to average to good to excellent. I rate his methodology as cruel.

cross the line

I've been known by a few nicknames in my life. When I first get noticed as a teenage player of some potential, it's 'The Boy from Balga'.

Later I become 'Tunnel'. People always assume it springs from some fondness for the Tunnel nightclub in Melbourne, a big dark haunt off King Street, popular with footy players, but I've barely spent any time there.

The name actually goes back to 1984. Me and a mate and a girl from school were 17, mucking around. I sugarcoated it, as young people do, and bragged about it one day to Corry Bewick, a scallywag older brother to Darren, and somewhat of a mentor to me. He roared with laughter and shook his head. *You're nothing but a tunnel cunt, Laidley.*

I didn't know what he meant exactly – *Tunnel?* – but it stuck all the same. It's obscure slang, apparently, for when two guys and a woman have sex, with one guy giving it to her from behind while the other's in her mouth. If the two blokes high five, it creates a tunnel above them. My experience was nothing like this, not even close, but people don't choose their nicknames and when they take hold they're rarely shaken loose. It's still what some people who know me call me. In 1996, after we won the AFL premiership, I got *Tunnel #7* tattooed on the outside of my ankle.

Yet the nickname the public knows is quite different. This one is born at the Kangaroos, in my first season. We're playing

Sydney at the SCG, and I'm playing wild football, racking up tackles and giving away free kicks. I'm lunging so desperately at every contest I even register two hit-outs. It's not unusual for me to cross the line in an off-Broadway game like this. In big games it's easy to reach peak stimulation but in small games it's harder, so my mental preparation becomes more exacting and focused. More intense.

Playing the Swans fires me up, too. They had been interested in recruiting me. They wanted me badly. It was my decision to go elsewhere, not theirs, yet I still want to show them what they've missed out on. It's a warm day, too – hot with a big blue sky, just like home. Where else would you rather be?

The ball is bouncing free in front of the interchange gates and I run towards it, while a nameless Swan runs in from the opposite direction. I love these moments in footy. It's a team game but contests emerge where it's one on one, me versus you. You might as well be a boxer in a ring – you can't leave until one of you is hurt. *Kill or be killed.*

I cream this other guy, lay him out fairly, and charge away with the ball as though he wasn't even there, like a car continuing on down the street after flattening a cat. That's when the commentators notice the display I'm putting on. That's when Peter McKenna comes up with a new term to describe me, something the public can latch on to, a verbal millstone I'll wear around my neck forever. He calls me 'the Junkyard Dog'.

I don't know if he means the American wrestler of the same name, or just some pit bull of the imagination, guarding rusty garbage behind a chain-wire fence. But it makes sense. Experts talk about addiction, like my father's to alcohol, and his father's before him to the same substance. Right now I have no such trouble with booze, no need to smoke weed and I've never even seen a hard drug up close. My vice is the work, the training, the game – it's the need to win, to dominate, to control something or someone, since I have no control over the secret that dominates my inner life.

People think they know what addiction looks like. The drowsy red eyes of a pot smoker. The sweaty twitch of a cokehead. The constant frantic nod of a speed freak. The hollow dark sockets around the stare of a junkie. What does it look like in me when addiction turns toxic, when I feed it and let it run free? It looks like a player with his socks down, chin forward, elbows up, lip curled, playing to hurt, and running off to goal leaving roadkill on the wing at the SCG.

McKenna is right. On the field, I'm giving in to all my worst impulses, and it's been building for a while. And so the Junkyard Dog reputation is spawned. People begin to form an opinion of me not just as a footballer but as Dean Laidley, as if the persona matches the person. It becomes something I have to live up to as well. I have to be that frothing attack dog every week now. If I'm not the desperate animal, raging and rabid, am I even playing?

Worse, the nickname begins to bleed into who I am. It infects me. Living in the Avondale Heights area I run into Bulldogs and Blues and Bombers all the time. I'm supposed to be a mature player – convivial with fellow professionals – but I'm not. We have a rivalry with Essendon, for instance, and it's fierce. In 1958 the Bombers accused North of cheating by playing too many men on the field, and demanded a head count. Kevin Sheedy later describes the club as soft, and executives Mark Dawson and Greg Miller as the pink marshmallow and the white marshmallow. Ever the shit-stirrer, Sheedy videotapes our training sessions at one point, too. But it mostly comes back to class. Blue bloods (the Bombers) versus blue collars (the Kangaroos). It's the haves against the have-nots.

If I see a Bomber at a party, I'm unfriendly. It builds inside me sometimes from the other side of a back yard – *Am I being fucking crazy?* – until my glare is enough to make them leave the barbecue. That's a win. I enjoy it. And hate it at the same time.

If any of my teammates use the term Junkyard Dog, I go at them. The more senior guys get away with it because I know they're winding me up, but one day a young player uses the term in earnest – which he probably means as a compliment – and I see red. I don't even know his name. I don't think he's played a senior game. I light him up anyway. I turn to him and spit, *Don't you ever fucking call me that again, cunt!*

There's only one person I allow to call me that name, and it's Wayne Schwass. I love playing alongside him. When you run down the race to play league football, you sense the teammates with whom you have a connection. You can tell who sees you and has your back. We look for one another on the field, too, ignoring what Denis wants and chipping it short instead, changing it up, finding each other through the guts of the ground.

We go back to Schwatta's house one night after a game. His place backs onto a golf course, so we get out the chipper and putter and play a few holes for free. A handful of his family is there, sitting on the deck singing songs together as the sun goes down. As much as Maori are seen as warriors, they're also a loving, soulful, smiling people. I appreciate these qualities in every long conversation with Wayne. That's why he's the only person allowed to call me Junkyard Dog.

Mostly he doesn't though. He knows better.

The end of the 1993 season implodes in predictably spectacular fashion. Going into the final round we're on top of the ladder, playing the Bulldogs, and we think we're going to win. Denis is so sure he invites Hawthorn legend Michael Tuck to join us in the rooms *after* the game, to talk to us about favouritism heading into finals.

My mum and my stepfather – Mad Carmel and Leif – have come across for this game and they're staying for the finals, confident we can go all the way. We stumble at the first hurdle, losing to Footscray, and I get reported. I tackle Tony Liberatore near the sidelines, and I'm on top of him when a pack forms. As I get up I see the back of his head just sitting there, and I crack it with an open palm. Why do I hit him? Because I'm a prick. Because he's a prick. Antagonist meets antagonist. Junkyard Dog meets Little Dog Syndrome. *Kill or be killed.*

I get up and trot away and he chases me. He's right in my face, hurling invective, grabbing at me with those grubbing little fingers and sharp nails. I lean into him, down to him, because he's fucking short, and he feigns a new blow, pretends I've given him a headbutt. He sprawls onto the ground, the fucking poser. I get a two-week suspension.

Worse, the shock loss bumps us from first place on the ladder. Instead of having double chance, we're now third playing sixth, in a knockout final against the Eagles. Of course it would be the Eagles.

We're still favoured, of course, but we've learned nothing from our hubris. The media team sends me out to do a Friday-morning news stunt with Lou Richards. We film it at Yarra Park by the MCG. It's a mock funeral for West Coast. I even dig a tiny grave for them in the grass. The national segment doesn't go down well in Perth.

We lose, and that's it. Our dominant season is over. I finish seventh in the best and fairest, my best result ever, but finals football eludes me again. After missing in 1990, and 1991, and 1992, I miss again in 1993. I wonder what I've done to deserve this.

restless

There's only one upside to this year, and it's the Christmas holidays. Craig Sholl invites us up to Echuca on the Murray River where he has a boat and we try waterskiing for the first time. We are all bitten by this bug. By the next year we've bought our own jetski and kneeboards and you can find us water skiing at Lake Eppalock. Eventually Echuca becomes our second home, where some of our best family memories are made.

Four times a year, Joanne and the kids travel back to Perth for a couple of weeks in the school holidays. They all need that connection to home – to parents and grandparents and uncles and aunties – and because I'm a professional footballer, I stay in Melbourne. Alone. In between training sessions and bonding sessions, weights sessions and massage sessions, I spend all spare moments in these weeks taking time to be me.

I don't have any makeup or clothes anymore. I got rid of them in the move east. Too risky to bring. I have to start again from scratch. I visit Highpoint most days, most often in the mornings when it's quiet. I talk to the perfume snipers and dress fitters. *This is for my wife. Yes, she's about my size.*

I begin to get a sense of my actual size, so I don't have to call on some random shop lady to give me her guesstimate. Forget the 34 waist or 102 regular. In women's sizing I'm a 12. In bottoms I'm a small, because my waist is still narrow. I'm a size 10 shoe, right off the shelf. I get some items home and they don't quite fit, and it's deflating, but mostly they slip on perfectly and it's thrilling. I build my collection slowly. And I wear it at every opportunity.

Sometimes there's a knock at the door and I shit myself. My car is in the driveway. A friend is popping by and they know Joanne and the kids are away. They knock and I stay deathly silent and still, not daring to breathe, pretending no one is home.

He must be out running, I want them to think.

Must have walked to the shops, I hope they reason.

Please fuck off and leave me alone, I pray.

Every 12 weeks for two weeks straight, this is my life. And then school holidays is over, and my family gets off the plane at Tullamarine, and I pack my existence back into a cardboard box. I put this cardboard box in the shed, and I bury it underneath other cardboard boxes, and sporting equipment, and tools, where no one will think to look.

My mood plummets then. The more I have this freedom the more I want it, the more I sense the loss when it's taken away. My year follows a rhythmic emotional cycle, in tune with term dates. Calm in the freedom of that happy fortnight of holidays. Flat when those holidays end and that freedom is curtailed. Grinding and yearning for weeks on end as a term begins. Delicious anticipation near the end of term as another fortnight draws near.

The more I do it, the more I want it. Is this an appetite that can never be sated? A thirst that can never be slaked? Why even use metaphors: is this a need that will never be met? My female side is growing stronger because the girl inside me keeps getting a look – a sustained look – at what her life might be like.

I know the next moment of freedom is never more than a school term away. I look in the mirror as I remove my makeup, and I speak to myself. *Twelve weeks. Three months. You can do that.*

But in the same breath I miss my wife and kids. I love our little family. The emotional toll of this wrestle with my identity – that restless pull – is a huge weight to bear. These are the times I absolutely hate myself.

Why am I like this?

not alright

In the pre-season of 1994, we play against Fitzroy in Sunbury, after 6 inches of rain has fallen. The ground is a lake. It's probably not even worth playing, but here we are, and here I am, lining up on a kid named Chris Johnson. He's a talented Indigenous player, all of 17 years old. He's good, too. He's grown up in the northern suburbs of Melbourne, in Jacana, and is freshly drafted after starring in the TAC Cup grand final, kicking seven goals.

I'm in a foul mood, coming off another surgery – for my ankle, this time – and not yet certain of my footing, and through the puddles and slop this kid is skipping and dancing away from me. Quietly, but with venom, I turn to him. *It's just a pre-season game. Ease up, you black cunt.*

He looks at me with a mixture of disappointment and disbelief. That's what I'll feel later, too. I should know better.

Balga is a rough little suburb in Perth, and it's part of a triangle of rough suburbs known as the KGB. Koondoola, Girrawheen, Balga. There's a strong Indigenous population here, probably stronger than in any Australian city. The kids I grow up with are part of the Noongar nation – the most dominant cultural force in Australian footy – the people of Polly Farmer and Barry Cable, Derek Kickett and Nicky Winmar, Lance Franklin and Paddy Ryder.

In the history of the AFL, Noongar players outnumber all other Indigenous cohorts in the league by a factor of five. Sheedy calls them 'the Zulus of this nation', because they don't back down. They have a word – *winyarn* – which means soft or scared. You just can't be winyarn. You have to stand up. That's my experience as a child, too. Many of my mates are Noongar, and the boys I play footy with, but I know I can run myself into trouble around any corner in my neighbourhood.

Like one Thursday night at the Mirrabooka Shopping Centre. Leaving the ice hockey rink and heading to the bus stop, I'm in a group of white kids that ends up fighting a group of black kids, like the fucking Sharks and Jets in a suburban Australian wasteland.

Another time, I'm in grade six at the Balga pool with my brother and we're wearing black T-shirts with schmick new transfers on them. Mine has a picture of Peter Criss from KISS, and it's my prized possession. Someone nicks the shirts while we're swimming. Dad picks us up and he's ropeable with us both for losing them. *You've gotta look after your stuff!* I'm beside myself and Paul is weeping. We jump in the car and head up Balga Avenue, and see a pair of Indigenous boys wearing our shirts. Dad pulls over and gets them back. He doesn't apologise to me or Paul.

That's our life in Balga. I play at Westminster Balga juniors with a Noongar kid who is the best player I've ever seen but he's troubled. There are times when he's let out of kids' detention to play footy with us. He never makes it to the higher level, and most likely that's because he's in a minority, facing uncertainty and confusion and intergenerational trauma, and has no sense – no evidence – that things can get better. I've seen this shit play out my whole life. I shouldn't be going around calling anyone a black cunt.

I can't excuse it but I try to understand where it came from. Maybe the way I'm caging myself is taking a toll, and this thing inside me is angry. Maybe the Junkyard Dog is becoming too reliant on white line fever for attention. Maybe reaching for a racial slur is the easy, lazy, nasty option when you're having a bad day. Whatever the reason, I carry the shame with me. It sits uncomfortably, like a stone in my shoe.

Four years later, when the Kennett government is knocking down state schools, they demolish Overland High School in Keilor Downs, and I buy a block of land in a cul-de-sac there, and build a house. I'm laying down turf for my front lawn one day, watering the grass and surveying this new street, when Chris Johnson appears in my next-door neighbour's driveway. I've moved in next to his sister-in-law.

I walk straight over. *Chris, what happened a few years ago was not acceptable. It was way out of line, regardless of anything that was happening on the field. It was horrendous. I'm so sorry. I hope you respect that – I certainly respect you.*

Chris is playing with the Brisbane Lions by now, and becoming a superstar, not to mention a leader for his people. He looks at me, nods, and turns the other cheek.

You know what? he says. *It's alright.*

I'm grateful he says so, but it's not alright. Not even a little.

On a summery day in April I get a taste of my own medicine. It's round 6 and we're playing West Coast at the MCG. We get thumped but that's not what stings about this afternoon.

I'm playing angry. I've abandoned my mantra of silence and instead I'm spoiling for something. There's a lot of lip in 1990s football and I've given plenty, but Eagles captain John Worsfold puts me to shame. Emotional assassination is the game he knows best. And here he is now, charging down to the opposite end of the field where he knows he'll find me. He makes a beeline for me more than once, and I can't quite hear what he's yapping at first, but then some words land on me like a body blow.

Is my mind playing tricks on me?

I can't be sure what I've heard but I'm immediately thrown, dizzy and dazed. I fumble. I fall. I kick the ball out of bounds twice. I can't get this out of my mind.

Did my teammates hear this? Will they think the rumours are true?
I want to jump the fence and run from the ground, or dig a hole on the wing and bury myself in it.

I learn what Chris Johnson probably already knew from multiple experiences – that these moments players create on field, these things we say to get an edge, they might just rip the heart out of someone, or lodge a prickle that gives them pain forever.

In 2021, John and I catch up for lunch at Steve's Hotel in Nedlands on the Swan River and we talk about many things. What I think I heard that day has niggled away at me for 25 years and it's time to clear the air so I take him back to the game.

He doesn't even remember it. He's quite a shy person, John, and he seems humbled right now. He looks me in the eye and winces a little.

If I hurt you, he says, *or caused you any grief or concern, I'm sorry.*

We've always had great respect for each other's fierceness, never more so than in this moment.

no justice

I'm not injured. I'm not dropped. I'm not suspended. I'm finally going to play in one of those games in spring, where they play the anthem beforehand, and everything is on the line. Finals football. It's finally here for me.

We play Hawthorn first, and we haven't beaten them in a decade. We almost don't beat them now either. The game finishes in a tie, 91 to 91. I'm playing on Paul Hudson, and the fourth quarter ends with the ball in his hands. We look at one another. *What do we do now?*

We shake hands and start to wander off the ground, but staff come sprinting on, telling us we're staying out there, playing extra time – two additional 10-minute halves to settle the winner. It's the first time in history this has happened.

For that next 20 minutes I sit at half-back, utterly untroubled. The ball barely reaches me. I enjoy the best seat in the house as number 18, The Duck, The King, Wayne Carey, chooses that moment to tear the game apart. We kick 3 goals 5 to nothing, and win by 23 points. We're one step away from a shot at a flag, if we can just win our preliminary final against Geelong.

We played the Cats a while ago, and they were good. Gary Ablett Snr is their menacing spearhead, jumping like a springbok, surging like a train. He kicked his 100th goal for the season against us that day at Princes Park, and thousands of fans streamed onto the field, as we knew they would. I stuck to our plan when the moment came, jogging to my teammates to gather as a group, but I was tripped by a supporter. The commentary from Dennis Cometti rang out: *Someone's taken down Laidley!* I'm lucky the cameras didn't capture what happened next, because I had sprung up and thrown a fist at the fan and caught him with a clean one. He knocked me over, I knocked him out. We lost by a point.

Now we get a chance at revenge. It's a storied encounter, this preliminary final. It's one of the handful of top games I play in, and I play well, too. The turnout is huge: 80,121 people, and that kind of crowd makes a sound you can't fathom until you're surrounded by it. It's a kind of aural vacuum, where you can't hear anything else. You can be 5 metres from a screaming teammate and have to read his lips to know what he's saying.

It's fast and skilled and brutal out there. I play on Brownlow medallist Paul Couch, and try to run him ragged. I see Anthony Stevens getting bumped by Garry Hocking, and I'm protective of Stevo, so I turn to the man they call Buddha and clarify things with him. *Put your head over the ball again*, I say, *and I'll kick the cunt off.*

We start well but kick poorly, 5 goals 9 to 3 goals 3. We're 18 points up but should have blown them apart. The Cats get rolling, kicking 7 goals to our 4 points, and we're down at half-time. The King is injured, too. He hurt his calf in that extra-time win over Hawthorn and has barely trained in the two weeks since, but he is nevertheless towering. 24 possessions. 14 marks. 6 goals, 4 behinds. On one leg.

It's close at the finish – scores are level with one minute and 40 seconds to go. The ball finds its way forward for Geelong and looks set to go out of bounds. I'm right there, mere metres away, when Leigh Tudor scoops it up and tumbles a sloppy left-foot kick directly over my head. I turn and watch as gravity does its work and pulls the Sherrin down steeply, over the outstretched fingertips of Mick Martyn, and into the hands of the man Martyn has beaten all day – Ablett – who marks directly in front of goal. The man they call God walks back, and takes his winning shot immediately after the siren. We've lost on the last play of the game. Cometti's commentary again matches the moment: *There is no justice in football.*

no one judges here

I walk off the ground after our loss to Geelong and the first thing I do is check my nose. I was hit during the game by a boot and a shin, and a layer of skin was scraped off in a downward motion. It's all scrunched up near the tip of my beak, held there only by coagulated blood. I feel like I've been in a street fight but I also want to see what it looks like. *I can't have some gross cut on my face if I want to be myself later,* I think. *How can I do my makeup over a wound like that?*

It's an idle thought, however – a distraction to keep my mind off the reality. I'm shattered. People look at the AFL and think it's a life of luxury, fame and fortune, but the calculus you have to do every week – evaluating what you get out of the highs, and what you have to endure with the lows – is an unsolved problem. Everyone wants to be part of the celebration – to sing that North Melbourne theme song, to join in the chorus – but no one wants to hear what it's like to walk off the ground after a loss like that.

I argue with Joanne later, about who knows what, because no real reason is needed, and take off into the night. I end up with Mick Martyn at the casino in the old World Trade Centre building.

Late night becomes early morning, and we're the only two people at our blackjack table, Mick remembering Ablett kicking the winner, me gingerly touching my bruised and bloodied face.

We aren't talking much, but there's comfort even in sad, silent company.

We might actually be the saddest sight in Melbourne. Maybe that's why security soon surrounds us. They probably don't know who I am, but Mick is a recognisable brute. They tell us to finish up and leave the premises and Mick explodes, pushing back his chair. *What the fuck are you talking about? We're playing cards – FUCK OFF!*

I talk him down as best I can, at least to the point where he can keep roaring on his way out the door, and storm out without a fight. It doesn't take much for these moments to become front-page news in Melbourne. He jumps into a taxi and heads off into the daylight somewhere.

I walk to the Megabar at the bottom of King Street. It opens at 6am, and after a sausage roll and a Coke from 7-Eleven, it's where I want to be. I like the eclectic mix of drag queens performing, trans people communing and clubbers coming down off a big night.

The doof doof music is throbbing, and I sit down in a corner and relax with my people. No one judges here. They don't care that I play football. They don't even *know* I play football. I'm not North Melbourne half-back flank Dean Laidley. I'm a 28-year-old with a fucked-up nose and black eye.

I'm hurting, and this is the medicine I need. I stay until midday, then walk back into my life.

that nagging need

Denis goes even harder at us in the new year. It's the only way he knows. He coached his side to 10 under-19s grand finals in a row, then an Essendon reserves premiership, and he keeps taking North Melbourne into finals, too. There's little surprise when he becomes a horse trainer in retirement – when he's 90 with a walking frame he'll want to win a footrace down Puckle Street. He doesn't like losing. Doesn't tolerate it. Can't really handle it either.

Football breeds that kind of personality. And while most clubs don't give two thin shits about the pre-season competition, North Melbourne does. We're a small club, with a small supporter base, and the longer we stay in the pre-season cup, the longer our membership campaign bears fruit. If we win, the prize money is $250,000, and those are make-or-break dollars down at Arden Street. This suits Denis just fine.

He coaches us into the pre-season grand final of 1995, and of course I'm not playing. I nicked my quad a week earlier against Essendon, playing on a 16-year-old named Matthew Lloyd. I'd heard he was hot shit, so I belted him all night. I elbowed his skinny ribs. I stood on his feet with my long stops. Initiation by intimidation. Getting injured is probably my punishment.

Most players wouldn't care about missing out on the chance for a piece of meaningless summer silverware, but I do. I'm 29 now, and that nagging need to win a premiership is consuming me. I don't know why exactly. Do I think it will fulfil me somehow? That it'll alleviate my gender issues? Or do I just see all the pain this quest has put me through and want reward for my suffering? *If I could just win one,* I think, *I could move on.*

strange people

The most infamous nightclub in Australia has been open for two years now, and I want to go. It's called Hellfire, and part of its marketing is little postcards with cartoons of women with whips and men with candle wax. BDSM is its brand.

It's meant to be dark and obscure, with masters and mistresses, velvet and leather and spikes, and people tied to crosses and racks. It promises a voyeuristic thrill – Studio 54 meets sex dungeon – and all the cool kids are going. I'm not interested in the sex but I'm drawn to the taboo. I want to peek into this part of the human race. A strange place that keeps strange hours for strange people – people like me.

Winter school holidays feels like my moment. Just thinking about going, planning the night I open my front door and leave my house as myself, is thrilling. My outfit is ready, my itinerary is sound and my route is sensible. Hopefully foolproof. But I have no way of knowing that after I drive down Epsom Road and through the Flemington roundabout onto Racecourse Road, a booze bus will appear.

I can't turn around. My red Ford station wagon gets waved into the left lane and my heart is beating a metre out of my chest. *Why do you do this to yourself? Why are you this way? Why have you taken this risk? Why? Why? Why? Fuck! Fuck! Fuck!* I pray I get a female copper, and I do.

Have you been drinking tonight? *No.*

Blow in this bag for me please. *No problem.*

Driver's licence? *No, I'm sorry but I left it at home.*

Have you got any ID on you? *No I haven't ... Oh wait, hang on!*

In the console is a bill with my name on it. It doesn't say 'Mr' and it doesn't say 'Dean'. Just 'D Laidley' and the address.

Thank you, you can go. *Phew.*

I turn down Flemington Road and into Queensberry Street, and drive past the small queue forming in front of Hellfire. I've planned exactly where I will park, in the side street opposite the opening – the shortest route possible to the entrance. I sit in the car and gather my thoughts. It takes me an hour to open the door.

When I eventually do, and finally begin walking, I feel like a sprinter moving towards the starting blocks. My nerves are a positive jangle waiting for something to happen. I walk for 10 metres and I'm a woman in the world, off to the hottest club in town, out to see things and be seen – and then I look up and recognise the man at the back of the queue, the one I'll have to stand directly behind if I want to go in.

He's an Essendon legend, a contemporary player, and I have to make a quick calculation. Is he open-minded? Or like-minded? Or here for a cheap thrill? Will he relate to me – or be repelled by me? Will he keep my secret or share it widely? I'm not fucking finding out. It's too close. Too much. I'm not ready. *Will I ever be?* I spin before he looks in my direction, clip clop quickly back to my car and get home even quicker.

It wears you down, this effort, these attempts. It tires you out. My kids are growing. My career is unfolding. My marriage is holding, just. My life is unspooling but in what direction and at what pace I don't know. All I can do is keep going, try to remain true – really, there's no other option.

retribution is the price you pay

At the end of 1995 I feel as though it's now or never. I'm carrying too much physical pain. Too many operations on ankles and knees, quadriceps and vertebrae. It's round 20 and I'm running across Princes Park against Carlton, and on that ground when the Blues are up it feels as though the crowd is sitting on top of you. I bounce the ball through half-back near the opposition race. I'm being tracked by Fraser Brown.

He's a slightly ridiculous-looking man. He has curly hair, possibly a perm, but he's tough and not a little mad, the kind of guy who takes the cap off a Crown Lager with his teeth. I kick the ball but Brown lunges and brings me down, swinging a fist at my lower back. He re-fractures L3 and L4, two of the bones crunched by Paul Salmon. It's a harder tackle than it needs to be, but I dish it out so I cop it back. Retribution is the price you pay when you're the Junkyard Dog.

I'm laid out flat on my back for two weeks ahead of the end of the season. If I try to rise the pain hits my nerves like an electric current, flickering in a web through the trunk of my body. The club doctor gets a guard for my lower back, to protect the healing fractures, and I begin to train again, and play again, through the final game of the year against Fitzroy, and the qualifying final against Richmond, and a semi-final against West Coast, until we're in the preliminary final once more, up against Carlton.

The Blues are in form, with ominous depth and balance, coached by the intense but savvy David Parkin. Denis talks them up in the media – *I'd hate to see the pressure on Parkin if Carlton lose* – and this seems stupid to me, and unlike Denis. But maybe there are other Kangaroos like me, going in sore, and he thinks we need a confidence shot.

It's a tough Friday night, rainy and cold for late September. We get to three-quarter time and we've had a great quarter. We're 18 points down but marching home with a wet sail. I walk into that huddle with absolute belief we're going to win. And we get beaten. By 10 goals. Ten fucking goals. In front of 72,552 people.

It's another failure at the penultimate step, and I don't take it well. I end up at Schwatta's house in Ascot Vale, climbing a pull-down ladder into his storage attic to hang out with Anthony Rock and Ian Fairley. It's a strange place to booze up, or maybe not. We hide in the dusty unfinished cavity of Schwatta's roof, drinking beers and talking shit. We get messy, and sometimes when we stand we miss the rafters and put our feet through the plasterboard ceiling, and laugh like fools. There are more than a dozen holes in the roof when we finally come down, in the late afternoon or early evening on Saturday.

We head to the Mansion, a nightclub near Albert Park, and after drinking and sitting we now drink and move. The boys rip their shirts off in the middle of the dancefloor, and before we know it Sunday morning has arrived and we're headed to Bloody Mary's on Commercial Road, and before I know it 10am has arrived and I remember I'm supposed to be on a plane to Perth with my family after lunch.

I go home with a looming hangover, and Joanne is hostile because I haven't been seen in two days. I throw down my footy bag, pack some clothes and we head to the airport. As punishment Joanne hands me Kane, who's four, and Brooke, who's nine.

Here you go, she says. *You can look after them today.*

I can't keep my eyes open, but every time I let them close I catch an elbow to the midriff. It's a long flight west.

I turn 30 during the early part of the 1996 season, and I'm struggling. I make myself violently ill at times through sheer self-loathing and worry. *What a waste of a career*, I think. *What a lack of achievement.*

I'm on summer holiday at Lake Eppalock outside Heathcote when the panic really rises in my belly. This is where we are usually at our family best, jetskiing and waterskiing on the lake by day and gathering together for a barbecue by night. One of our group consoles me. *Bad luck last year – two years in a row*, they say. *Such a shame.*

I know they think they're telling me I've done well, that they feel for my loss, and that I'm not responsible, but it doesn't matter. Chance or fate being responsible seems worse to me. It's a trigger. I go days without eating or smiling, and I go no more than a few minutes without dwelling on some darkness or another. I don't have a name for this emotion yet, but I'm suffering from anxiety.

fight, flight or freeze

Coaches come up with stories not just when they want to inspire but when they want your attention. People follow narratives. It's the one weapon a storyteller possesses: every human needs to know what happens next. Denis tells us a story at the start of 1996. It's about something called 'the wildebeest syndrome'.

Wildebeest are members of the antelope family, with curved horns and slim legs and a long beard. They're known for roaming the plains of the Serengeti. But they're different from other hard-hoofed beasts on the savannah, insofar as when they get hunted down, and it looks like they're cornered, with no escape, they don't put up any fight. They surrender. They basically lie down and accept their fate, as gruesome as that is when you're being hunted by hyenas.

Denis tells this story, and goes to great lengths to align us, the players of the North Melbourne Football Club – at least during the past two preliminary finals we've lost – with these wildebeest who resign themselves to slaughter. We all have three options when cornered: fight, flight or freeze. He says he knows we're not wildebeests. He knows that we can fight, and that we will fight, that our time will come.

He's a good coach in this way. He reads and watches documentaries and borrows material wherever he can. I flick through the bookshelf in his office, for instance, and find a famous book, *When Pride Still Mattered*, about the life of American gridiron coach Vince Lombardi. I ask if I can read it and as I turn the pages I realise that I've heard all this before. I guess it's not the greatest crime, to conceal the source of your IP.

It's around this time in AFL history that teams begin considering modern tactics – that balance between guarding a man and guarding space, favouring the corridor or the boundary, deciding when to fight and when to run. Denis becomes known for 'Pagan's paddock' – using the space behind the forwards, instead of in front of them.

In the tactic's simplest form, Carey leads up at the ball then hook leads back to goal, turning his opponent around, leaving our champ streaming back into unprotected space, with the goal in sight. I don't think anyone takes as many flying-back-towards-goal marks as Wayne. If any of those small forwards – McAdam, Romero, Rock – sit even 15 metres behind his back shoulder, Wayne absolutely pastes them. It's *his* space, and with good reason. He doesn't lose a contest. It's a funny thing to play with someone who always wins the 50/50 ball. It's like having a trick coin up your sleeve. Flip it all you like, but tails never fails.

Denis is a good teacher, too, great at drilling us with his technique, and making it work for the champion at his disposal. We practise his attacking drills on the baseball grounds behind the Melbourne Zoo. I hear the baboons hooting and calling at feeding time. (No wildebeests.) We learn by repetition – almost rote memorisation – and by 1996 we've been repeating his methods for four years. The geometry of his game plan is tattooed on our brains.

There's talk this season about North Melbourne merging with Fitzroy. It's more than talk, actually. We get on the bus after a round 13 win against Fremantle, and the club powerbrokers come on board for the ride. *At the end of 1996*, they say, *we will be merging with the Fitzroy Football Club.*

We are all stunned, and we're all thinking the same thing: *Who on that Fitzroy team plays in my position, and will they take my place?*

They have talent. Brad Boyd. Chris Johnson. John Barker. Jarrod Molloy. Stephen Paxman. Martin Pike. Those guys will force their way in, forcing half a dozen of us out. The bus is all furtive looks and hushed, worried chatter.

And yet almost as soon as it's announced, it's walked back. The merger is off. North will remain North. When the eventual merger between Fitzroy and Brisbane is announced, the short-lived Fitzroy and North Melbourne plan will become known as 'the superteam that wasn't'.

This sounds like an extraordinary run of events for a football club to endure, but you learn quickly at the Kangaroos that there will always be chatter about merging and folding, relocation and debt. You can feel defeatist about that, letting thoughts of existential doom wash over you, resigning yourself to your fate, freezing in the face of your fear and waiting for the end to come, like the wildebeest do. Or you can fight and survive, as we do, and that's a great mindset to have charging into the tail end of a footy season.

don't underestimate relief

They say footballers require a singular focus to win on the biggest stage – that you need to devote every inch of your being to the task at hand. You can't possibly survive – let alone thrive – without total tunnel vision. But we're playing in a grand final now, and I call bullshit. All throughout this finals series so far, I've been hedging. Calculating every decision and calibrating every move.

Earn your spot, I tell myself, *but don't get injured.*

Play right up to the line, I figure, *but don't fucking get reported.*

Do anything for the win, I think, *as long as you can still get to training.*

But now grand final week is here, and the clichés don't do justice to the mood in Melbourne, from the smell of grass to the sound of fans clapping at open training. It's all sausages sizzling and face paint on kids. The ball zips up and down the field and people who've never seen it in person look on, and they *ooh* and *ahh* at every great kick. You begin putting on a show, feeling fast and fresh and strong. *Jeez, we're crisp tonight.*

I can be uptight and tense about it all – letting my newfound anxiety burn – or I can embrace this as a reward. In junior football I won the grand final in every single season except the year I had glandular fever. As a senior player, I've never even made it into the grand final.

There's excitement everywhere. I arrange flights for family to get here, but I won't let any of them stay with me for fear of distraction. I grab my 10 allocated tickets from the club. One is for Dad but he doesn't come. My dad has never seen me play an AFL game. Seeing him this past decade has mostly been a box-ticking exercise. I go back to Perth, visit briefly, say hello and leave him be. He's living by himself in Osborne Park, and struggling. The years and his drinking have caught up with him.

It's hard to let go completely though. I see other fathers in the change rooms after a big win and wonder if one day that'll be him. Whenever something big happens in my life, I ring him. I get drawn back in. I remember riding in the tray of his ute to watch East Fremantle as a kid, and I feel that connection or debt.

When I was playing a game in Perth he usually still wanted the free tickets, so he could sell them or give them away. I'd get them for him. You do these things for family, don't you? You make these concessions to appease something in yourself. I do it to make myself feel better. Or to let myself know that I've done everything I can.

I awake on grand final day at 9am, the same time I awake on any game day. I have the same breakfast – a cup of tea and two bits of toast with Vegemite. I still have my toast cold, still smeared with butter, still dabbed with dollops of yeasty brown goodness. My pre-game dinner the night before was the same as usual, too: a bottle of SportsPlus, a bowl of spaghetti bolognese and a bag of chicken Twisties.

I get a bit anal about my rituals. I always take my Musashi amino acid supplements – and let it be known that no one fucking touches them. I make sure I have the same locker in the change rooms – first on the left as you walk in. I make sure

I find the same seat in the briefing room – back row, right side, against the wall. I wear my lucky undies, too – a pair of mud-stained, yellowing Y-fronts with holes. They're disintegrating after so many years of use so I have to wear another pair of newer undies over the top.

My personal warm-up never changes and it begins earlier than for most players, because I'm a veteran now. I stretch my broken back. I get on the exercise bike and roll my broken knee over and over. At half-time I never sit down, always standing, always moving, always afraid that if I stop I won't be able to start myself again.

I want this day to be the same as any other, but it's not. I can hear everything today. The sound is muffled but even down in the rooms you know bands are playing, you know F-15s are doing flyovers, and you know the retiring players from around the league are being driven around the oval in convertibles, saying goodbye. My daughter tells me later that they had those inflatable tube-arm men on the ground, and the North Melbourne inflatable tube-arm man wouldn't inflate.

You know the production is in full swing up there, and you can't help letting your mind drift up into the yawning maw of the stadium, even though you're supposed to be focusing on your coach, reading the mood of your teammates, listening to the creaking whispers of your body, and the frailties of your mind.

The noise is what stands out most. People talk about the roar on the first siren, but what I notice is the way the crowd sustains it – the way it keeps bubbling and hissing and spitting as the first quarter unfolds, and the way that quarter unfolds so quickly.

We're under siege in the second quarter, and I come off my man to cut off an attack from the Swans. I'm standing in the hole. It's the most vulnerable spot you can be in, because those big key forwards behind you don't give a fuck about your health and safety. The bear in the square is happy to maim you, and that's never been more true than with this forward, the goliath Tony Lockett. He hurts people. Has done his entire career. Some of these brutes caution against standing in their space – *Stay there and you better fucking watch out!* – but Lockett doesn't trouble you with warnings. Does a great white make any sound before it bites? Lockett warns you just by swimming in the same water.

The ball comes in and I'm tracking it, and I'm open, and I have to stretch for the ball, and that means I'm exposed. *Something's behind me here. I'm in dangerous territory.*

I get my fingers to the ball, take the mark with outstretched arms, and fall to the ground with a spin, just fast enough to feel the hurricane full-forward blow by me. I put my body on the line and live to tell the tale. I swoop and scoop and play on with the footy. I don't know it yet, but Kangaroo fans will want to talk to me about that moment for the next 25 years.

It's a nice moment to follow you around.

The Swans skipper, Paul Kelly, has one of the other kind. There's a point in the game when they're in control and he streams out of the middle. All he needs to do is hit the leading Lockett on the chest and they'll be five goals up, hard to catch, but he scrubs his kick along the ground and out of bounds. I'm glad I don't have to live with that moment.

We win. The manner isn't important, not on this day. This day is all about the outcome. There's a photo taken of me as the game ends, printed on the back page of the *Herald Sun* the next day. It's me, Schwatta and Anthony Stevens. Stevo in the background with a dopey, euphoric smile, and Schwatta with his hands in the air, triumphant. He looks big and proud, but although he masks it well he's plagued by depression and he'll talk later about being outright suicidal in those moments.

If Schwatta looks exultant, I look the opposite. I'm falling to my knees, sinking into the surface of the MCG. I'm supposed to feel elation but I feel only relief. *Only* relief? Don't underestimate relief. Relief is a cool wet cloth on a bad burn. Relief is passing the exam you knew you would fail. Relief is knowing your kid is alright after a late-night phone call about a head-on car crash. Relief is testing negative. Don't underestimate relief.

a fucking mirage

It's been months since the siren rang and I can't shake the moments immediately afterwards: walking off the ground with a premiership medal – gold, for the 100-year anniversary of the league – and realising that the emptiness is still there, as dark and cavernous as ever. I thought a flag would settle some disturbance in my life, but the whirlpool in my stomach is twisting and churning as much as ever.

I drive to a function with Denis and he knows I have a year left to run on my contract, but he asks the question all the same. *Are you ready to go again?*

I lie to him. *Oh yeah, absolutely*, I say. *I want that again.*

I even sign a contract extension, taking me through to the end of 1998. But in reality I'm gone. I'll never be the same because the quest will never be the same. I thought the premiership would be an oasis in the desert and instead it's a fucking mirage. But the money for 1997 is guaranteed, so I take my cheques and front up for another pre-season.

The club has put together a big presentation and invited wives and girlfriends, and it's all about back-to-back flags. It's the last thing I want to hear. For the first time in my career I have no motivation. Footy used to be something I could devote myself to fully – a distraction that kept my other self at bay. And now? Now I use every private minute to be myself.

The kids are at school and Joanne is working full time as a

marketing manager for agricultural magazines and the *Stock &
Land* newspaper. She does the long drive down to Port Melbourne
every day and I walk out to the back shed and get to the bottom
of the pile where my cardboard box is buried.

I put on a touch of makeup, a denim skirt maybe and a short-
sleeved top. I try on my outfits and take little photos of myself
in the mirror, in the era before selfies exist. I walk around
the house like this, playing music. I make myself a sandwich.
I sit around in front of the TV and put on ESPN. I'm dressed
as myself, as the person I want to become, while watching the
Cincinnati Bengals.

I've followed them since the 1970s, since the days when you
could only see American football at 1am on Channel 9, through
those years when Don Lane had his show on the ABC. I love
the way each position is so specific and articulated, the way
a defensive lineman's job is to kill the quarterback, even if it
means they can go through their entire career without ever
touching the football itself. I love set plays and the way the clock
can be milked.

I've been to a game on a trip to the States – sitting in the stands
to see the LA Rams against the Atlanta Falcons at Anaheim
Stadium, baking in the 35-degree heat of southern California.
Now I watch my Bengals in full drag makeup, sinking into the
couch cushions with a cup of English breakfast tea.

I convince Dad to come to Melbourne. It's late January, the
hottest week in 100 years, they say, and we're moving in to our
house in East Keilor. We hire a big tandem trailer, fill it up and
hook it to our little all-wheel-drive Daihatsu Terios.

Dad helps out with everything, hauling boxes and hanging
pictures. We assemble the new pool table together. We put up
a new washing line together. We connect the sound system

together. We've never been a pair to talk much. Now we talk by working – communicating by passing a tool, lifting a box, having a beer, sweeping a hallway, sharing a pizza. It's the best week I've had with my father in my entire life.

We play our first practice match of the year at Waverley, and Dad comes. I'm 30 now and it's the first time he's come to watch me play since I was 15.

It's an intraclub game, where we play against each other. I play okay, and get through unscathed. Then I'm sitting in the rooms with ice on, and he appears out of nowhere. It's what I've always wanted, but a strange fear sweeps over me.

He doesn't really know anyone, doesn't know where to stand, and I feel embarrassed by his awkwardness. I'm annoyed, too, because it shouldn't be this way. He should be used to this, because he should have been here all along.

My birthday is coming up and we've made invitations for a party. Dad starts handing them out to everyone there, even though he doesn't have the first clue of who's who in the zoo. I've had a great week with him, and I'm glad to have that, but an entire childhood is a hard thing to shake.

pointlessness

The ending comes in small successive whimpers, rather than a bang.

I play a semi-final in the pre-season cup against Geelong, but I've hurt my back waterskiing, and get benched. When I come back onto the ground my man kicks a couple of goals to win the Cats the game, and Denis is furious.

I play round 1 anyway and deliver a terrible kick to Wayne Carey, and he dives and injures his shoulder. It's in a sling when he comes to my birthday party, and the mood is dark. Denis calls me and gives me a spray for the first time ever.

I'm not putting my body where I need to. I'm not finding the energy required. But it feels like a subconscious choice, as if I'm slower in the head than the body. Either way, I fall back to the pack.

I injure my thigh in round 5 and miss four games.

I come back through the reserves against the Bombers, and Mark 'Bomber' Thompson is coaching, and he tags me with an American project player. I have the flu, so this novice tagger playing a foreign sport beats me.

I get back into the seniors and do my thigh again. Soft tissue injuries come for us all one day.

I play Hawthorn at the MCG and there's a loose ball between me and a Hawk. The Hawk gets there faster and lower than me.

I go to tackle and he breaks that tackle, and I think – actually, I probably know – *that's it.*

I play Collingwood the following week and I end up on the bench. Princess Diana dies. I know this because I'm sitting on the pine and watching the news broadcast on the big screen at the MCG, because who gives a shit about this game of footy anyway.

We're into the finals but I suspect I won't be playing. Or maybe I will, because my record in finals is strong. It's Thursday night and Denis walks into the locker room and right for me. He grabs my arm and that's how you know he's got something to say. *I can't go with you, son.*

And that's that for the season.

I go around again anyway. There's $170,000 for me if I continue into 1998. I tell myself it doesn't matter if I play seniors or reserves, my pride can handle it. I steel myself for that. *You've done this before – you've gotta dig in here.*

Instead I withdraw from the club over summer. And instead of being myself once a month, I'm being myself once a week, twice a week even, for just a single snatched hour alone. The more comfortable I feel in myself the more I hate the game of football, the idea of football, the pointlessness of football.

Martin Pike has joined the team, and Byron Pickett, too, and they have the run and aggression I used to have. They're younger, meaner junkyard dogs. We split up into teams to do drills, and I'm in the B team.

Injury finally puts me out of my misery. I'm doing simple lane work in Parkville one night and my left thigh rips apart while leaping for the ball. The scans say it's an 8-centimetre tear, probably 10 weeks on the sidelines. I'll need another month after that in the reserves. The earliest I'll be back playing in the ones is the middle of the season. I ring Greg Miller.

I'm out. That's it. I can't do this anymore.

I'm happy at least that I haven't become one of those players who is pushed out. I'm content to have read the writing on the wall. I'm not going to feel any pain at my absence from this life. I'm not afraid of moving on to the next phase.

No more pressure. No more anxiety.

I'm done. Done.

Finished. Finally.

What do I do now? I have no idea what my life looks like after football.

I'd studied a little online to become a stockbroker. Trading has interested me since my days at R&I Bank, when I used to get calls from people at the Bond Corporation and the Parry Corporation about fluctuations in the overnight markets, but it was always an unlikely path.

I try a few things out. I start a graduate diploma in sports business at Victoria University on Tuesday nights. I work as a selector for the Western Australian State of Origin side. But like so many ex-players the thing I know best is footy. I'm institutionalised.

I become a development coach at the Kangaroos, working with the likes of Cameron Mooney and Kent Kingsley. I'm the runner for the reserves team, too, under coach Tony Elshaug. On Tuesdays I coordinate a development day about football skills, and the skills you need for life after football. What would I know about life after footy?

The seniors team makes the grand final but loses. Denis brings in a raft of new assistants at the end of the year and I'm given the flick. But I know what I want to do with my life now. I want to coach.

I interview everywhere.

Sydney is my first choice. I've kept in touch with their coach, Rodney Eade, and he's keen to bring me up there. The wage is wonderful – $120,000, plus $500 a week towards rent. I'm horrendous in my interview. I have my resume, notes, plans and insights in front of me, but I freeze and miss my opening.

Mark 'Choco' Williams interviews me at Port Adelaide, but I suspect he's not really interested in anything other than intelligence gathering. He spends our meeting mostly pumping me for information about North Melbourne.

I interview at Essendon, close to home, where Sheedy is under the pump. They're the most incestuous of all clubs, the Bombers, so they appoint favourite son Terry Daniher instead.

Leigh Matthews gets in touch about a possible job in Brisbane, and says he'll call again in a few days. But a few days pass, and more pass, and Chris Johnson is starring for the Lions, and I hear through friends that what I said to him – that racial slur I'll never be able to unsay – was neither forgiven nor forgotten. I'm no chance for that position.

Jobs in second-string competitions are a possibility. A part-time role with Box Hill. A coaching director gig with a junior academy in Tasmania is on offer, but I haven't done my coaching certificate level II, so I'm not even considered, and that makes me fume.

The Western Jets – one of the Victorian junior pathway teams – reach out. They want me on board and I give it a shot but the job won't put food on my table. I leave a session one night wondering where my life is at. *What am I going to do? What the fuck is going on?*

can't it be fun again?

Things aren't good at home. I'm despondent and anxious. Rejection and aimlessness create a crisis of confidence. I feel impotent. Joanne and I have been gradually drifting apart. We're basically living in separate rooms.

That summer we go on holiday to Paynesville and Lakes Entrance. We camp in the sand. We wave to dolphins from jetskis. We're supposed to be there for weeks, with other people, but early one morning Joanne says we're leaving, she wants to go home. We hit the road and something is amiss. We pull into McDonald's in Bairnsdale and the kids go inside to eat and play. Joanne turns to me. *I'm pregnant. I'm fucking pregnant.*

I think back, and remember. We've been ships in the night but there was that one evening … We had both been to different Christmas parties, ran into one another at home, and, loosened by liquor and holiday spirit, it happened. Now there's a baby coming.

We were both overjoyed the first time we fell pregnant, and the second time, too, but this time we're so distant. Maybe the baby is exactly what our family needs. We talk about how on earth we can make this work, sitting on the back patio for days, but it feels like weeks.

This is our child. There's no way that I can … I pause … *We need to pull our heads in and reconnect, and give it a real go. We've grown up together. It was fun. Can't it be fun again?*

Seven months later, little Molly Rose, my baby girl, is born at St Vincent's Hospital.

I need a job. Missing out on the Sydney position eats away at me. I start thinking of what I might have been able to do for myself in a city that large, with that kind of anonymity. AFL isn't the parochial beast there that it is in Victoria. I tell myself I should look further afield, into those places where people pay more attention to the Steeden than the Sherrin.

A phone call from Weston Creek Football Club in Canberra feels like serendipity. *Would you be interested in coming here for three years? It's a full-time role as a playing coach, while working in development for the AFL in the ACT.*

Joanne puts the offer in perspective. *You need to take the job. If you don't, I'm concerned about your mental health, and physical health, your outlook on life. I'm worried about your future. Our future. It's not going to be easy, but it's what we need to do.*

She doesn't say it, but I suspect there's another thought running through her head. *I need to get this lunatic out of the house for a while.*

Kane is in primary school, Brooke is just starting high school and there's also the baby coming. I would have to go to Canberra by myself.

I'm conflicted. I don't want to leave my family. I love them. I love us.

I'm a homebody. I love my space. I love my castle – this two-storey red-brick beauty with black grout and a terracotta roof. I love the bold block colours on the walls, the burgundy and burnt orange. I love the marble-top kitchen island and the white tile splashback. I love the pool table and six-person hot tub. I love the track lighting and the signed photo of Dennis Lillee and the framed poster of Ayrton Senna and the beautiful old wine barrel I stained and varnished. I love being upstairs with the kids in their bedrooms and playrooms. I love their fish tank, which cracked once, spreading water and goldfish all over the floor.

Football was painful, always, and this house was my reward. It was *our* reward. I can't conceive of leaving it. But I do, because Joanne is right. I worry about what will happen if I don't.

people love war stories

The first time I drive north, it's waterworks all the way. Through Kilmore and Seymour, past Baddaginnie and Benalla, beyond Euroa and Glenrowan, I don't stop crying. I can't believe I'm leaving, but I'm saving myself to save my family. I think about my childhood often and don't want what happened to me to happen to us.

I bring my favourite chair with me, and an old leather couch we've been moving from place to place since Perth. A mattress on the floor will do for a bed. The club has supplied me with a house to live in, and I'll be staying with two young players from country Victoria – kids who played for the Murray Bushrangers but weren't quite drafted in the AFL. I visit the shops every day to buy those basics you need for any house – all the condiments and cleaners a pair of kids from the country wouldn't think to bring with them.

I have my dog, a Siberian husky named Sheira, with me. She eats two raw chicken wings for breakfast every day, and sleeps in my room, and sometimes in the Canberra winter she gets me up to go pee in the middle of the night, and I stand at the door freezing because it's dropped to minus six degrees and the little bitch changes her mind at the threshold and goes back to bed.

A guy at the club works for Qantas, so I'm able to get cheap flights, which helps me get home as often as possible. I really miss the kids. I often just drive down the Hume Highway, too, and Joanne and the kids come to visit in school holidays. The most I would go without seeing them is a fortnight.

There's work to do. This team hasn't won a game in three years, reserves or seniors. I make hundreds of calls to attract new players, and coax older champions out of retirement. I lean on my name – AFL premiership player Dean Laidley, who has contacts at every AFL club, who played with Wayne Carey and learned coaching from Mick Malthouse. You make whatever gravitas you have count, and people love war stories.

I set strong boundaries, train the players hard and put a few noses out of joint. I go to the nth degree, hoping they will, too. On our footy camp I play them a video of Kieren Perkins swimming to gold in the 1500 metres in Atlanta, from lane 8. People have written him off, I tell them. But he's done his training. He knows he's ready. He knows it will come from within.

We play a team called Eastlake in round 1. They're tipped to finish on top, with a boom recruit, Jack Aziz – a VFL legend from Werribee. Ten minutes into the game I try to corner a bouncing ball on the centre wing and clash with an opponent. All of a sudden I can't breathe. Maybe I'm just winded? It gets worse throughout the quarter, my gasps getting more and more shallow.

An ambulance arrives and they tell me it's a punctured lung. It's three minutes until quarter time. *Can you just wait a minute for me?* I ask. *I want to speak to the boys.*

The paramedic is unimpressed. *You can die from this, you know.* I know. *Yeah, just give me a minute.*

I tell the boys about my injury, and I talk to them about how we've trained, how we've learned to make our teammates better, and how faith in themselves and one another will be enough.

danielle laidley

In the back of the ambulance I suck on a morphine whistle. My lung has collapsed. In hospital they thread a needle the length of a shoe in between my ribs, and draw the air out of the space in my chest cavity as I scream. The club president rings me a few minutes later, on the siren. He's in tears. We won. We fucking won.

my heels are clicking

When I don't go home to Melbourne, I don't always know what to do. Once I go to Sydney. And I go out as myself. The game ends and I jump in my car with a bag full of clothes, and I drive until I arrive at a cheap hotel near Kings Cross.

I step out into the city dressed as me, and the anxiety courses through me. After half a block, it subsides a little. After two blocks, I'm watchful but smiling. After four blocks my heels are clicking and I drink in my new surrounds.

I love how big this city feels. There's something in the topography. The strange streets that curve and dip. The absence of the Hoddle grid. The buildings of sandstone instead of bluestone. Sydney feels somehow more muscular than Melbourne. I walk through the Emerald City scared to be alone and happy to be anonymous.

I head to the Taxi Club, where people welcome me. *Come up again soon*, they say. *Stay with me. Next time we'll do this and that and the other.* But I never give out my number. I never really let them know my name. I'm still a secret I have to keep.

I stretch myself thin between playing and coaching, between Melbourne and Canberra and sometimes Sydney, between these roles and states and versions of myself. Heads. Tails. Dean. Danielle.

I drive back to Canberra early one morning after a night in the Cross. It's 4am when I get in my car to leave Sydney. More than a handful of times I nod off behind the wheel and begin to drift. The rumble strips on the edge of the highway save me from crashing.

no boundaries

Halfway through the year, the football media jungle drums are beating. They say Mick Malthouse is coming back to Melbourne. I write him a letter, explaining where I am and what I'm doing, and where I would like to go. I hear nothing. It was worth a shot.

I keep an eye on his side, West Coast, as they charge into the finals but lose to the Bulldogs. Weston Creek makes the finals, too, and we also get knocked out. I'm driving back to Melbourne when the phone rings. *How you going, Tunnel? It's your old coach here.*

Is that Rob Wiley?

Did Rob Wiley fucking coach you? It's Mick!

We talk for 15 minutes. He read my letter. Mick is a family man – he understands the decision to leave my family to support my family. He thinks leaving the city to learn my craft in the suburbs shows how far I'm willing to go. He has something in mind for me – a role that might offer less money but better experience.

I'm coming back to Melbourne, Tunnel, he says. *I can't tell you what club. But they're big and fat and lazy, and they've got a millstone around their neck. We've got a lot of work to do. Do you want a job?*

Our first game together at Collingwood is on New Year's Eve of 1999. It's the Millennium Match, and we're playing Carlton against a backdrop of fireworks and Y2K hysteria. The Blues have just come off a grand final appearance – the Magpies off a wooden spoon.

A young full-forward, Brendan Fevola, is lining up against us in just his third game. He's only 18, and had stopped at a friend's party on the way to the game, where he'd had two cans of bourbon and Coke before pulling through the McDonald's drive-thru for a pair of McChickens. He kicks 12 goals and we lose by 88 points.

Don't worry, says Mick. *It's not as bad as it seems.*

He's calm and it's easy to see why. He's still young and combative. He's coached the West Coast Eagles to a flag, so he has a solid reputation. He's the biggest recruit of the off-season, to the club with the biggest supporter base in the country, so there's certainly pressure, but it's also a club on its knees. The expectations for immediate success are low.

He sees positive flourishes even in that 88-point thumping. We've been coaching for five weeks, not a long time to bed down new tactics, and yet he sees the players attempting his game plan. Things won't instantly become automatic and seamless, but the fact that they're trying his new methods means the group is teachable. Active listening is all he wants from them. And from me?

There are no boundaries, he says. *Your role – your only role – is to keep getting better, to improve and to learn, to bring ideas. The best ideas should win.*

Nathan Buckley is the captain and he immediately buys what Mick is selling. He can see how we want to change the culture, and he leads that change on the field. Even in the warm-up before a game the other players see his intensity – the pressure he puts on himself to hit the target every time, not allowing himself to be sloppy just because he's stretching out his legs.

Their work ethic spills over into me, reigniting that disease of addiction. I'm given a platform to chew up as much football as I want. I go to three or four games every weekend. Depending on the fixture, I try to study our opposition for next week, and for the following week. I write reports and find footage for players. I prepare and deliver defensive line meetings, and prepare and deliver the team meeting for the reserves. As soon as AFL teams are announced publicly on Thursday night, I call Mick and pick his brain about the team we're playing, and how they might line up. He will know some of them personally, and I will, too, and our web of knowledge criss-crosses and strengthens every tailored strategy.

I feel straight away that he trusts me. I feel grateful, too, relieved to be back home. I pay my debt with work.

little truths

The Netscape Navigator browser launched in 1994, but computers weren't ubiquitous then. That took time. By the year 2000 I'm still just exploring what they can do. I have my own PC at work, and the temptation to look up something other than statistics is strong.

I feel safe in my little nook at Victoria Park, so I start exploring. I begin reading about people who live with this feeling of their outsides not matching their insides. I research this word – *transgender* – and read all about the Stonewall Riots, and the murder of Rita Hester.

I make a profile in the chat forum of Yahoo Groups and I enter virtual rooms to talk to people like me here and overseas. I have my chat tab open all day at work, so I can pop in between sipping my tea and coding game tape and looking over injury lists.

Each forum thread builds another bridge off the isolated island I've been living on. I meet a girl named Christie who's just beginning to transition. When I put on my face it's still often heavy, like a drag performer, and I share a photo and she tells me I have to do less, make it more subtle, make myself real. But I can't. For me it's not just a matter of being myself – I need to use the makeup as a disguise, too.

But mainly I consume articles about how it feels to be transgender. I look for little truths and try to recognise myself.

A web entry that describes transgender women as sensing that their frame and body are more feminine than masculine. *Me.*

A thread in a chat forum where every trans girl says she would rather go shopping than hang out at the pub with the boys. *Me.*

An anonymous post describing how anxiety leads to bad behaviours and relentless shame. *Me.*

A research paper that discusses gender dysphoria. *Me.*

An article warning people who fight against their identity: the longer you carry it and conceal it, the stronger it'll become. *Me.*

Me. Me. Me. Me. Me.

My name is Danielle. That's how I refer to myself now, at least when asked in the right company. I've finally found the right company, too. It's the punters at the Greyhound Hotel, that art deco queer haven at 1 Brighton Road, St Kilda, right opposite the town hall. They have drag shows here on Wednesday nights, so I drive down, made up and dressed up, and slink into the bohemian heart of Melbourne, where I guess I belong.

It's 2001 when I first visit, when I finally decide that I've spent enough hours as myself at home, watching the Bengals in a dress on my couch. It's time to be myself in the world, albeit under cover of darkness.

My heart is thumping and pulsing and the cold sweat is made worse by my luck – another encounter with a booze bus, this one on Canterbury Road in Albert Park. I kept putting off leaving the house and so by the time I arrive, well after midnight, it's almost closing. I barely have time for a lap of the bar when the lights come on. A group of trans girls spot me and say hello.

Why don't you come with us?

Where are you going?

The Peel.

And with that I'm tailing strangers to the door of the most noteworthy gay club in Melbourne, on Peel Street in

Collingwood. Walking in this door is scary, and it has me scanning, scanning, scanning, not for people I know but people whose eyes backtrack to mine, as though they know me. I'm looking for that flicker of recognition, the surreptitious whisper to whoever they're with.

Eventually I sink into the comfort of a corner where the foot traffic is light, where we can smoke and joke and I can sip a drink but not too many. I still have to drive home. It's a good time but a vigilant one. Here I am again, just like I was at Three Faces, *uncomfortably comfortable.*

This is the way it goes for me in the early years of the new millennium. I take my chances. Mick soon promotes me to senior assistant, and I begin travelling interstate more frequently. I'm in Brisbane because we're playing the Lions, and I bring my kit of clothes and cosmetics, and I go out to a place in Fortitude Valley I've been told about by the girls from the Greyhound. It's called the Sportsman Hotel, and it's a dirty rotten pub that's seen a million sweaty drag shows. It's friendly and warm and I feel as though I can relax here.

But I really can't. No matter where I go in this country there's always going to be someone from Melbourne or Adelaide or Perth or Hobart who follows the national game, and who can look through my makeup and see the beauty spot above my lip, then scan my jawline and my build and know who they're seeing. I'm talking to a trans girl and a drag queen when a bloke approaches. *Can I have a photo with you?*

Nah …

Come on, he says. *Just one pic.*

I don't pose for photos when I'm like this. I don't like the look on his face either. I don't trust his smile. I ask him where he's from.

Melbourne.

I put my drink down and walk straight out the door.

reading patterns

The AFL coaching merry-go-round begins before the season ends, and at the end of 2002 there's a pair of top jobs on the open market. Terry Wallace is sacked as senior coach by the Bulldogs, and Denis Pagan moves to Carlton, leaving the Kangaroos job vacant as well. It's grand final week and Collingwood is playing, and I apply for both.

I don't have to scramble either. I've been working on a presentation all year in case an opportunity arose. Each week I find an hour or two and polish my PowerPoint. I develop manuals about draft selections, development, culture and leadership. I compile significant statistics from the past 15 flag winners. I'm ready.

I interview with the Bulldogs on Wednesday afternoon. At first I think they're doing it out of courtesy, but then I'm in there – at David Smorgon's offices in Park Street, South Melbourne – and I can see I have them. They're interested. I'm asked to come back and see a headhunter, whose last question is how much I think I'll be paid. *$300,000 a year sounds right.* We leave things there.

The North Melbourne interview is Thursday and it lasts for five hours – a grilling in the conference room of a hotel not far from Arden Street. I get through to Friday afternoon, after the grand final parade, and I'm spent. You could pour me into a bucket. But exhaustion makes me sleep, and adrenaline gets me up, because we've got a premiership to win.

Brisbane is our opponent and they're on top of the ladder. I've been watching them all season, making trips to Queensland to scout them, and to visit the Sportsman Hotel once or twice. I'm at the end of my third year as a full-time AFL coach, and I'm adept now at reading patterns and knowing how plays will unfold before they do.

I know where their stars – Jason Akermanis and Nigel Lappin and Simon Black and Michael Voss – will stand, and run. I build impediments to block and blunt them. I make sure the fearless Scott brothers can't drop off at half-back.

We set traps. We plan attacks. We hang in and defend and tackle like crazy and it's ours if we want it, until a cruel snap in the final two minutes seals it for the Lions, who win by 9 points.

Best laid plans …

We have the mournful post–grand final dinner as a team and then we go out all night. Both the Kangaroos and the Bulldogs have told me they will let me know by Sunday, and Sunday arrives and I haven't slept.

I eventually get a call from David Smorgon. I've missed out. I learn later that the job was mine until my $300,000 contract demand became a deal-breaker for the sons of the west.

No matter though, because I meet Geoff Walsh in a cafe on Bellair Street in Kensington, and he offers me the job as senior coach of the North Melbourne Football Club. Two years at a touch over $300,000 a year. By the time I finish coaching there I'll be earning $700,000 a year.

I feel giddy, and go home to break the news to Joanne.

What? she screams. *I don't want you to coach!*

It has never dawned on me that she might not love the idea of me taking on a role more public and more demanding than any I've had before.

I do it anyway. Apart from anything else, I have a family to support. And I don't know what else I would do.

there are questions

Within weeks I'm reintroduced to the North Melbourne faithful at their best and fairest night. It's held at the Palladium room inside Crown Casino, and after meeting players and assistants, volunteers and staff, it's my turn to make a 25-minute speech.

I'm talking to the crowded room about a changing of the guard when my phone begins buzzing in my jacket pocket. I contextualise the season and am talking about losing experienced players but being given a chance to groom high draft picks and grow the future when the phone vibrates again. I share my own connection to the Shinboner spirit and my wish that we might bring it to a new generation and the phone just keeps on nagging me. I talk about unity. *Buzz.* I talk about strength. *Buzz.* I talk about community. *Buzz.*

Finally I step off stage and get a chance to return the calls, which have been coming from my brother in Western Australia.

My dad has just died.

His esophagus burst.

He bled to death on the kitchen floor.

I don't know which passing emotion to catch. They all slide by and circle back. Distress becomes sadness becomes anger. Regret definitely shows up.

The powers that be tell me to do what I need to do. I get in my car and cry all the way home. I fly back to Dad, and grasp at every memory of our relationship, our attempts to relate and our failures to connect. There are questions.

What could I have done to make our relationship better? Why did I make my visits to him in Perth a box-ticking chore? Could I have done more to wake him up from the sorrowful slumber his life became?

We cancel a planned holiday to Bali and instead I help my brother organise a funeral, which in itself is tough. I speak to my brother sparingly, maybe once every few years. It's not a strained relationship but it is an absent one – not built for this kind of thing.

The funeral is held at Pinnaroo Valley Memorial Park. Dad's cremated and given a small plaque up on top of a hill overlooking a lake. I deliver a eulogy, with little idea about what to say.

I talk warmly about his seat at the Malthouse Tavern in Balga – but I don't talk about how bad it got at home after those flagons of goon.

I talk about the way it felt to walk alongside him on the way to WAFL games – but I don't talk about the matches he never came to see me play.

I talk about his strength atop the roofs of so many houses stretching through the suburbs of Perth – but I don't talk about him kicking me out of home at 12.

I talk about the things that gave him comfort and solace – not the addictions that shaped his life.

After the service, I take three red roses off the coffin, and later I have them bronzed. I guess I just want something I can hang on to, from the man who pushed me away. I want a tangible connection to the true David James Laidley, as much as to the one I knew.

all about the healing

It's 12 October 2002 and a bomb is detonated in a busy Bali nightspot and two North Melbourne players, Mick Martyn and Jason McCartney, are caught in the blast.

Back in Melbourne, we get reports that both players are OK but in hospital. Those reports are revised and refined quickly: Mick will be OK but Jason is a mess. He's flown by medical plane to Darwin. Soon I'm standing in front of his bed at the Alfred Hospital in Prahran, but I don't recognise him. He's a mess of wounds and weeping sores, seared and swollen pinkish skin. His voice is scratchy and stifled by painkillers. I don't know how anyone comes back from that.

I turn my attention to Mick, my former teammate who's been slowing down these past few years. When he's recovered enough from a wound to the scalp, I make the tough decision to let him go. I call him in to the club to break the news with our football manager, Tim Harrington, and CEO, Geoff Walsh. I warn them to let me talk it through, but Tim speaks out of turn.

Mick, unfortunately it's time, he says. *We need to give opportunities to younger players. At this point, it's all over for you.*

Mick doesn't say much, but he's building to something. He's 13 games away from 300. He's recovered from the horror of a terrorist attack in Indonesia. And now he's being delisted in the old social club upstairs. I can see the anger in his breathing, and the rise and fall of his shoulder. He stands, picks up the round trestle table we're sitting at and flings it into the air. It lands on me. *GO AND GET FUCKED!!! I've got options!*

The situation with Jason McCartney is no easier to deal with. Jason is a player who would definitely have been cut from our list, too, but that can't be contemplated given what he's endured. He slowly emerges from hospital and ends up coming to training. He has compression bandages covering every limb. He jogs laps while we do drills. After training he takes off his bandages, showers, then applies his creams and salves and wraps fresh gauze on his arms and legs and neck. He progresses through running and weights into contact drills.

We make an award in his honour. A number 5 guernsey is signed by everyone and put in a frame, and every week we give the McCartney Award to that player who goes above and beyond, overcoming obstacles to perform. If you win, you bring it along with you to training and game day. It stays with you for the week as a reminder.

My first pre-season in charge of a team is all about healing. We're all fragile.

there is no hiding

It's been said that the senior coach of an AFL side becomes the sun around which all the club orbits. You set the tone, direction and rhythm within your own sporting solar system. And usually, you have a little time to do this without pressure. New coaches are appointed when a team is struggling or fractured or rudderless, so they're given a grace period to get it right.

But for me – in the first 11 rounds of 2003 – there is no hiding. There is only a sequence of public and private highs and lows.

In round 1 we surprise St Kilda by winning, and I play unknown former rookie list defender John Baird on Saints champion Nick Riewoldt. The former keeps the latter goalless, earning himself a single Brownlow vote – a beautiful quirk in football history that no one could predict.

In round 2 we play Geelong at Kardinia Park – the toughest away assignment in football – and the Cats ooze young talent in Jimmy Bartel, James Kelly, Gary Ablett Jr and Cameron Ling, yet we shock them with a four-goal win.

In round 3 we play the Lions – the reigning premiers – in Melbourne, and we're in front during the final seconds, until a misguided third man up from Adam Simpson leads to an ugly snap from Michael Voss that tumbles through for a single point, and we play out a draw, 109 to 109. We get hearty pats on the back but we don't want them.

In round 4 we get flogged by Fremantle at Subiaco – an interstate game in which the Dockers take control against a young team sapped by a big few rounds. From here on in, this season is less about football than people.

In round 5 we're playing Carlton. It doesn't help that Denis Pagan has gone there for a truckload of money and it's built up in the media all week long as 'Dean versus Denis', protégé versus master. Denis loves the spectacle and gamesmanship. We hold a joint press conference and he shows up late, keeping me waiting for an hour. I'm annoyed, and I let that sway my pre-game speech. I ask Glenn Archer to talk to the boys about how Denis abandoned the club, abandoned them. It's my mistake, because they can't play against a coach – they can only compete with the players and tactics in front of them. Fevola kicks 8 goals against us and we lose by 9 points. I'm embarrassed and wrathful.

In round 6 we play Adelaide – a match that's been looming for months. I've really been dreading this one. 'Grudge match' doesn't begin to cover what's coming.

In March 2002, 14 months before that round 6 game with Adelaide, I walk in the door of my house and Joanne is standing in front of me. *Have you spoken to Anthony today?* She means Anthony Stevens. I'm with the Magpies at this point and he's with the Kangaroos, but we're still incredibly close. We've been on family holidays together. We've lived 100 metres apart. His wife, Kelli, is close to Joanne. *I think you better speak to Anthony.*

I don't know exactly what's happened. And when I do know, I wish I didn't. Last night there was a party at Glenn Archer's house, and the truth of an affair between Kelli Stevens and Wayne Carey emerged. It shatters the group. Shatters the club. Long friendships – forged over a decade in blood and sweat and laughter and tears – are suddenly over. In one evening the heart is ripped out of the North Melbourne Football Club.

The story sets a new record for engagement. It holds the front page – not the back page – of the *Herald Sun* for 14 days straight. Of course Wayne is no stranger to that limelight. He's been flirting with trouble his entire career, starting a fight here, pinching a breast there. He's the best player in the competition, which is reason enough for an outsized ego, but in his case it's also fed and watered, enabled by players and coaches and administrators. When Wayne was 21, Denis would read us the riot act about our recovery after a night match. *Don't you boys go get on the piss this weekend!* he would say. *You know there's only one player who can get away with that: number 18.* There were rules for us and there were rules for Wayne. It seemed as though no one could tap him on the shoulder and say, *Hey mate, don't do that.* He was too good to reprimand for the bad.

There's tension in the air, and it fizzes and pops. It's Friday night at the Docklands stadium. Round 6. Wayne is wearing red, blue and yellow as the star centre half-forward for the Adelaide Crows, and Anthony is still bleeding blue and white as the new captain of the North Melbourne Kangaroos. Forget 'Dean versus Denis'. Tonight is 'Carey versus Stevens'. This is 'the Rooboy against the 'Roos'.

Arms are cocked for fighting. Heads flinch. The atmosphere is unpleasant. The Rooboy kicks the first fucking goal of the game, and we lose by 54 points. Leigh Colbert is the only player to shake Wayne's hand.

Wayne made a mistake. He made a few. We all do.

a small, small thing

Wins and losses come and go in rounds 7 and 8 and 9 and 10, and then we're at the halfway mark of the year, heading into round 11 against Richmond. There's no rivalry here, but it's yet another significant game.

Jason McCartney is striving but he's also struggling, and he comes to me. *I'm cooked*, he says. *I can't do this anymore.*

I understand. *You can breathe. You can move. You're alive*, I say. *Footy is a small, small thing. You've taught us something big.*

He looks me in the eye. *If I wanted to retire, would you give me a last game?*

There is no question. *Of course I would. You can play this week.*

We decide to keep his retirement a secret until game day. It turns into a difficult week.

We have a rule at North Melbourne about no player appearing on *The Footy Show* on a Thursday night before a Friday-night match, but when Eddie McGuire hears that Jason is playing a comeback game he wants him to go on the show. Jason asks my permission. *I'm not going to say yes or no – it's your decision – but you know my thoughts*, I say. *I'll leave it to you.*

He goes on TV, and I judge him harshly. But maybe it's the right thing to do. The news that Jason is playing immediately turns Friday night from a private appreciation into a public celebration – a full house with caps and T-shirts. Richmond's coach, Danny Frawley, finds a man whose wife died in the same bombing, and has him speak to the Tigers before the game. I can't quite nail why but this sticks in my craw.

I put Jason on the field near the end of the first quarter, and the roar when he runs onto the turf is so warm and organic. He stumbles around the ground, having trouble finding the ball. He gets a few touches before half-time and it's a relief. We're behind on the scoreboard near the end of the match when Jason roars to his teammates, *I'm fucking retiring! It's my last game!* It's the news all the boys have been expecting but didn't yet know for certain and they lift for him, and he kicks two goals and has a hand in one other. We win by 3 points and the fairytale is complete.

There's still half a season left to play.

chopping up my soul

A coach is a storyteller, a motivator – a person who uses words and plans to extract effort from athletes. You have to be able to convince them they can when they believe they can't. But you need people to do that favour for you, too, it turns out.

People spotted this about me at Collingwood, when my behaviour could be broken into two modes. I'm either introverted and withdrawn – looking to leave group settings as quickly as possible – or I'm a volcano erupting over every issue – major or minor, real and perceived. Their media manager confronted me about it one day. *If you're ever going to be a senior coach, you've gotta cut these mood swings out.*

Then I become a senior coach, and I'm no closer to the stability people want from me. Donald McDonald is my assistant coach at one point, and later my boss as football manager. I walk into his office one time – during a bad time – and the look on his face is confused, almost plaintive. His eyes are pleading with me for an explanation. *What are you so angry about?*

Hiding myself is becoming too hard. I'm putting too much energy into concealment – so much so that I become inscrutable. Jess Sinclair, a young player, goes on Triple M radio to chat with the usual blokey panel. It's Dermott Brereton, Eddie McGuire and Sam Newman, but in this setting they go by whatever ocker moniker has just stuck, meaning Derm, Ed and Foss. Tomorrow it could be Purple, Chief and Kinga. The day after that might be Duck, Dipper and Browndog.

How's the new coach going? they ask.

Jess tells them it's going well, and he adds that the players have given me a new nickname. They don't call me Junkyard Dog or Tunnel. They call me 'the Bible'.

Why? ask the radio boys.

Because he's hard to read.

The joke sends these professional special comments men into stitches. They get Jess onto *The Footy Show* that week and prompt him with the same question, so he can repeat his winning line for a live audience and the people watching at home. I play it up at training, too, hauling him up in front of the playing group in a team meeting that turns into a light-hearted biblical sermon.

I tell Jess he's the Judas to my Jesus. *You betrayed me!*

We all laugh and bellow but behind my eyes I have a single thought. *I wish I could tell you. I wish I didn't have to hide.*

I've always thought of what I do to protect my authentic self as compartmentalisation, but that's not what it is anymore. I realise now that I'm breaking myself into bits – sustaining my life by chopping up my soul.

a dangerous untruth

There's angst in my house now. I've got the job and I'm in it constantly, and Joanne doesn't want me to have it, which makes sense. She sees me coming apart at the seams. I've been speaking with some of my trans friends back in the chat rooms, and they sense it too.

Can we ask you a question? they type.

Of course.

Do you coach North Melbourne?

Yes.

Well, know that you're safe with us. We know what you're going through. If you ever need anyone to talk to, we're here.

I stare at the console and sigh, and then I'm crying. I tell them I'm going to leave my marriage. It's not fair on either of us.

No no no, they say. *There's ways you can do this and get through.*

Like what?

Why don't you introduce it into the bedroom?

I don't think about the idea much over the coming days and weeks, then one night Joanne and I go out together for a few drinks. We come home and the timing feels right.

It works. It's nice. Playful. We make excited small talk later about how much fun it was, trying something new, fooling around together. Lingerie, bras, stockings, garters, knickers. This feels like heaven – this alignment of both my selves. But I also think about the way it must look from Joanne's perspective.

To my wife, it must seem like something new for us as a couple – as if it's *our* thing rather than *my* thing – and that's a dangerous untruth. I feel even guiltier about my deception now, but I run with it all the same, because I can't waste this opportunity. I can't take it for granted or let it slip.

I also have to pace myself. I can't make my needs obvious, can't push too hard or too soon or too often, in case Joanne fully figures me out.

For now at least, I have to restrict my true identity to an occasional, innocuous twist. That's the bargain I strike with my soul.

I am 35 years old.

not bad for a boy from balga

There are upsides to coaching. I start taking little Molly to work with me some days and she immediately makes herself at home. Mick Mathouse set the standard for including family in the football club that absorbs so much of the players and coaches' time and attention so when it's my turn at the top, I encourage that inclusiveness too.

There's no denying that the money I'm making is good, and it gets better near the end of 2004 when I present my vision to the North Melbourne board, explaining to them how our premiership window opens in 2007. I have their backing to implement a plan, and I have a new contract with more years, more cash, big bonuses for making finals, and bigger ones for winning them.

Even winning our first pre-season game will now come with a $25,000 bonus. It's easy money, too, because so many clubs don't care about those games, using them only to try untested players, experiment with positions, or blow the cobwebs out for the veterans on their list. For the Kangaroos, winning those games means more attention and more members, so they place a premium on late-summer success. Suits me fine. I'm now earning around $550,000 a year, with the promise of more. Not bad for a boy from Balga.

I come home one day and Joanne has spread one of those community magazines out on the kitchen table – the ones with the real estate listings. There's a one-page advertisement for a big house in Chusan Close in Niddrie. We go from inspection to expression of interest to sold. We move into our mansion with a pool and pool boy and cleaners.

We spend money like crazy. We invest in residential bricks and mortar. We try the share market. Accountants set up various trusts. We buy toys, too. A new boat. A holiday place in Echuca. Two jetskis.

At the end of each season we go overseas. We visit the United Kingdom, so I can spend time with English Premier League clubs like Fulham and Charlton Athletic and Manchester United, and learn what they have to offer. Joanne has read the Dan Brown novels, so we design our own *Da Vinci Code* itinerary. She wants to see the crypt at Westminster Abbey, and I sit outside and read the paper before realising how stupid it is to fly halfway around the world to read *The Sunday Times*. I chuck the newspaper in the bin and wander inside, and am completely floored by the grandest cathedral of them all. We go see Churchill's underground bunker for coordinating the war effort. We do the Buckingham Palace tour.

We visit Ireland and stay in bed and breakfasts all the way around. It's winter. It's always winter in Europe if you're an AFL coach. You have to wait until your AFL career is over if you want to see Santorini in summer. We visit a little pub where a large American family is having a reunion, and they're loud and brash and basically own the joint, so we get hammered with them on pints of Guinness. We walk the darkening streets and the mist is rolling in and it feels like something from a movie. *Don't go near the moors.* We go to the cliffs of Dover and can't see through the fog of our own hangover or the fog that has settled on the edge of the island.

We fly to France and take a bus tour up to Reims, the champagne-growing region, and pop into Piper-Heidsieck and

Mumm and Moët & Chandon. A pickpocket tries to take $1500 from my back pocket on a train in Paris, but I grab him by the throat. *Where's my money?* We fight in the carriage, fall out onto the platform, and the gendarmes come around the corner and arrest him. We end up in court, where he gets three months' jail and we get 1500 euros compensation.

We walk down the River Seine towards the Eiffel Tower, and look out at Montmartre from the top. We visit the Louvre, and the *Mona Lisa* is sort of underwhelming, but the history, the place – the free pass we've been given to access this wider world – it blows your mind at every turn.

Despite the tensions, the Laidleys know how to have a good time. And life can be wonderful.

We have a rule at home. I have to be there at 6pm, because 6pm is dinnertime. And at dinner we turn off the TV and we ask, *How was your day, and what did you do?* Phones vibrate and go ignored.

In the new house I set up an office. This is where I'll do my work, away from everyone. But I feel disconnected there. Instead I sit at the dining table, where I can be a part of my family's life. I want to see which $1 pirate DVD from Bali Molly is watching. I want to be able to pop out the door to where Kane is on his skateboard attempting a kick-flip. I want to wander into Brooke's bedroom, where she's working on her latest psychology assignment. *Don't you psychoanalyse me!* I joke. *You won't like what you find.*

I enjoy the interaction and I usually don't start work in earnest until 10pm anyway, when the house is largely silent. Then it's just me and Sheira. She sits by me and growls to be let out. My gorgeous wolf bolts into the yard to pin down a bird or a rat in the night, and presents me with her prey on the patio.

weight of my own making

I need to spend more time with my players. It's 2005 and my working week needs to change so I'm not consumed by meetings and match-committee and managerial functions. I need my feet on the field.

We tweak roles in a way that allows me to spend more time with my boys, chatting to them while they're doing weights, working with them at one-on-one skills practice. The only problem is that this doesn't so much lighten the workload as shift it. I simply feel the need to do more work at home instead.

I'm working at the kitchen table past midnight most nights. Every week I watch the previous three matches by our upcoming opponent, and take notes. I make statistical comparisons between them and us, searching for correlations and outliers. This data only has value, of course, if I can present it with clarity to the players. When I stay up until 3am and present to them in a meeting at 8am, I'm not sure that's possible.

I get sick a lot. I catch colds, too. I feel headaches. My energy ebbs and my motivation dips. I'm laden with a weight of my own making. I need sleep. I used to take sleeping tablets when I played. Not often but on every road trip. Strange room, different schedule, foreign bed: Stilnox was my friend.

I turn to those pills again now, to make sure I'm resting well in the small windows I give myself to close my eyes. I slowly grow addicted. One pill becomes one-and-a-half becomes two. And that becomes three, with a glass of bourbon and Coke.

There's a long hallway between the kitchen and the bedroom, with maybe 20 metres between them. I know when I've taken my Stilnox that I have about 10 minutes to get to bed, or I'll end up passed out on the floor. Sometimes I get to my long walk a bit late, and I crash and stumble down that hallway like a steel pinball ricocheting from paddle to paddle.

I usually make it though, and collapse into my self-induced general anaesthetic. Morning seems to come quickly, because slumber wears off suddenly. Fast asleep turns to wide awake without warning. It's a horrible feeling, rising from oblivion to eyes wide open.

On Sunday 4 September 2005, the day of our elimination final against Port Adelaide, I walk into the change rooms of Etihad Stadium and my football manager explains that Saverio Rocca – my biggest, tallest forward line target – is at the hospital with his wife, who is due to give birth. I cannot believe I am only being told now, with the first bounce approaching. *You're telling me this three hours before the game? What I am supposed to do?*

I call big Sav.

How's it going?

It's going well.

What do you want to do? I'm happy with whatever you choose.

I want to play.

Well, how long do you think it'll be?

Might be an hour.

Okay, I say, *I'll back you in.*

We're not far away from beginning our on-field warm-up and it's hard to imagine Sav making it to the ground in time to play. But this is what he wants. I have an idea. Our furry North

Melbourne mascot – the Roo Ruckle – is a police officer in his day job. I sprint to where he's performing on the sidelines for the kids in the grandstand. *Can you organise a police escort from the hospital, to get Sav to the ground as quickly as possible?*

He does. And he gets into trouble for it later. Sav gets to the ground halfway through the first quarter and plays.

It's my first final as a senior coach and we lose by 87 points, demolished by the Port Adelaide Power.

surrounded by silence

Sometimes Joanne and I head to Sydney together before the season. We go to the beaches during the day, where I dress as Dean. We go out clubbing at night, when I dress as Danielle. If anyone asks my name, Joanne laughs and says 'HC'. *Hot Chick.*

We go to Stonewall and Arq and the Taxi Club, and for a while our arrangement feels to me like the best possible version of this thing – like something we can both manage. It's like a game, like playing dress-ups.

After partying all night I wake up hungover in a hotel room, and a text message is glowing on my screen, waiting to be read. *YOU'RE NOTHING BUT A GAY CUNT.*

It's come from the father of a girl who goes to school with my youngest daughter. I don't understand, but I'm wide awake now and losing my mind. I'm too paralysed to respond.

Two hours later another text comes through. *Sorry folks, that was my son – he's grabbed my phone and sent that message to everyone.*

It was a practical joke. A shit one.

I come home from work one day and Joanne says she's heading to Echuca. We have a holiday house there, but she's going to meet Kelli Stevens, who wants to catch up. Kelli has something to share – something she's known for a long time.

When I was coaching in Canberra at Weston Creek, I lived with two young players. One of them knows the Stevens family well. And that player, Joanne now learns, rummaged through my belongings. He went into my bedroom and found a suitcase, and found my clothing and makeup, and told people about it. This means that Anthony – my friend and teammate and captain – has known or suspected something about me for five years.

Joanne plays a straight bat, pretending that this news is all a surprise to her, while noting, too, that this is our private life. Then she comes home the next day and tells me what's happened. This is, I imagine, the first time she realises how deep this thing runs within me. She asks me if I'm gay.

No, I say, *but I have this genuine issue with my gender. And at some point when I am comfortable – or when we are – we need to go and see someone about it.*

Yet we don't make any plans. We don't call any experts. We don't discuss it later. It's like a question has been asked but both of us would rather leave it unanswered. The truth just hangs in the air, surrounded by silence.

On grand final day of 2005, the Swans play the Eagles, and it's Joanne's 40th birthday, so we have a big party that starts mid-afternoon – a short while after Leo Barry wins the flag for Sydney – and gathers a bit of pace after dark. We haven't been in our new home long, so it feels like a good chance to celebrate and warm the house.

It's a nice spring night but beginning to cool, so I fire up the outdoor gas heaters, and people gather around the pool. Anthony and Kelli are there, and at some point I hear a commotion. Another guest has started calling Kelli names, trolling her subtly and not-so-subtly over the Carey affair. I try to settle things down. *Right, I don't care who you are or what it's about, but not tonight, not at my house.*

I go back inside, and return to preparing the food and fetching drinks and tweaking the playlist. I hear a crash and the fight is on. I sprint outside to stop it and lose a thong, stand on broken glass and slice a great gash into the arch of my right foot. I jump into the brawl, blood gushing from my wound, and I'm not sure who I'm fighting – maybe both of them – but I end up wrestling with Anthony, each of us grabbing the other in a headlock. I can barely breathe as we roll around on my back lawn, and when it's all done we each have a black eye.

I'm exhausted from finishing fifth and getting beaten in our first final. *It's not acceptable – it's my wife's birthday!*

He's exhausted from finishing his career and almost losing his marriage. *It's not acceptable – my wife's been slagged off!*

He withdraws from me. I withdraw from him. We don't know it yet, but our stubbornness is going to cost us many years of friendship.

The footy doesn't stop, of course, after the season is over. We need a key defender, which means I need to visit Hawthorn's full-back, Jonathan Hay, in Byron Bay. He seems in a good place mentally. We don't yet know about his depression or bipolar disorder. We only know we can complete a huge deal with the Hawks to get him, but I have to visit him first.

I don't know whether my team is coming or going.

I don't know whether my marriage is dying or evolving.

I don't know whether my friends are with me or not.

On Monday morning I board a flight for New South Wales, wearing big sunglasses dipped over the shiner glowing on my cheekbone. I'm on crutches, too, to take the pressure off the cut that's severed two tendons in my foot. It's 10 centimetres long and 2 centimetres deep, and shaped like a question mark.

we're all hurting

I can't get myself going anymore. I spend almost the entire 2006 pre-season in bed, depressed and depleted. I get this way when black clouds linger. I try to sleep it off. My senior assistant, Darren Crocker, takes training most days and makes my excuses. Sometimes I go into the club and watch, more bystander than anything else. I'm a pantomime coach.

When I finally realise that I need to do my job, I focus on the last game I watched, the grand final between Sydney and West Coast, and I study both teams. I see what football has become. It's a stoppage contest, where bigger bodies count and tackles rule everything. I decide that's what we will try to match.

We begin specialised tackling training with the Melbourne Storm. If the Swans and the Eagles want to wrestle everyone to death, then we'll be ready. We visit the NRL club to learn from some of its finest, like assistant coach Michael Maguire, football manager Frank Ponissi and retired prop forward Robbie Kearns. We do recovery sessions with them, and build relationships.

The former mixed martial arts guru John Donehue is the Storm's 'dark arts' wrestling coach, and he comes to Arden Street to refine our grappling skills.

We work on developing our own tackle statistics, too, so we can better track our progress. We don't just register tackles anymore. Now we count missed tackles. Broken tackles. Gang tackles. Tackles to the ground. Tackles that lead to scores.

People begin recognising what the game has become. Stories start appearing in print about how the Sherrin is now in open play for the least amount of time in the history of the game. Pundits bemoan sequences within matches where one stoppage leads to another and another, until the spectators are watching five, six and seven scrimmages in a row.

The AFL takes note and takes action. They tweak the rules to keep the ball moving. They store spare Sherrins in baskets behind the goals, so that play can restart more quickly when a ball is kicked into the crowd. They instruct field umpires to throw the ball up immediately in play, and boundary umpires to throw it in more quickly, too. These adjustments help make footy a transition game again, and it catches us on the hop. We've spent our summer bulking up and it becomes a liability.

If the ball escapes us at stoppage, we have no running power to match. When we get in front in games, we invariably get outrun and overrun. Halfway through the season we've won two and lost nine, and if it weren't for a recent contract extension I'd get the sack.

Every now and then, the universe grants you a dose of perspective. The club has invited a special visitor to join us at training. It's a young boy, Luke, and today, 5 May, is his 13th birthday. Eight days earlier his father was stabbed to death.

Luke's aunty has told the club his story, how he and his dad were members of the cheer squad. She drives him in and he's apparently most nervous about meeting me, the Junkyard Dog, the notoriously grumpy coach he's seen in all the press conferences. He's grown up around tough people, but in Luke's mind I'm tougher than all that. I'm someone to be feared.

When Luke steps out of the car, I bend low to meet him and give him a hug and a smile, and tell him he's my right-hand man for the day. Wherever I go, Luke comes too, out onto the field and into inner sanctum meetings and up through the club. I introduce him to the stars – to Glenn Archer and Boomer Harvey and his favourite player of all, Daniel Wells.

At the end of the day I say goodbye, and Luke leaves, and I don't give him another thought. Not until 16 years later when, as a 28-year-old man, he finds my number and texts me, thanking me for my compassion – and showing me kindness in return.

I learn that that day was one of the few positive memories in Luke's dark and troubled teenage years. It's one of those happy moments he leans on to see him through his struggles.

When you coach a football team, no matter what level, it's easy to forget that you're a figurehead people turn to and take their cues from. People listen to you, and your impact is felt through gestures small and big. And sometimes you need a reminder about the power of that gift, about how what you give to others resonates beyond the moment.

This guy has been chipping me all night long. It's only three weeks after Luke's visit, and we're playing the Saints at the Telstra Dome, and getting done. I'm trying to focus on that but every time I walk up or down the aisles of the grandstand I hear this supporter – a bloke in his late thirties maybe – unloading on me.

It's getting hard to block him out, but I keep myself in check. When the game ends, he hurls a few more jeers at me and I stop, and I look at him.

We're all hurting, I tell him. *Please come downstairs with me, and see the hurt and the effort.*

It defuses the tension, but he looks at the security guards behind me and in front of me and shakes his head. He doesn't want to do that.

Are you sure? I say. *Come down and I'll show you what I mean.*

He shakes his head again. *Nah, nah.*

The whole exchange is captured on camera and broadcast nationally. It might have been a footy media talking point for a day, if that, but on Monday morning at 6:30am it becomes something so much bigger. I get a call from our CEO, Geoff Walsh.

The man from the match was hit by a train after the game. He took his own life that night at 1:15am, on the Frankston line near Seaford. I feel sick, and dizzy. Geoff meets with the devastated family and offers them professional support services, and they stress to the club that what happened at the game was unrelated to his passing. I speak to the police and they assure me of that too. I call the parents, too, because I want to make sure they are okay, and they reinforce the same message, that their son had been ill and suffering. But I can't shake the nausea, because who really knows.

The story breaks soon enough, and the incident is quickly twisted into a bitter confrontation, with me as an aggressor. A media scrum sets up camp outside my home and takes photos of my children leaving for school. We're prisoners in our own home.

We organise a press conference, and I find a way to slip out of the house unseen. Our place backs onto a creek, so I scale my back fence and run down to a side street where a club staffer is waiting to pick me up and ferry me to Arden Street.

I sit down in front of the cameras and I want to be heartfelt and authentic – to offer the most human response I can to a loss I can't comprehend – but the language you need to use around suicide and self-harm needs to be so precise, so sensitive, and it's too easy to slip up, so I keep my eyes on the written statement in front of me.

I try to explain my devastation. I try to say sorry without assuming blame. People always talk about how footy isn't a matter of life and death, and they're right. I'm not equipped for this moment. Is anyone?

hands off the wheel

This season can't get any worse, but it's going to try. We play Sydney at the SCG in early August and it's Glenn Archer's 250th game. We're down by a heap and looking to lose by a lot more again when Saverio Rocca offers the side a choice. *We can embarrass ourselves, or put some pride into it and pressure the scoreboard!* he roars. *We can fucking win this game!*

Sometimes it's best when coaching to step away and take your hands off the wheel. When you can tell they've made the decision to fight, you don't want to accidentally change their minds, so I skip any motivational talk and offer them only a sketch of how they might win.

We're going to use the whole ground, open up the play, and create a vacuum of space in which our best footy can happen – and sure enough Simmo and Harro and Wellsy and Boomer get to work, and we start winning and spreading and scoring.

Late in the game the ball hits the heel of a Swans player and pops out of bounds on the full, giving us a shot on goal. It's a shot favoured by a left-footer, so our small left-footed forward, Corey Jones, runs 40 metres to get to the ball before anyone else. The umpire lets him take the kick, even though he shouldn't – many other players were closer – and Corey launches from his favoured side and the ball curls in an arc through the goals. We win, with seconds left, and are in raptures.

I come down from the coaches' box through the crowd at the SCG, and the Swans fans all around me are incensed. I have a fist raised high anyway. A win on the road always sets the senses firing.

Soon after I notice a group of Sydney staff and officials on the bench, clustering and milling, but I can't tell what's going on. I only find out later that one of their head trainers has suffered a heart attack and died.

The more passionate and parochial Sydney fans blame the Kangaroos, for exactly what I'm not sure – an ill-gotten free kick maybe – and soon they take to blaming me specifically. The letters start rolling in to the club within days.

You should hand back the four points.

You're an absolute disgrace.

You disgust me.

We lose to Adelaide in South Australia in round 16, and I'm sapped. I need time to myself. I don't eat with the players or coaches – I just go up to my hotel room and spend the evening alone.

I fly out of town early the next morning, headed for Sydney. Ostensibly I'm going to watch Sydney versus Richmond, scouting a future opponent, but in reality I just want to go out in Kings Cross by myself. I have two bags with me, one for Dean and the other for Danielle. The bag for Danielle goes missing, and ends up in Melbourne. It's locked so there's no damage done, but I can no longer go out. I watch the footy, go to bed early and fly home to Melbourne the next day, lethargic and annoyed.

My personal assistant calls me. Arden Street is smouldering. The club has been hit by an arsonist at 4am, for the second time in as many months. The old Arden Street betting shed was razed in the first fire, along with two club vans. This fire destroys the portable buildings that house our gym, bootstudders' room and assistant coaches' offices. The players' lounge – their TVs and couches, PlayStation and pinball – is all gone.

We're only two thirds of the way through the year, but the final third of the season disappears with a splutter and a sigh, and I'm thankful for that. I need a break.

look through the storm

A new year requires a new approach, so we start pre-season early – with player surgeries as soon as possible and a training block before Christmas that includes our training camp. It's not like other camps. It's not led by me at all.

The players are taken mostly out of my care and handed over to the Special Operations Group of Victoria Police, otherwise known as the SOG, or the Sons of God, or the Soggies. They're a group of elite counterterrorism cops, trained to respond to sieges and conduct mobile intercepts. And they subject the players of the North Melbourne Football Club to the most gruelling training camp I've yet seen.

We meet at the club and the boys are bussed down to Port Melbourne beach for a horrendous five-hour fitness session, slogging through the sand until after lunch, then it's back on the bus and up to the Dandenong Ranges, where they're split into groups. Over the coming days they're given increasingly less sleep, not quite enough food, and ordered to perform complex tasks with minimal instruction. On one night they have to stand guard, on a rotating watch shift. By day three half the squad are so tired they begin to fall over. That's when the gut-wrenching exercises with iron bars begin. These iron bars are three feet long and an inch-and-a-half thick, and every player has one. They're instruments of torture.

I seize a moment immediately after that camp, when they are waterlogged and beaten down. We've returned to Arden Street and I make them stand at the edge of the oval. I place the 1996 premiership cup – the one I won with this club – in the centre of the oval. From the boundary line it looks tiny. *How far away that must look, with what happened last year!* I bellow. *But it's never as far as it may seem!*

I bring them in a bit closer, step by step, metre by metre, as the rain tumbles down, and I tell them to remember that what they're playing for is always in their grasp. Always.

You just have to look through the storm and you'll see it, I say. *It's always within reach.*

I take the players back to those iron bars every time someone is late or a session is missed that year. In round 3 we play poorly against Hawthorn. I watch the boys walk into the rooms and I bark, *Where's your fucking bars?*

This time, the captain, Adam Simpson, says enough is enough.

Nah, fuck you, he says to me. *We're not doing this anymore.*

And I'm with him. I've been waiting for the day when this side would take control of their own preparation. My speech now takes them back to that cold day when we returned from the camp, rain drizzling down and wind whipping at any exposed skin.

Look through the storm, I remind them. *Success is never as far away as it seems.*

When I first start coaching North Melbourne, the plan of the day is for the city of Canberra to financially back the cash-strapped Kangaroos, and in exchange we play three games there each year. Next we're offered a contract by Gold Coast to play those three games there, and we roll our pre-season camps into the bargain. Not long after, the relocation rumble gets even louder – we should shift to Gold Coast entirely. On offer are a raft of draft picks and a new stadium – a package worth $100 million dollars. Our club is now split, divided into camps, the movers and the stayers.

The league CEO, Andrew Demetriou, is calling me, asking me to come and see him. He wants to show me this big bound book with all the benefits of the move spelled out. I'm a young coach with little to no resources. The sunshine and beaches and new equipment and fresh outlook seem seductive. We lose our first three games and I'm ready to pack.

I reckon we're cooked, I tell the other coaches. *But I'll tell you what we're going to do. We're gonna have some fun, we're gonna work hard, and we'll see what happens.*

I tell the players the same thing. *Let's make this a fun place to be,* I say. *Look after each other. Make sure your teammates are okay.*

We talk about not carrying the burden of what might happen, but instead focusing on each moment and being present in whatever that looks like. We don't know it but we're practising mindfulness. We shock the league – and ourselves – by winning 10 out of our next 12 games.

I'm sitting on the balcony of my hotel room in Queensland one morning before a night game against Brisbane. I look out at Surfers Paradise and sip my tea in a light balmy breeze. I see families playing in the surf and sand. And this is when it hits me: if we move here we will have to uproot 60 families, 70 families, possibly more, and bring them into this foreign land. Every bit of togetherness and goodwill we've built will be destroyed. Players have started coming to me, too. Glenn Archer. Daniel Wells. Michael Firrito. Josh Gibson. They all say the same thing. *If the club moves to the Gold Coast, I won't be going.*

I stay away from relocation meetings as much as possible. I make no public commitments to my position either way. The chairman, Graham Duff, offers me a three-year contract extension, but I decline. I want to see where everything goes.

Graham steps down and James Brayshaw takes his place, and he begins fighting the AFL push. The press finally corners me and asks what I think of this pledge from James to pay off debt and right the ship – or go down swinging – and my lack of political skill sticks out like dogs' balls. *Let's see what happens*, I answer, smiling, tongue in cheek. *I'll believe it when I see it.*

I'm called in by the board, grilled and given a whack. I whack them back.

There are no resources underneath me here – none, I note. *This club has had four chairmen and three CEOs in seven years. You want me to have trust in the organisation, but the organisation doesn't have trust in itself.*

With no continuity and no foundation, I have no guarantees, and I offer none either. I'm irate, to the point that I meet with Carlton and talk to their coach, Brett Ratten, and their CEO, Greg Swann, about a head–of-coaching position at the Blues, with less stress and slightly more money. In the end I sign on with the Kangaroos for two more years, but we add a clause to the deal. In round 14 of the final year of the contract, both parties – club and coach – need to give an immediate indication of whether they intend to stay together or go their separate ways. Either yes, we're going forward, or no, it's time to go.

Too many coaches go into the tail end of every season without any such certainty – with a sword swinging over their neck each week. I'm not going to put myself through that. I'm already dying a slow death. I'm 40 years old and feel as though I have one foot in the grave. If the coach is the sun around which a club orbits, I don't know how much longer my flame can flicker.

hold your head up high

I'm driving home from the final game of the 2007 home-and-away season and we've won, finishing in fourth place, earning ourselves a double chance going into the finals. I should be on a high – even if we lose the qualifying final to Geelong, we'll still be playing in a semi-final. But I'm arguing with Joanne over something trivial, and I take it too far.

I pull up on Dudley Street, just past Festival Hall. I put the car in park, grab my bag, open the door and walk away, leaving her there. I'm not going home right now. In fact, I don't go home all week. I check in to a boxy little hotel room in Parkville and begin thinking about our final against Geelong.

I go to work every day, and my anxiety soars. On the way back to my room each night I buy a frozen meal from the supermarket. I sit in the hotel sweating, struggling to sleep. I've always been proud of my preparation, but I do nothing this week. Nothing at all. The team has fought so hard to give themselves this opportunity, and I spend the days in the lead-up staring at the ceiling.

The work falls to the football department, or whatever is left of it. Adam Simpson is my captain but also a de facto midfield coach. Two other assistant coaches come in each day, working full-time hours on part-time salaries. I know winning this week will be like climbing Everest in shorts and a T-shirt, and we're beaten by 106 points.

Walking downstairs to see the players afterwards, I don't know what to say or how to say it.

By this point in time I'm no longer the Bible. I'm easy to read. I'm Dan Brown. I'm Dr Seuss. I'm Coaching for Dummies. I'd been given a book a while back – *Surviving and Thriving with Generation Y at Work* – and it became a manual for reading and reaching these boys. They know my mannerisms and my tone only too well.

And they are my boys. I look at them now and think of all their stupid nicknames – like Shagga (Shannon Grant) and Leroy (Leigh Brown) and Dish (Drew Petrie) and Patch (Leigh Adams) and Spitta (Andrew Swallow) – and I can't help smiling.

I feel like I've been run over by a Mack truck, fellas, and I wasn't even out there, I say, facing the room. *But we've had a ripping season. We've had fun. We've worked our backside off, and because we did we have another opportunity next week. We get to have another go, to dispel what they're going to say about us in the paper and on radio and TV. We have a second chance. Let's use it.*

I meet the players at a restaurant on Errol Street and explain why I'm confident we'll beat Hawthorn. We have a formula that works well against them – the right personnel for the right roles. Adam Simpson can quell the creativity of Sam Mitchell. Leigh Harding can stop Clinton Young from gathering uncontested marks through the wing. Brady Rawlings can block the drive of Luke Hodge. Josh Gibson knows how to corral Lance Franklin.

After picking at our meals we sit in a square facing inward, eyeballing one another. I begin talking about my feelings because I need to reach the boys and that's what Gen Y does. I let them know that I think I've let them down, but I don't detail exactly how or why.

I ask who's seen the movie *Saving Private Ryan*. Most people have, and most of the time they think of the bloody opening scene on the beach at Normandy. I have a different moment in mind, closer to the end of the film, when they're sent to save an important bridge from being bombed.

Remember how they were prepared, and set, and waiting for the enemy? Remember how they played a little music, and sat quietly? I say. *That's where we're at, boys. We've got everything set. We're together. We're ready.*

By the time the game arrives I have little left to say. I've spoken to them about using their strengths – focusing on whatever makes their game special and bringing that to the field, dazzling me with their speed or strength, talent or tricks. I actually bring Denis Pagan along, and ask him to speak to them. The players probably think it's a conceit – an effort to shake things up and do something different. In truth I just need to lean on someone else right now.

We win by 33 points in front of 74,981 people, and then I'm cooked, and they are, too. This was our grand final. We play a preliminary final the following week but we're running on fumes.

Fourteen players need pain-killing injections to take the field. Port Adelaide monster us by 15 goals, and I can live with the result.

The one thing I detest, though, is watching Power spearhead Warren Tredrea bowing to the crowd, lairising and showboating when the win is secure. I believe in winning gracefully and professionally, and his theatrics make me apoplectic. This is Glenn Archer's last game – he deserves better.

Glenn had a horrible season the year before, when I thought he should probably retire. But we came up with a plan to get him through 2007. I didn't take him interstate, letting him rest at home instead. I didn't play him in the reserves, because there was no point. If he felt off, he would sit down with me for a week or two and rest. When he felt strong again, we would play him, often in daring five-minute bursts through the midfield. I didn't make him come in on Tuesdays for skills training, because I wanted him fresh.

One quirk emerges during this time, and it's something I'm not expecting in a veteran as tough and uncompromising as Glenn. Every Monday morning he comes into my office to catch up and shoot the shit, but all he really wants to hear is, *Well done, Arch,* and all he really wants to ask is, *Who am I on this week?* He wants validation and a challenge.

People talk about motivation always coming from inside. They say it means nothing if you're relying on credit bestowed by others. But inside of every man on the field is a little boy, and that little boy once sat on a muddy change room floor, and his coach singled him out for his effort – *Great job today, son, hold your head up high* – and that made him feel good inside. It's a team game and a club effort, but each of us is the star of our own story, the protagonist of our only life.

i feel thin

One year later, and things are tough again. We've been grinding against expectation all season long, stumbling near the finish, beaten by Port Adelaide in the last round, falling out of the top four and into an elimination final against Sydney in Sydney. The game is being played in a flood, and we're up at half-time by three goals. It feels as though the most important hour of my life is approaching, and of course it isn't, but this is the trick the game plays on you in the moment.

We get overrun by 35 points, and I've never felt so gutted. Later I argue with the new football manager at the airport. It's about something inconsequential, but our tempers are frayed.

As I digest it all in the coming days, I question what this position is doing to me. The answer is obvious – what my wife always knew it would do. *I don't want you to coach!*

The rhythm of the last few years suddenly feels unhealthy. In pre-season I fill myself up on intel and hope, which I spend each week on my players, while my mood bounces and drops on every win and loss. I fortify myself for the final matches of the year and place outsized importance on what 22 men do to 22 other men. I collapse and recover and do it all again. It's madness.

I reckon that's it, I tell Brayshaw one morning. *We're staying in Melbourne, we've got development programs in place. Maybe it's time to step away and let someone else come in.*

He doesn't think so. He thinks I'm right for the role. We have a new CEO in Eugene Arocca, and he tells me that support is coming, that they're looking at luring Nathan Buckley away from Collingwood or Scott Burns away from West Coast, and inside I laugh grimly, because bringing in assistant coaches of that calibre isn't a move designed to support me so much as succeed or supplant me.

I go away to the United Kingdom on another study tour. At a Champions League match I meet Gordon Strachan, a former star soccer player with Dundee and Aberdeen, Manchester United and Leeds United, who's now coaching Celtic in Glasgow. We spend a week together and I feel as though I'm learning again.

I need to. The AFL is in a state of transition away from more than 100 years of playing simple man-on-man football to something altogether more complex. Tectonic plates are shifting. Geelong and Port Adelaide are playing a new brand where they fold back their defensive zone. Alastair Clarkson is creating his 'cluster' while Mick Malthouse is leading the 'forward press'.

I feel as though I understand the game better than ever before, but I'm not convinced I have the innovative spark. I feel thin, and I wear it on an increasingly gaunt face. I throw myself into it all again, launching an attack on the 2009 season, but I only get halfway through the year before I begin thinking about that round 14 clause in my contract. A decision is coming.

It's round 12 against the Crows, in Adelaide on a Sunday evening. We arrive on Saturday, and after settling in to the team hotel and going through our meetings and meals we turn in for the evening, but I can't sleep.

I go for a walk and it turns into a sprawling wander, from 2am to daybreak. It rains and rains and I'm wearing a cotton hoodie that gets soaked through. No one can recognise me, or so I think. Twelve years later a supporter comes up to me and says he saw me on that lonely walk, and thought I looked distressed, and always wondered if he should have stopped to ask if I was okay. I would have answered the question as I always do. *Thanks. I'm fine.*

Three goals is all the team can produce that night in a sad 44-point loss. It's Adam Simpson's 300th game. Mine too, although for me it's 151 as a player and 149 as coach. The club doesn't notice my milestone but Simmo does. He gathers the match ball, signs it and puts it in a glass case with a plaque, and hands it to me.

Back in Melbourne I get set for my quarterly presentation to the board. I open my laptop ready to type out my plan. I open a new file and before I can begin typing my right arm reaches forward, almost as if it's acting independent of my mind. My hand clutches the laptop screen and pushes it closed. I hold my palm flat on top of the computer for a minute, and walk away from my desk for the last time.

a new day

On Monday night, players come around to my house and we have a party. It's a strange occasion.

I can already feel the way the cord is cut – the fact that I will not see them this week at work, or the week after that, or any week ever again. When you spend so much time devoting yourself to something in such complete alignment with others, it's disorienting to even consider a new direction.

I get pretty loose that night, drunk on a heady mix of relief and cheap beer sculled out of boots. When dawn starts to break, I'm sitting in my back yard with Daniel Pratt and Michael Firrito and they're smiling.

Bloody good night, they say. *Why weren't you like this when you were coaching us?*

There are so many reasons. The time away from family and friends is draining, and the denial of self becomes obligatory and total. The spotlight is another issue, through the loneliness it creates and the way it keeps you on guard, ever vigilant – bone weary and bloodshot and suffocating.

I look at these guys and I think back to the first time I walked into the North Melbourne Football Club, when Greg Miller told me that the Kangaroos are rich in cultural capital. It's not the buildings or the crowds or the lights and action and uniforms. It's everyone around you. When you have a job in clubland, you pour an unbalanced emotional equity into your working life –

into all these people. That's why it drains you and yet that's what you'll miss most of all.

The weight is gone. The sun is coming up.

A new day is here. Maybe a new person.

I want to feel immediately lighter but I'm like a chip to seagulls. SEN Radio wants me to work with their callers. Channel 10 wants me for a special comments job. *The Footy Show* is eager to have me as a guest.

I speak to practically every AFL club. I go to a pub in Fitzroy to meet Ross Lyon, who wants me to do some opposition analysis as his Saints head towards the finals. I talk to Brisbane about a job supporting Michael Voss in his rookie coach year. But Port Adelaide is the most interesting and interested.

I meet their entire coaching staff, led by Mark 'Choco' Williams. They've isolated various North Melbourne games I coached, and want to understand my strategies and positional moves. *Why did you do that then? How did you think of that?* I talk to them about my method, playing each game on the whiteboard, wargaming all possibilities, listing all contingencies. I tell them all the answers because I no longer have any intellectual property to protect.

I know Choco well. We sit together at coaches' association gatherings, because you're seated in alphabetical order, and N for North is always next to P for Port. I take the job in South Australia, coaching his coaches. He sees the game differently from me, so I'm also there as the yang to his yin, to try to achieve a balance between his flowy, showy footy and my desire for a defensive shitfight.

The family is going to come with me. We fly over and pick out new schools for Kane and Molly. One of the Power board members is in real estate, so we begin househunting. But it feels wrong.

Joanne and I aren't doing well. She suspects my gender issues are more than some passing sexual novelty, and the moment that dawns on her she shuts down. I don't blame her one bit. We sit and talk about it but it's not working between us. In the new year I make a decision and let her know. *You're staying,* I say. *I'm going. By myself.*

I'll be in Melbourne every other weekend anyway. We can pre-book cheap flights so that Molly and Kane can visit all the time. Brooke is old enough now to drive across and visit her dad as part of an adventure with friends.

I pack up my car with some clothes, an Esky, a few pots and pans, a mattress and not much more, and I drive to my new townhouse in coastal Glenelg. There's a pub called the Watermark Hotel only 50 metres from my door in one direction, and a Coles supermarket 50 metres in the other direction, and the beach across the street.

I unpack and stare at all my belongings. I go to the supermarket before midnight to buy all the basics, and as I walk through the doors I run into former player and coach Graham Cornes, the most South Australian footy figure the state has to offer, who grins and shakes my hand with vigour. *Welcome to Adelaide!*

something of a game

I get to be myself now most days. And some days, all day. The move has been restorative for me. I go into Alberton and work with the coaches at the football club each day, and then I drive home to my beachfront flat, to be myself, by myself. In 2010 I spend perhaps 70 per cent of my spare time as Danielle, and it's wonderful.

I jump online to grow my wardrobe – I know all my sizes now – in between reviewing game tape and oppo presentations.

I apply false lashes, because mascara is too difficult to remove in a hurry, while I annotate staff contracts and annual reviews.

I try out a nude lip gloss or a light pink lipstick while composing an email to CEO Mark Haysman.

I put white shimmer on my eyelids with a dark purple highlighter around the edge, and then I cook my favourite meal, Vietnamese pho with stock and poached chicken, bok choy, bean shoots, spring onions and a little chilli – but not too much because I get heartburn – on a base of flat noodles with a bowl of rice on the side.

I pop on a miniskirt, leggings and sandals with a nice crop top, and chat on the phone to midfield coach Matthew Primus about how our draftees are faring in the SANFL.

I try out big draggy makeup that will disguise my jawbone and the mole above my lip, and I turn on the TV to watch *RuPaul's Drag Race* on Foxtel.

My clothes are strewn everywhere. My makeup station is a mess. I shower and shave and moisturise while playing music and sipping bourbon. I'm home and I don't have to worry about hiding my things or locking the door, and there's a calmness and freedom about my life that I've never had before.

Life is something of a game now, or at least it feels that way. I've always liked the idea of a flutter, and now I have time to indulge in some harmless betting. I study soccer mostly, sifting through reviews and previews of games in England. I develop a system of factors for determining winners. If a team ticks five of my set boxes against an opponent, I bet on them.

And I win. I win quite often. I get a good price on Nottingham Forest one day – you always get better betting prices on teams in the Championship than the Premier League – and pocket $5000, and that sets me on a path of betting big and spending big.

I buy myself a human-hair wig, which costs me $2500 – blonde with feathering, a lace front, which means you glue it down to your scalp at the top of the forehead – and a special wig stand, too. I win more bets and buy more wigs. This is my indulgence now. Wavy and straight. Shoulder length and down to the dent of my buttocks. I try a short dark wig once, but it doesn't work with my bone structure or skin. I like lighter hair. Call me a natural blonde. We have more fun.

I reach a point where I don't even need to draw down on my wage. I make enough gambling to get by. Port Adelaide is paying my rent, so my salary becomes my savings. Still, the wagering gets out of hand. Of course it does.

One day I bet $10,000 on LeBron James and the Miami Heat to win. It's a stupid bet, too. They're so heavily favoured – paying $1.10 – that I'm basically risking ten grand to win one grand.

That's gambling for the thrill, not the money. With five seconds to go they're five points down. But basketball has the unique ability to elongate the final moments of any game, and this one stretches with foul shots made and missed until a buzzer-beating three-point shot from LeBron ties it up, sending it into overtime, which the Heat wins.

I tell myself I'll never do that again, then I do exactly the same thing a week later, betting on the Los Angeles Lakers this time. Only this time they lose.

Port is losing, too. It's not a good year. By the middle of winter they're on a nine-game winless streak. The club powerbrokers want to meet with me to ask what I think is going on. I guess that our preparation started too early – that we didn't ease into our season. They've heard a rumour that I'm going back to West Coast to coach there, but there's no truth at all to the whisper. They ask if I want to coach the Power.

That's so disrespectful, I say. *I've come over here to support Choco, my friend, and not to dance on anyone's grave. Be respectful enough – if you want to ask me – to ask me when you don't have a coach, because I'm not here to do what you're asking to anyone, let alone a mate.*

Ten days later they sack Choco, and come back to me, but I want none of this place or these people. I want to go back to Melbourne.

the banged-up and broken state of things

I begin a foolish piecemeal work arrangement, committing to a midweek radio show on SEN, two days of leadership consultancy work through a company run out of Brisbane and Sydney, and two days still with Port Adelaide, helping their new senior coach, Matty Primus, find his feet.

A standard week might include flying to Brisbane on Sunday night, flying to Adelaide on Tuesday morning, then back to Melbourne on Wednesday night, with a day off on Thursday to see my kids before flying to wherever the Power is playing that weekend, and then back to Melbourne before it all starts again. I left South Australia to be closer to my children, and have managed to end up somehow further from them.

When you become a parent, you have no idea of the responsibility that will follow, how you will worry yourself sick about your kids forever, turning yourself inside out when you know you could have done things differently, better, when you know you didn't put them first but you couldn't see another way through the mess.

I cling to my marriage and the idea that making a good home for my children means having a mother and father under the one roof even though I'm not really there. I am clinging to this life raft as much for myself as for them and it's not working for anyone. I can barely look after myself.

Then one day it seems like I wake up and my children are making their own way in the world. Without me. Despite me.

Brooke is now a woman, all of 25. I've seen her grow into herself as a girl with a fierce work ethic. She studied psychology at university and wanted to give back, so she became a teacher. Her boyfriend from when she was 13 is now her husband. She doesn't drink or smoke. I know she idolises me, and is proud of me, but I idolise her, too. We sit for hours talking about the world. I goad her – *You're institutionalised, my dear* – and she turns around and gives it right back. *Where have you been all your life if not in the AFL institution?*

Kane is now 20. I know he has felt the pressure of being a sportsman's son. His friends would come over in primary school and want to kick the footy with him and with me. *No,* he'd say. *Not interested.* He was an athlete though, on his own terms – a state high jumper and local footy player. But his passion is music. When he was 15 he saw a friend spinning records on a DJ deck at a party, and decided to get his own set, becoming a DJ of some note in the city. The nightclub underworld drew him in, and he found trouble inside himself. There have been late-night phone calls. There were times when I put my head on the pillow and thought I'd never see him again, blaming myself for not being there more. Absent for a good reason is still absent.

Molly, now 12 years old, changed our clan forever. She's bold. She sings and dances with abandon. She has always loved costumes – fairy dresses and tutus and tiaras when she was little. She's the youngest, yet she's the one who drives our boat in Echuca. She grew up inside the North Melbourne Football Club. I'd take her to work with me and she'd run in the doors at 7:30am and I wouldn't see her until 6pm. She'd be front and centre at all of the games, singing the song, and go to school on

Mondays – *I saw you on TV, Molly!* – as the proudest kid in class. Now I know she sees the distance and the separation within her family – the banged-up and broken state of things – but I hope she remembers when we were whole.

The Laidleys visit a family lawyer, and we sell everything. The house, investment properties, stock. We buy a house for Joanne and the kids in Essendon and put aside pots of money specifically for weddings and education. I put a deposit on a new house in East Keilor. It'll be built 500 metres from where we were. Four bedrooms, two lounges, two bathrooms and a study.

After 24 years, my marriage is officially over. I feel homeless.

i can't outrun this

I bump into Scott Watters one day. I haven't really seen him since we played together at West Coast, so we catch up over coffee. We talk about senior coaching. He wants to be a senior coach now, and asks me if I would want to do it again. *Not really*, I say. *But if the right opportunity arose, I might.* We strike a bargain – a curious little pact. If one of us lands a senior job, we'll bring the other one along for the ride.

It's 2011 and the travel for my consulting work in Brisbane and Sydney is too taxing. The constant flying into and out of Port Adelaide isn't much better. I jettison both jobs. That's when Ross Lyon decides to leave St Kilda. Scott applies for his position and talks to me until the process is complete. *I've got the job*, he says, *and you're coming.*

I'm the new midfield coach for the Saints, and it's a glittering midfield to lead. Lenny Hayes. Nick Dal Santo. Brendon Goddard. Leigh Montagna. Jack Steven. I don't much like the commute – in fact I hate it. East Keilor to Seaford without any traffic at all takes a little over an hour, but try getting there at any time between 7am and 5pm and it might as well be two hours, occasionally three.

Near the messy end of Mad Monday in 2012, I've had my lunch with the coaches and staff, so I drive across to the bowling club in Port Melbourne where the players are partying. Tall forward Justin Koschitzke is drunk, and he turns to me.

Are you a cross-dresser?

I look him in the eye, furious but also terrified. There are people around.

No, I'm not, I say. *Give me more credit than that.*

He looks at me, wobbling on his back foot. *It's just what I've heard.*

I look back at him, feet firmly planted. *Okay, but we hear a lot of things. And I am not.*

It's never mentioned again, but for him to bring this up means some part of my gender dysphoria is common knowledge now, an open secret. He's heard this from someone and they've heard it from someone else, but who is it who knows? And what exactly do they know? What are they saying about me?

I plot the perfect distraction – an American holiday schedule. I'm going to see the New York Giants at MetLife Stadium. I'm going to Boston to see the New England Patriots against the Miami Dolphins. I'm going to San Francisco to see the 49ers take on the Seattle Seahawks. I'm going to visit Los Angeles and stay in Hollywood. I'm going to Las Vegas, too.

Vegas becomes my happy place – the city I visit most years, where I can completely be myself. I go onto websites where I can create a profile and meet like-minded girls, just to go out and have fun. I become friends with trans women in Sin City and they know me for me, not the player or coach of some niche sport from another hemisphere.

I'm surrounded by thousands of people at a Halloween Ball near the Hard Rock Cafe, and I feel free. That's when I hear an Australian accent behind me. I don't know this man and he doesn't know me. We don't speak and he's probably not even aware of my presence. But it reinforces once more that wherever I go and however I dress, there's always a risk of recognition,

danielle laidley

and a rumour being passed onto one person and another person, until I'm faced with another Justin Koschitzke moment.

I can't outrun this. I begin not to even try.

In 2013, I meet more and more people in Melbourne's trans community. I connect with them on websites. I go to the Greyhound and the Peel and DT's Hotel in Richmond. I still drive because I never want to drink too much and lose my inhibitions or control. I don't want to catch cabs either, because I don't want to find myself waiting on a busy public street on a Saturday night, desperately trying to hail a taxi in high heels and a black pleather bustier.

On at least a dozen weekends throughout footy season, I can be found in the queer nightclubs of Melbourne, being myself. I go to talk. To be accepted. To feel welcome.

a trip to the moon

I'm reunited with Mick Malthouse in 2014, as his assistant coach at Carlton. I don't want to be at St Kilda anymore anyway. The drunken question from Koschitzke is part of it. That fucking commute, too. Scott Watters is sacked as well. And at Carlton I have an opportunity to work with my friend and mentor, 10 minutes from home.

In my first week on the job we head to the United States for a high-altitude training camp in Flagstaff, Arizona. High altitude is all the rage right now, but I think it's overrated – sports scientists run amok. I've been on one of these trips before, to Colorado with the Saints. The camp was good because the players and coach needed to bond and the setting was beautiful, but the benefits of thin air seemed marginal to me, at best.

I get homesick on these camps, too. It can be a three-week commitment, which means time away from being myself. I want to be home, where I can be Danielle again. I have it in mind to try something new. A risk not yet taken. I'm not sure I'll go through with it, but I hope I will.

I step out of my apartment in Moonee Ponds, dressed as myself, and walk downstairs to the street. It's around 11pm on a weeknight, and I have something I need to do, somewhere I need to be. I get in my car and drive south on Ascot Vale Road, then right at the big roundabout onto Epsom Road, and in less than five minutes I've arrived at my destination. Showgrounds Village Shopping Centre.

I'm not headed to any nightclub. I'm not doing a first dramatic lap of Subiaco Markets. I need bread and eggs and milk and tea. I'm doing my grocery shopping, and I'll be damned if I have to do that dressed as Dean forever. The Coles here is open until midnight, and it's quiet at this hour, less crowded, although the overnight shelf stackers have started putting their boxes out in readiness for a long shift stocking the store.

I wander up and down the aisles wearing wedges, a long dress and a wavy wig. The bread they won't sell tomorrow is down to $1 a loaf. Thirty cans of Coke is only 19 bucks. I hold on to my trolley and feel as though I'm at the bridge of a great ship, steering myself in the direction I want to go. At the register I look the cashier in the eye and smile, and I make small talk, and I emerge into the night with everything I need for breakfast. Errand run.

One of the things I've always hated about having a public profile is walking into a place and knowing that people recognise you. That starts almost immediately when you play league football and doesn't stop when you do. Someone turns to their friend and you catch that twisting head in your periphery. A whisper. A nudge. A point. A snap on the phone. Soon people step into your space for a conversation about footy – the last thing you want to talk about with a stranger on the street.

Sometimes it's fine, when they offer something like *You know, mate, I really loved watching you play* – it feels good to hear that, and then you can both talk for a fleeting moment before the little interaction ends. You watch them walk away and you know they're smiling about their chance meeting with that person who used to play football, and you know they're going to tell a friend about it, and you don't mind giving a little of yourself when it means so much.

But most of the time you feel like an animal in the zoo, exposed and degraded by your albeit limited fame. Dressed as Danielle, no one notices who I am or used to be. No one asks me to compare Ablett to Carey. No one wants to know what really happened with Adam Simpson and the rubber chicken condom sex video episode.

And so I'm free now, to go out and live my life. I throw on an outfit I like, jump into my black Mazda Tribute SUV and head to Kmart for a few bargains, or to OPSM to get new lenses and frames. I like going to Savers, the big second-hand clothing store on Sydney Road. I pay my bills at the Brunswick post office. I take a number and get in line at Medicare at Airport West.

Every errand feels like a trip to the moon. It feels like my life is slowly settling into something resembling a new normal, as if my cloistered existence is opening up. I am in transition.

saying the loud part quietly

I've read about hormone replacement therapy for years now. There's estrogen and progesterone and a whole suite of testosterone blockers. There are injections and pills and gels and ointments. I'm not ready to go to a doctor or a psychiatrist or an endocrinologist. I'm not ready to tell the world about myself yet. I'm saying the loud part quietly, whispering my truth keystroke by keystroke, self-diagnosis by Dr Google. I do my research as best I can.

I order testosterone blocker tablets that come in a brown glass jar with cotton wool in the top. I take one big white pill per day, a minimum 50-milligram dose. You can take estrogen orally, but you risk getting deep vein thrombosis or blood clots or liver problems, so I settle on transdermal patches instead, the equivalent of a low 2-milligram dose daily. They come in a little blue and green box of eight.

The excitement and adrenaline when these medications arrive in the mail is incredible. To know that they will make changes to my body – reversible if you are on them a short time, but permanent if you stay on them long enough – is exhilarating. This feels like a step towards releasing the girl inside me, towards aligning my outer and inner selves. I barely wait five minutes before swallowing my first pill – *gulp* – and applying my first patch – a sticky rectangle about the size of a small stamp, which I put on my hip or backside and replace after three and a half days.

One day I'm at the shops with Molly, trying on a shirt, and she sees one of the patches. *What's that?* she asks. *What's it for?* I tell her it's medication, but she's a teenager now and has follow-up questions. I stay vague and hope she thinks it's for giving up smoking.

The gender-affirming hormones quickly have an effect on me. Basically, they lower the male part of my being and raise the female part, because we all have both inside of us.

I've always had very low body fat, but the estrogen has other ideas, and all of a sudden I start building little fatty deposits on my hips and bum. I feel a layer of softness settling over my entire body. My skin becomes smoother. My hair becomes finer. Straight away I feel my breasts starting to grow, budding like a teenage girl in puberty.

I've always dreamt of having breasts and filling out a nice bra. I quickly reach the point where work shirts – those branded Carlton FC polos – are getting too small for me. If anyone looks closely at me on TV, they will see the strain across the chest. In summer I begin wearing a women's sports crop top underneath, to smoosh down my new boobs, and in winter I wear big puffy jumpers and jackets.

The testosterone blockers have their own way of working. My facial hair stops growing. I lose my libido, too. No more morning glory even. I find this daunting. Some transitioning women hate looking at the male part of themselves anyway, so to them it's a relief. But to me it's confronting.

The side effects of taking estrogen can include depression and hot flashes – the symptoms of menopause – and I feel myself begin to transition emotionally as well as physically. After three weeks, I come home from work one day and begin crying. About what? I have no idea. But I weep and sob uncontrollably. It goes on and on, for days and days. Sometimes I cry and begin laughing at myself at the same time. *What the fuck are you crying about, Dani?*

I stop taking the medications after five months. They've had an impact but they're also getting expensive. While this kind of therapy will one day cost about $40 a week, in the middle of 2015, going through an internet pharmacy without consulting a medical professional, I'm paying $400 a week.

I also stop because I realise that hormone replacement therapy isn't the silver bullet I had hoped it would be.

I thought it would be like magic dust, sprinkled over my head and transforming me into Cinderella, removing all confusion and pain. In some ways it's done the opposite. It's given me the beginnings of the body I want – the one I imagine for myself – but I don't feel different inside. The sadness and alienation are still there.

The issue of my gender seems to loom larger than ever now. I start to question everything about myself. *Is this for me? Is this my pathway? Where do I belong?*

I've carried this feminine part of me all my life and grown it in secret, nurturing it when I could, and all of a sudden it feels as though it's rejecting me. *Am I really a woman? How would I even know?*

bang

Things are going badly for Mick in season 2015. So badly that I get called into the office of the Carlton CEO, Steven Trigg. He asks me the same question the Power did when Choco Williams was struggling there – *Would you like to coach the side?* – and I tell them the same thing I told Port Adelaide – *You have a coach, and I'm not here to dance on anyone's grave.*

Mick gets the sack, and his assistant John Barker is given the job temporarily. Brendon Bolton takes over from him. He visits all the peripheral football department staff except me. I walk into the office of football manager Andrew McKay, a man who had committed to keeping me at the club, and I get given the sack. I pack my gear and leave. After 28 years in the system, this is the last day I work in the AFL.

All coaches and players know that there's a bullet with their name on it somewhere. Mine was finally loaded into the chamber, and aimed at my temple. *Bang.*

one night i say yes

I've never been much of a drinker, but I give it a shake in my football retirement. It gets a little big on me, and fast. My gambling is becoming an issue, too – as if betting $10,000 on a basketball game didn't already qualify as an issue. In the summer of 2016 I basically end up a bit lost, and that's bad timing because I'm about to be introduced to drugs.

I smoked pot in high school, of course, and have seen more serious substances now and then in football, but not as much as you might imagine. Drugs weren't part of my football club. In the early days playing for North Melbourne, Wayne Carey and Glenn Archer made it quite clear that if you did cocaine, you wouldn't have any place on the team. As a coach I like to think I had my finger on the pulse of the playing group, and I saw no signs then either. I used to have tough conversations with our leadership group about the weighty, personal problems of the boys on our list, and not once did they bring up drugs.

Hovering over all of this is knowledge of the pain addiction wrought on my father and grandfather and those around them. So I've stayed away from substances, afraid of falling into the same cycle.

But now, leaving football, winding up alone and a little embarrassed by where my life has led, I suddenly find myself in places and with people where it's normal to enliven life with illicit fuel – or to numb your pain with a naughty sedative.

I'm out and about and get asked if I'd like a line of blow, and I say *No*, and I'm asked again another time, and another time I say *No*.

One night I say *Yes*. It's as simple as that.

I'm at my holiday house in Echuca and there's a black dinner plate in front of me, and on the plate is a pile of cocaine. I cut it with a credit card, split it into rails and snort it with a short plastic straw. Those first few lines are everything I've been looking for. I feel 10 feet tall.

When I want to drink I can do it all night long and the next day, too, and not pass out. When I'm feeling withdrawn and frightened, I can become sociable and chatty, and jabberjaw until dawn. When I feel defeated by life, I can suddenly see limitless possibility and all the ideas I'll ever need to succeed.

I'm sure there are people who can use coke occasionally and have no thoughts drawing them back to the drug in the days and weeks that follow. But I want that euphoria and calm and confidence again quickly, so I go back quickly and I go back often.

It's a weekly occurrence at first – I tell myself once a weekend only. Then it's both nights of the weekend, because what are weekends for? Then I decide that a weekend is comprised of Friday and Saturday and Sunday nights together. Soon I throw a sneaky weeknight into the mix. All of a sudden I'm chasing a good time constantly, looking for a daily chance to disengage with the world. This is how my drug habit is born.

learning on the job

I see the job advertisement online, and it doesn't seem a likely landing place for a former AFL player and coach, but I submit an application in early 2016 anyway, and within weeks I become a learning and development consultant for the Department of Justice.

I work with custodial staff on the prison floor, with new squads of officers at academy level and with general managers in important jobs. I develop, write, facilitate and deliver leadership programs. I administer the Myers-Briggs Type Indicator personality test and the Neethling Brain Instrument and conduct Emotional Intelligence 360 degree feedback sessions.

I also go from being a person who has all the solutions – *who is asked questions because I have all the answers* – to someone who has little core knowledge and no broad understanding of the business. I'm learning on the job. I have no idea who does what within the department or where the hierarchies begin and end. I've never had to lean so heavily on people for direction.

My skill set is strong, however, based on teams, culture and high performance, and I very quickly learn that prisons are a lot like footy clubs. Ninety per cent of the time things go smoothly, but when there's an incident you need to perform at a very high level or face consequences. Even the media reporting on both industries is similar. When something goes wrong you'll be on the front page immediately, but when that excellent little community program has a big win no one will notice.

I get to know my new workplaces. I start with the Melbourne Assessment Prison, once known as the Metropolitan Remand Centre, a scary and bustling concrete beast where offenders wait to see where they'll be sent, like triage for criminals.

The worst go to maximum-security facilities like Barwon Prison and Marngoneet Correctional Centre. Some will stay in the Karreenga protection unit because they're child sex offenders or former police officers or likely to get beaten up or killed in the mainstream population.

There's the Dame Phyllis Frost Centre for female prisoners, and then there's the low- to medium-security places, prison farms like Beechworth Correctional Centre where they grow vegetables, Dhurringile Prison where they raise sheep, and Langi Kal Kal Prison, where they farm cattle.

I have a special white pass that allows me to walk unescorted through most spaces in the justice system, and I drive all over Victoria, spending no more than two days in any given week in the office.

I still get to coach people every single day, too – from prison officers to supervisors and operations managers – only without the risk/reward, win/loss dichotomy of football. I love this job. I stay for years. I make lifelong friends.

Before I began the role, I would see a criminal on the news and spit my reactions – *Mongrel, lock him up and throw away the fucken key* – and there are career criminals and recidivists to be feared, but there are also people who've made one single, dreadful mistake, and they deserve the chance to ensure that slip-up doesn't derail the rest of their life. I now work for a place that creates avenues for building skills and repairing self-esteem while serving punishment and paying penance. People can learn from their mistakes. This is the place that gives them that opportunity.

patient bastards

On holiday in Las Vegas, my substance abuse goes into freefall. I'm there for six days and I do not sleep. I stay at the Cosmopolitan with friends from previous trips. We rent a stretch Hummer and go exploring this adult playground on a locals-only tour, avoiding the tourist traps.

One friend lives in an apartment on Dean Martin Drive, and her home is a polyamorous one, shared by three girls and one guy. I stay with them at one point. They're protective of me, as the only trans girl in their circle. They feed me drugs and I hoover them up all too freely.

We go to a festival – Life is Beautiful – and listen to Lionel Richie and OutKast. I walk 10 kilometres in high heels but I feel as though I'm walking on air. We are buzzing, blasted to the eyeballs and by the end of the night I'm demolished. The last night in Vegas is always a big one.

I sleep the entire flight home, and my problems are waiting for me in Melbourne. I can dodge them on holiday but they're patient bastards. I start looking for new acquaintances in the city who can find drugs for me, to calm my restless mind. What's that song called? 'Novocaine for the Soul'. I need more contacts and go deeper into dark parts of town. My good friends now are dealers.

I stay up late and sleep even later. Early in 2017 I come home from work one Friday at 4:30pm, and start drinking immediately. At least one thing hasn't changed – I'm still a bourbon and Coke girl. Jim Beam white label. No ice.

I play records while I get soused. Music that reminds me of family. Midnight Oil. INXS. Joe Camilleri. 'I'm on Fire' by Bruce Springsteen. It's the soundtrack to a hundred Gippsland car trips and a thousand Mallee barbecues. 'Brown Eyed Girl' by Van Morrison is my favourite because it makes me think of Molly Rose's beautiful big brown eyes. I play these records over and over by myself, dancing in my first-floor apartment in Moonee Ponds.

The songs and booze mingle with my gender issues and my gambling woes, the whole toxic mix given energy by the fact that I'm not eating or sleeping. Earlier in the evening I told someone I was going to self-harm – not so much a plan but a sense of being fed up, of reaching the end of my rope, and that it might as well be tonight. I turn off my phone, not interested in being talked out of the moment, and I go back to drinking.

Past midnight and I'm fading. I go to my medicine cabinet and find the downers I'm looking for – the Valium and the Xanax – and I down both bottles. I swallow them all and sink sadly into my own annihilation.

Or so I think. My body has other ideas. I wake up vomiting violently, and to the sound of my door being knocked on – beaten in really. It's the police. They've been warned that I'm a risk to myself. I drag myself along the floor to the front door and open it. They want to take me away for observation but I won't go.

I can't, I tell them. *I'm too scared. I know it'll make the news if I go with you.*

Over more than an hour I slur and beg and talk them into letting me stay, but I need to have counselling. They hand me a phone with a bright and sympathetic girl on the other end.

She talks to me for half an hour while the police wait. They really want me to go to the hospital with them but I'm not even considering that. Eventually they let me be and leave.

I close the door finally, and fall to the floor. It's dawn on Saturday, the start of another long weekend.

I get help, of sorts. I have a friend, Greg Ryan, who used to be my personal assistant at the Kangaroos, and who has become a dependable mate in my life. I don't tell him about my gender dysphoria but I do tell him about my drug use, and how I feel completely wayward since football ended, and how everything came to a head in a suicide attempt or a cry for help last week.

I'm struggling, I say. *I feel close to the front of the queue.*

Greg reaches out on my behalf to Greg Buck, our old club psychologist. I meet him in a cafe in Footscray and he welcomes me into his home. His wife is so kind, and kindness is a salve in such moments. I talk to him on and off for a month. He knows me and my methods from the club and he explains how my avoidance feeds all of my problems, hampering my chance to talk and connect and heal. He refers me to a psychiatrist friend in Church Street, Richmond, who I see once a week for the next year. He asks the same question first every Monday.

Did you indulge on the weekend?

Yes.

How much?

Not much.

Well, it's not much to you, but it's a lot to anyone else.

He explains how I might think I'm dousing my pain, smothering and silencing it, but in fact I'm only creating more trauma. Not only that, I'm weakening any defences I might have. I'm tiring myself out, making myself more susceptible to traumas with which I can no longer cope.

I used to feel like I had one foot in the grave. Now I feel like it's two feet and one arm, with more to come. I'm holding down a job and putting on a show by day, but every night I come back into my apartment and collapse in a heap.

is the cross–dresser there?

I have a villa in Bali, in Seminyak, and I have a plan. I want to live there for six months, and in Melbourne for six months. I want to go from the Indonesian dry season to Australian summer on an endless loop. I don't think that will happen, but I am spending more and more time at the villa, negotiating extra annual leave from work.

Rick Olarenshaw gets in touch with me. I know him from playing against him, when he was an Essendon onballer. He fell out of love with footy and eventually hated it. I'm more ambivalent in that regard. Only a year ago I spent time helping coach a suburban side in Frankston North, the Pines Football Club, and found the entire experience rewarding. I struggled with the demands of football at the elite level, and it caused me grief and at times cost me my sanity, but I'm not sure I ever hated the game.

Rick lives in Bali now. He's found his way back to footy, coaching the Bali Geckos, and he wants to know if I'm keen to help. I don't even know what he's talking about, but I soon learn. AFL Asia is a wildly popular competition, fielding teams made up of locals learning the sport and expat Aussies who miss having a kick. The Geckos play out of the mammoth Finns Recreation Club in Canggu. I help Rick out with coaching and training, using an interpreter to talk to the local boys about ball drops and tackle technique. Every second weekend the team flies out to a different country for a match.

They play the Jakarta Bintangs and the Thailand Tigers, the Singapore Wombats and the Cambodian Eagles, the Lao Elephants and the Macau Lightning. An AFL Asia Championship is held every year, too, and this year it's in Kuala Lumpur. A representative team including many Geckos is formed – the Indonesia Volcanoes – and we head to Malaysia for the round robin competition. It's played on an equestrian field with four ovals marked on the vast grassy space. Buses arrive carrying teams from Myanmar and Japan, Hong Kong and Beijing. Rick gives me the title of Director of Coaching.

We sneak into the final match but the founder and spiritual leader of the team – Hitchy – has been riding the bench. My advice to Rick is to start Hitchy on the ground. He might tire quickly, but his emotional presence will carry a lot of weight, and if he hits a few early contests hard it will go a long way to carrying the team over the line. He's in the top handful of players on the field in the grand final, and we win, and the teams all converge on the grandstand as the darkness and humidity gathers. The tropical rain falls in a torrent until shallow lakes form on top of the grass, and one by one the players sprint into the long puddles, seeing who can slide the farthest. If my infatuation with footy ever faltered, I'm back in love with it now.

On the bus back to the hotel I post videos online and type a big, excited story about the day on my Facebook page. We sink beers and cheer and go up to our rooms to shower before dinner and a night out in the capital. I check my social media post and see that it has hundreds of likes and dozens of comments, but one stands out.

It's from a guy I played against and coached against – and never particularly liked. And it's another one of those moments that make it clear how many people know something private about me. The smiling profile picture of Jason Akermanis has popped up in my feed with a single snarky comment. *Oh, is the cross-dresser there?*

what's this?

I've been living authentically as myself for two years now, except at work, and except with my children, but in February 2019 that all changes in a click.

Kane has more than a clue about what's going on. He's lived with me on and off and seen my room, where I don't hide my dresses or wigs, and where I have one of those makeup mirrors bordered by light bulbs, like something you'd find in a backstage dressing room. It becomes something known but unspoken and unacknowledged between us.

My girls, however, have no idea. Until I fuck that up. It's Sunday morning and I'm off my head again. Too many bourbon and Cokes, too many drugs. I'm being taught to use Snapchat, the social media messaging app, and am having fun experimenting with it. I'm taking selfies and saving them to my phone. I don't have my glasses on – because a girl's gotta look her best – and this has consequences. I can't see properly and I think I'm pressing *save* but really I'm pressing *send*.

Me pouting with lipstick. *Send.*

Me with chin lowered, eyes up, and a come-hither stare. *Send.*

I have no idea what I'm doing until a friend from Perth texts me. *What's this?* he asks. *Why are you dressed up?*

I understand what's happened now – my mistake – and pretend I've woken up after a masquerade ball. I plead social media ignorance.

Had a few too many after the party, I say. *Just mucking around online.*

Then I realise who else has received the messages. Brooke and Molly.

This is how they find out their father has gender issues, with a few photos beamed into their hands, sent with no warning, no context, no explanation. They're disgusted. They lash out. They go silent.

I can't blame them one bit.

a little plastic baggy

My drug use becomes a daily habit now, and it's not just routine cocaine use or occasional ecstasy anymore. I'm doing ice. Methamphetamine. I first had some three years ago, on one of those trips to Las Vegas.

It's the night of a massive Halloween ball. I've heard all the bad things about this mean little drug, but I want to try it anyway. I buy a gram – a little plastic baggy filled with crystal rocks. They sell the pipes and gas lighters you need to cook it up at any petrol station on the Strip.

I spark the lighter and draw in the silvery smoke, and the high is like nothing I've ever felt. My body tingles all over. My senses are elevated. I'm coherent and extremely horny and I have a dry mouth. I also look incredible. I'm wearing a tailor-made black PVC bodysuit with fluffy cuffs at the end of the sleeves, a cut-out chest and zipper all the way up the back. A micro mini skirt covers my bits. A suspender belt and stockings accentuate my legs.

I party all night on the strength of one hit from that pipe, and I throw the other three quarters of the gram in the trash in the morning because I'm headed back to Melbourne. I write myself off in a Los Angeles bar and then fly home with a fresh habit forming.

Back home I learn that the difference between cocaine and ice is the finish line. With ice, there isn't one. You just keep going and going, stocking your pipe and continuing. Your benders bleed from night into day, day into night, ad nauseam ad infinitum, so long as you have the money.

This isn't about my disease of addiction anymore – it's not about some obsessive trait inside me that demanded tunnel vision in football, or drove me unhealthily into my work, or even created my cloying dependence on a depressant like alcohol. This fucking thing has a physical and psychological stranglehold on me. I know it will consume me. If I let it take hold, it'll lay my soul to waste.

LEFT: The long hair I refused to cut – I loved my white-blonde locks.

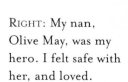

RIGHT: My nan, Olive May, was my hero. I felt safe with her, and loved.

ABOVE AND RIGHT: Mum
(Carmel) and Dad (David)
split up when I was six and
my brother, Paul, was four.

LEFT: Mum and
Leif got married
in 1979. I lived
with them in their
caravan after Dad
kicked me out,
when I was 12.

WARRIAPENDI PRIMARY SCHOOL MAY 1973

I made friends with Donna Leckie (circled, centre-front) in Grade 1.
Two left-handers seated together. Two DLs.

WESTMINSTER - BALGA J.F.C. U.11s 1977

Tom James (centre-back) was the first coach who took me under his wing.
He treated me like a son. I'm in the front row, fifth from the right.

LEFT: Year 9, feeling rebellious. I developed this photo in class.

BELOW: I won best first-year player at 16, in the under-19s for West Perth. Footy became the path I was on but I often wondered if I'd made the right call.

ABOVE: When I was selected for the under-15s state team, they made me get a haircut.

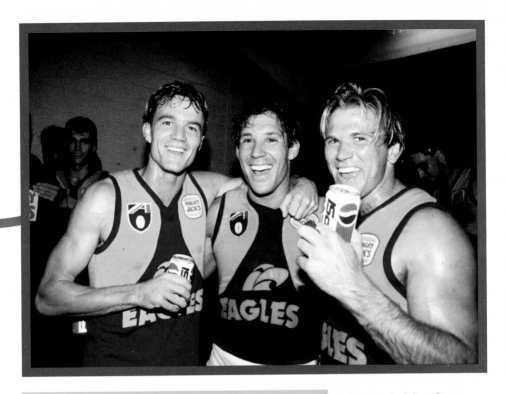

ABOVE: As West Coast
Eagles players, we were
kings of the town. 1990,
with Dwayne Lamb
(centre) and Chris
Mainwaring (right).
(*AFL Photos*)

LEFT: I arrived at North
Melbourne at 25,
suddenly a senior player
but also just a skinny kid
from Perth. (*1994, round 15,
AFL Photos*)

LEFT: With my great friends Anthony Stevens (left) and Wayne Schwass (centre) as the siren sounded on our 1996 premiership. I felt only relief. (*AFL Photos*)

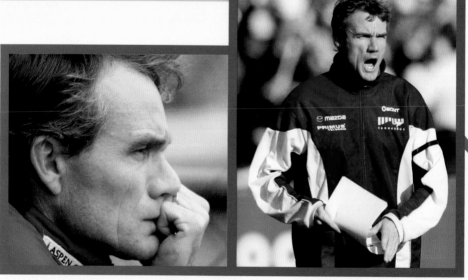

The boys at North called me 'the Bible' because I was hard to read. My coaching behaviour ranged between introversion and volcanic eruptions. (*Left: 2008, Lachlan Cunningham/AFL Photos; Right: 2005, AFL Photos*)

LEFT: 2016, Las Vegas, a massive Halloween Ball. My PVC bodysuit was tailor-made. This was my first time on methamphetamines.

RIGHT: In late 2019 in Bali, I was ready to mark my body. My tattoo tells the story of how I've felt my whole life. *(Courtesy Tina Smigielski)*

By 2022, I felt comfortable representing my two tribes – the football and LGBTQIA+ communities. Tossing the coin at the AFLW Pride Round match at Arden St, alongside Emma Kearney (left) and Alicia Eva (right). *(23 January 2022, Dylan Burns/AFL Photos)*

My sibling bond with my brother, Paul, has never been stronger. *(Scarborough, WA, April 2022)*

With Donna Leckie – together is our favourite place to be. *(Courtesy Kaity Leckie Photography)*

fallout

Retired footballers always complain about their aches and pains. We spend a decade or so sprinting faster and jumping higher than most people can, invariably colliding with the hardest parts of each other and the ground, tearing muscle fibre and snapping ligaments and cracking bones. Then we allow surgeons to slice us open and saw and drill and stitch and bandage – and we're meant to be good as new.

People love the idea that when a bone heals it becomes stronger in the place where it was broken. It's the kind of thing that gets printed on inspirational posters. *Whatever doesn't kill me only makes me stronger.* That might be true in the spiritual sense, but when it comes to the skeletal system and the calcium that gathers at a break site – particularly in the vertebrae of my lower spine – there's no evidence at all that fractures heal with strength.

In middle age my neck and back are racked with pain. I can't get off the couch because my body is screaming. I have fibromyalgia and depression, and my doctor prescribes a heavy dose of prednisolone – a powerful steroid – as well as a small therapeutic dose of antidepressants. An unhealthy lifestyle is partly the cause of my pain, but it's not just the stress I'm causing to my tired body. This is also the fallout from a bruising career.

Paul Salmon broke my back first, followed by Fraser Brown, both accidentally. There's one more accident though, in 2004. I'm helping Shannon Grant recover from injury by training one on one with him. We're doing drills at Arden Street one dewy morning when my left foot slips and my body slides out from underneath me. I'm airborne for one second then my back hits the grass. *I'm just winded*, I think. *Let me up.*

I try to stand and keep falling. I can't breathe. I get into the change rooms and collapse. They take me straight to the club doctor and race me into imaging for scans, while my body turns numb.

Our neurosurgeon comes in to consult, and he holds the scans up to the light box. He looks at me and looks at another scan. He looks at a final slide before turning my way. *If you weren't standing there right now,* he says, *I would say I'm looking at the scan of a person who's going to be in a wheelchair for the rest of their life.*

I've split T4, T5 and T6 down the middle. I rest for a week or so, but I'm walking and moving and the pain seems manageable. Being the dickhead I am, I get strapped and front up to training. I stand on the sidelines for our match at Victoria Park that weekend.

It takes me three years to fully recover, although 'fully recover' is an odd thing to say, because my back is never the same.

My bank account is dwindling now. I throw money away on my habits, and money is taken from me by bad people, too. When the latter happens I don't go to the police, because I don't want my name entered into their system. My pad becomes party central. I rage all weekend and have no idea who is in my house at any given time.

I'm not sleeping anymore. That sounds like something people say when they're going through a bad time. They talk about insomnia – about wakeful nights and blurry mornings. But this is something different. I'm doing ice so often now and tearing through so many multi-day benders that sleep becomes optional. In the year 2019, I miss more than 150 nights of sleep. Not only do I damage my body with these binges, I deny it any chance to rest and recover.

Recuperation is not my concern. When I want sleep I find another way. I've begun taking GHB – gamma hydroxybutyrate – a nervous system depressant. Some call it a date rape drug, because it can be used to knock someone out, but others know GHB as liquid ecstasy, or fantasy. It takes euphoria to another level, but there's a fine line. Take too much and you can knock yourself out, or die.

I take it sometimes when I need to wipe myself out. I wake up on the floor of my kitchen, or the bathroom, or the hallway, and the TV is on and the music is blaring. I'm in an altered state. I look around at this mess and think Joanne is going to kill me. When she's not in the bedroom I check the bathroom, and then the spare room, before I realise I haven't lived with my wife in eight years. I stay awake and start using again.

There's another street name for this drug, and it's the one I use. It's a jumbled initialism, mixing up the order of the letters GHB to stand for something else. I think it suits my situation now. I know it does. The other name for the drug is Grievous Bodily Harm.

fuck it

I think tattoos tell a story. They're one of those things in life that reflect a moment, if not an entire personality. I find a design I like and keep it to myself for years. Finally, in late 2019, I'm ready to mark my body.

The design is a woman's face, but you can't see most of it. Four sets of hands are reaching out from behind her, covering her eyes and cheeks and grabbing at her chin. There's a tattoo on her neck – meaning a tattoo within a tattoo.

I take this image into Celebrity Ink in Kuta. The tattooist doesn't like it. He says the proportions are wrong and the styling is off – there are too many hands, too much going on.

Go have some lunch, he says, *and come back in a couple of hours. I'll redesign it for you.*

I apply numbing cream to the large section of my outer thigh where the ink will go, and when I return he's pared everything back. Fewer hands. Black and grey shading. The only colour is a dollop of red I insist on for her full, pouting lips.

Her hair is pulled back by one set of hands, her eyes covered by another, with a final set clasping her cheeks. It takes five hours. The first two are a breeze, but when the numbing agent wears off the final three are agony. I don't mind. I feel like earning my mark.

I love how it looks. It signifies how I've felt my whole life. I see a girl who's hiding, who's in pain – who peeks into the wider world and wants to speak but is being held back. I see a woman who's avoiding and despairing. I see sensuality and secrecy. She's beautiful, really, this chick.

It feels as though my two lives are getting closer now, like trains barrelling in opposite directions down the same track. The locomotives are cruising towards a collision and there's no pumping the brakes or switching tracks. Something is coming and I know it's going to hurt. I start seeing two counsellors.

Maureen and Jane work at a clinic on Royal Parade in Parkville. They change the name on my records, because of my paranoia.

One weekday, we wander down to the back of their office and file into their private space. I explain all my issues but dance around the one that matters to me most. They're both scared out of their wits that I won't be around much longer.

I keep coming back. I guess I like them. Maureen is a vibrant young lady with all the empathy in the world. She has that skill of sitting silently and listening yet drawing things out of you at the same time. Jane is a mother-type figure – all care and love and concern – who checks on me daily and makes sure I'm taking my medication.

One day I'm seeing Maureen and I don't know why but the truth comes out. Something inside me just takes over. It's Monday afternoon after a bad weekend, off another week-long bender. Containing my gender dysphoria is taking up too much of whatever bandwidth I have left. Am I bottoming out? Maybe.

We're talking about family and work and drug use when it finally dawns on me that I'm wasting my time by not addressing the crux of everything – the centre of who I am and what I'm becoming.

Fuck it – I can't do this anymore, I say. *I know what my issue is, and I can't manage it alone anymore. I have gender dysphoria. I have had it from a very early age.*

Maureen looks at me, offers a sad smile and a knowing gaze. And she says the most wonderful thing. *What do you want me to call you?*

She goes downstairs and gets Jane and Jane moves immediately to next steps. *We have to get you in to see someone now,* she says. *Straight away.*

They organise everything, from an endocrinologist in Heidelberg to a gender psychiatrist in West Melbourne. I have a road map. Finally it's come out. Not to friends or family or colleagues, but to people who can help.

i need a hit

North Melbourne names its top 150 players of all time and I'm on the list. In July there's a presentation night being held at Atlantic on South Wharf, and I don't want to go but Cade Brown, a friend from Canberra and crazy Kangaroo fan, is coming down. We meet outside the function venue and walk in together.

We make our way to our table where past players from my era are already seated, guys like Matthew Larkin and Brett Allison. It's hard because I feel them all staring at me. *Is this paranoia, or do I look like shit?* I wonder. *Maybe it's both.*

I'm wearing men's clothing and hate it. I decide I'm not staying. I'm there long enough to hear Peter Chisnall, a member of the 1975 premiership team, make an emotional speech imploring us to stand up as a footy club and move forward – to thrive rather than survive. But I don't stay for the ceremony or presentation. Cade shakes his head at me on the way out.

Mate, you're unwell, he says. *You've gotta look after yourself. Come for a visit – come to Canberra? Or I'll be back down in a few weeks and will look you up.*

But I don't want to see anyone. I'm invited to the North Melbourne best and fairest night at the Showgrounds in October, and that pans out even worse. I'm being honoured with life membership of the club, and they've given me an entire table for my family. Kane and his girlfriend Alicia are there. Molly, too. Brooke and Justin and my grandson, Jet. Cade flies down from Canberra. My old friend Greg Ryan comes along. Despite everything I've done, they all still come.

I have put these people through so much – this night should be my thank you to them. It should be a proud, joyful evening and instead it's a grind. I don't want to be there. I'm off my head on ice, in fact. I've been smoking all day and all night prior. I look like shit. I'm distant.

Ben Buckley makes a gracious speech about me. I've written my own speech, too, because if I'm going to be here then I want to talk about what I've learned through playing and coaching 300 games of football.

The host of the night is TV sports reporter Tony Jones, and I really fucking dislike this guy. I remember him in press conferences at the club, always finding a way to big-note himself, to stand out at the expense of others. I stand can't him. *Bighead*, I think. *Poser.*

He calls me up to the stage and I take Jet with me. Jet loves the lights, and the cameras are trained on him so he sees himself on screen, smiling and waving. He loves this moment. I mumble answers throughout a short Q&A, and while I'm waiting for *Would you like to say a few words?* things switch to *Thanks for coming up.*

I don't know if this is a club decision not to hand me an open platform, but I want my time to be grateful and thankful. It's frankly all I want out of the night, and I don't get given it. I walk off the stage with my grandson and my medal and plaque, and I seethe.

As soon as the event finishes, we have a photo taken and I leave. We should all be going out together to a late-night restaurant or bar for a celebration or nightcap. That would be normal. But I want to go home. I want to be out of this suit suffocating my body, out of this tie strangling my neck. I know I'm letting everyone down and I do it anyway. I need a hit.

tell me your story

It takes six weeks to get my first appointment with an endocrinologist, but it's finally here. I'll be seeing an award-winning and world-renowned specialist, Dr Ada Cheung. I drive to where she works out of a medical centre in Heidelberg. I don't know where I'm going, and I mean that in all possible ways.

I'm dressed as Dean but still petrified of running into someone I know, in case they guess why I'm here. I take a lift up to Ada's floor and turn left down a thin corridor to a waiting room full of people. I make my way to the receptionist. *I have an appointment for Laidley.*

She taps away at her screen. *Ah yes, Danielle. Please feel comfortable coming to us any way you wish.*

I sit in the corner with my back to as many people as possible. I pick up a magazine and pretend to read. It might be upside down for all I know. But I'm finally here, I'm finally doing this.

I've googled Ada extensively, read some of her research into transitioning and mental health. She's young but I sense in her a determination to help and heal. She appears and instinctively knows not to say my name into the room, silently waving me over instead. We go into her office, where her file contains all the referral information she could need from Jane and Maureen.

She looks at me. *How are you going?*

I break down and begin crying, overwhelmed by such a simple question.

She looks at me and nods. *Tell me your story.*

I go right through every crib note from cradle to nearly the grave – my family and fear, confusion and shame, drugs and despair. I don't mention football much, and it begins to occur to me that the game I've devoted so much of my life to actually isn't central to who I am inside.

Ada is an adept listener. She finds pauses in my story – all the right moments – to affirm what I'm thinking and feeling with the weight of clinical expertise.

What you described just then is gender dysphoria …

That's a very common reaction …

There are ways we can address that …

My nervousness subsides and I can almost feel the anxiety rush from my body, as if every screaming cell in my system is suddenly quiet. My 40-minute session becomes a three-hour consultation. She runs me through an array of tests and pledges to go through my results and her notes, and then meet with me again soon to review. I cry tears of sadness, tears of joy, tears of anger and tears of laughter. I walk out of there floating.

I'm shaking with excitement at the idea of professional assessment. All the things I've felt will be explained. All the questions I've asked myself will be answered.

I told Ada I've been self-medicating with gender-affirming hormones, on and off, so she starts by examining my testosterone levels. My levels are low already, it turns out, making the small dose of testosterone blockers I'm taking more or less appropriate. She walks me through every chemical facet of my being exactly, and prescribes a new regimen of medication she thinks I should take.

She also presents me with a simple summary – something I can pass on to others if I like. Imagine gender dysphoria on a scale from zero to 100, zero being a state where you can function normally and are happy in your life and gender identity, and 100 representing people who can't bear to see themselves in the mirror because their sex is so discordant with who they feel themselves to be.

After evaluating our therapy and testing, she says, *I see you as a 75, at a minimum.*

I take this moment to get a few other things off my chest. I explain my experience in football, from playing AFL to coaching AFL to forever being a public figure whose identity is bound up in the AFL. Ada asks why I don't consider moving interstate and all I can offer is a rueful laugh.

It doesn't matter where I go in this country, there is no place I can live as myself without being hounded, without being splashed across the newspapers and the nightly news, I say.

I know I can't go on the way I am any longer. But I don't know how I can be myself either.

It turns out there's someone who can help with that.

His name is Dr Jaco Erasmus, and he's head of the Monash Gender Clinic, run out of offices in West Melbourne. I drive in there as myself in early 2020, and I'm terrified. I can't find a parking spot and there are people everywhere on the streets – and this is my neighbourhood, too, where I might run into someone I know at any moment.

I find my way into his office and sit opposite this soft-spoken South African man. He's talked to Ada and knows my story, but I share my journey again in shorter form.

Don't pull away from it, he advises. *We're here to help you be yourself – whatever that looks like.*

I tell him I want to transition, and he walks me through the various options in front of me, beyond hormone replacement therapy into gender confirmation surgery.

There's breast augmentation if I want to enhance my bosom with silicone implants. There's vaginoplasty, where the penis is inverted – its tip becoming a clitoris and the scrotal skin becoming a labia. Those are only possibilities, Jaco reminds me. Not everyone gets surgery, and surgery does not define your experience as a transgender woman nor make your transition any more or less valid. People think if you're a trans woman you want your dick lopped off as soon as possible, but it's so much more complicated than that.

Jaco refers back to my test results, too, and reminds me that what I have – who I am – is not a psychological disposition but a medical condition.

It's summer and sunny when he walks me through these concepts and more, and I start to imagine a world where everyone knows. I feel myself articulating and imagining next steps.

How do I let my family know?

How do I let the football world know?

How do I let my workplace know?

I don't like the phrase coming out of the closet. I prefer stepping into the world.

topple and fall

Unfortunately the world is shutting down right now. The Covid pandemic has reached Australia. I'm working hard from my home office with Zoom. I'm going to medical appointments by Google Hangouts. I'm keeping in touch with the outside world by FaceTime. I buy an investment property online.

Parts of me are highly functional but my drug use is still highly destructive. I do my drugs in my ensuite bathroom, which I call the naughty room. I have a little fan there for ventilating the toxic smoke. The naughty room is the only place I want to be.

I attempt self-harm for the second time in my life on a Sunday. I've been awake for eight nights, and I'm a volcano. I can hear voices and then I can't. I hatch a plan and I set it in motion.

I get out of the shower and spend a few hours getting pretty. I've bought new lingerie, including a new bra that fits me perfectly.

I think of Michael Hutchence, because how he went is how I'm planning to leave. I have a big belt – black leather with a large gold buckle – and I make it into a noose, which I loop over the handle of my bedroom door.

I pile cushions into a little stack, a couple of feet high, and I perch myself on top, legs stretched out, ice pipe at the ready. Being awake for a week on this stuff you can't really get any higher – you just keep yourself going, avoiding the crash. I take more ice tonight than I ever have before, and by the time I'm ready for the end the smoke in the room is so thick I can't see myself in the mirror.

I set my phone against my bedroom drawers and press record. I don't know why I want to capture my final moments on film. Drug-fuelled psychosis, I guess. I have my computer out, too. I email people, some with sweet goodbyes but also lashing out at anyone who I think has done me wrong.

I've usually shied away from the act of suicide in the past. It's like that feeling you get when standing at the edge of the train platform, knowing it's within your power to jump down onto the rails before the carriages come rushing past. It's like leaning up against a high balcony rail, knowing how little it would take to topple and fall. Self-preservation usually spooks you in those moments, pulling you back from the precipice, but I feel none of that now.

I'm ready for the euphoria and the silence that I get from GHB, my liquid ecstasy, my Grievous Bodily Harm. Usually I only take 2 millilitres and then no more for two hours. I'm disciplined in that way. *Disciplined?* How deranged has my thinking become?

I'm confident a bigger dose will see me fall off my pillowy perch and the leather mechanism above me will do its work. I load the syringe with much more of the drug than usual – 12 millilitres – and squirt it into my mouth. Did I mention that it's the most disgusting, horrible, loathsome-tasting shit ever? It is foulness.

And then it is solace.

I feel that familiar slipping as the drug takes hold, but can't quite pinpoint the second it takes me down. You know that moment before surgery when the anaesthetist knocks you out?

They count backwards from 10, through 9, then 8, and 7, and when you wake up you never really know how far you counted before you fell.

The stupor sneaks up on me in that way, and all of a sudden I can't see my phone or feel the pillows or even sense the tightening noose.

I'm in darkness now. I'm comatose. I'm nowhere.

no, no, no

Things go mostly to plan. I blow out and begin choking at least. And yet my body revolts, rousing me ever so slightly back into consciousness, until I'm kicking and thrashing. My roommate and I are separated by a single wall and she hears me banging, gasping for air. I've locked my door but she forces it open, causing a further tightening of the noose, but she frees it from my neck. She slaps me and screams at me and makes sure I'm alive and awake.

Her name is Jada and she doesn't deserve this memory.

We meet on Grindr in 2019. She's a beautiful trans girl with dark hair and sad eyes, and she pops up on my grid 500 metres away, and we start chatting. I ask her over on my birthday but she skips the party and comes over at 5am in her dressing gown and ugg boots. We talk for hours and she tells me her whole life story.

She's one of four, the youngest. She's the youngest of four. Her mum left when Jada was three or four. She was brought up by her abusive father. Jada had drug and alcohol problems from age 13, but she left the family and got herself clean. Flew to Melbourne by herself and transitioned alone. How's that for courage?

I make up my mind then and there that I'll help her to live her best life, tapping into whatever network I have in this city. I don't tell her about my life in football right away, and when I do I have to remind myself that she's a queer kid from Queensland

and isn't likely to know anything about me or the game I love. Playing in premierships and coaching champions – she shrugs at all my biggest moments. To her, they do not define me.

Jada is escorting when I meet her, taking men down to the Maribyrnong River and into grimy car parks in Flemington, and I don't like it. *You're gonna get killed, darling.* I let her move into my spare room a few nights a week. I don't mind if she sees a john here when she needs to, so long as she's safe. Eventually I give her a key and I come home and she's doing the washing and cleaning the kitchen.

She becomes the person I share everything with – the only one who sees it all. She finds me on the floor of the naughty room after every bender, and tears me a new one every time. I love her for giving me a clip.

We live as best mates. Me 52, her 22. She's the first person in my life to call me Dani. I'd give her my last breath.

She gives me back my breath right now. She doesn't need to do CPR but she shakes me into the world and she launches at me too. I'm dribbling shit from my mouth and she gives me a mighty spray. *What the fuck are you doing to yourself? I fucking told you to get off these drugs!* Jada would probably make a good coach.

I lash out at her for interrupting my plan. *I don't care*, I moan. *I can't do this anymore.*

She switches gears and sits there with me on the floor, both of us lying back on that toppled pile of pillows. She brings me down, nurses me through the moment and puts me to bed. I drift off and she stays and watches over me as I sleep the sleep of the living.

Jada believes I need treatment for drugs and alcohol – *Trust me, you need help to sort this out* – and she would know. But I'm not hearing any of that right now. I'm like fucking Amy Winehouse – I say *no, no, no.*

this is what i look like

I have a work meeting on Zoom at 8am the next day. I should skip it – *I just tried to kill myself* – but I need this job. I don't put my camera on, so they won't see me looking like death warmed over. But I don't put my camera on most of the time, actually, because I prefer to be myself. There's only one person at work who knows why my screen is usually black. Her name is Erin.

We're on the same learning and development consulting team, and she's writing a new program to deliver to a few management cohorts. She asks me to come into the CBD office at 22 Exhibition Street one Friday afternoon in February, to be the audience for her dry run, listening and asking questions.

She gets her PowerPoint presentation going, and the topic areas drift to holistic health and mental wellbeing, and in that moment I have so many thoughts about my own struggles, I blurt it all out. I tell her about my depression and anxiety, and my childhood, and my drug use – and I can see she is engrossed in my story. Erin is a queer girl, a really cool chick. I tell her there's something no one in our team knows – that I've been diagnosed with gender dysphoria.

Your whole life, you've had this?

Yeah.

Since you were a child?

Yeah.

And you've lived your life and done what you've done, with all this hanging over your head?

I pick up my phone and show her an image of me as Danielle. *This is who I am*, I say. *This is what I look like.*

She envelops me in a hug. *I love you.*

And now we're in this online meeting together with our colleagues, the morning after I've tried to end my life, and I think it might be time that someone else in my team knows and understands my problems. I do need help. Maybe Jada did get through to me after all. I'm mostly silent throughout the meeting, but I text my boss privately in the chat thread. *Can you stay online afterwards?*

When everyone else has left the meeting I tell him what happened the night before. He is nothing but sympathetic and concerned and supportive. In fact I end up in counselling all afternoon, a direct referral he organised through work, paid for with their employee assistance program. There's no judgement – only consideration.

I fall deeply into two days of talking with people and figuring out my next move. I have a planned appointment with Jaco on Tuesday afternoon, but I forget and miss it, and my phone is switched off or to silent or is being used when he calls, and that means he can't reach me for 30 minutes. When your client has a history of self-harm, that's a problem.

He has no choice but to call for help, in this case a CATT squad – a crisis assessment and treatment team from the Royal Melbourne Hospital. They're banging on the door of my apartment in under an hour. CATT squads are mobilised all over the state by medical professionals, tasked with helping anyone who has self-harmed, or might be about to.

I open my front door and find myself staring at two psychiatric nurses, two paramedics and two police officers.

I have to explain to them why I missed my Zoom meeting and why no one could reach me. The police and paramedics feel fine leaving in 15 minutes – but the nurses stay for four hours. They ask questions and offer advice until they feel satisfied enough to leave their cards with the phone numbers underlined.

I feel empty when they're gone. I can't take in all this professional advice. People are giving me guidance and recommendations and warnings and insights and it's all well meaning but I can't apply all this knowledge. I can't even compute it all.

The psychologist at the Kangaroos had a way of describing these kinds of overwhelming scenarios. It's like driving up the Tullamarine Freeway and trying to read the number plates passing on the other side of the road. Your mind will blow up quickly attempting the impossible. Sometimes you need to ignore all that traffic, keep your eyes on the road in front of you, and let the busy world drive on past.

head miles

Where the fuck did it all go wrong? I've been talking to people, telling them my story, consulting professionals, beginning therapy but none of it seems to matter. I'm sinking into debt and the drugs are sapping what's left of my spirit. I feel stretched and opaque. Again, I haven't slept in a week.

I know I need to get off this dance floor in my head but I can't.

It's early Friday night, 3 May 2020. I'm in the ensuite of the main bedroom at my apartment. The naughty room. And it's a mess. A towel rack ripped from the wall in a rage. Chips in the porcelain basin. Bright red nail polish splashed on the cupboard walls and across the floor tiles. A wall filled with holes, created by aimless vengeful haymakers.

My makeup is on from the night before, or maybe the night before that. I'm wearing my favourite wig, the human-hair one. Gas lighters are strewn across the floor in front of me, as well as a few baggies with crumbs of white powder inside. The rubbish bin is overflowing. Towels smeared with my makeup lie in a soiled pile in the corner.

I've spent a lot of time sitting still in here this week, going nowhere except around and around in my mind, doing head miles. My stomach is a dirty washing machine, thrashing and splashing. I'm shaking constantly, too, not even realising that my hand is scratching away at the premiership tattoo on my right ankle.

I get in my car, a gunmetal grey Mazda MX-5, and speed around Melbourne all night. I see the darkness in Footscray and the sun rise while driving through Elsternwick. I cover real territory, too, ending up on the Monash Freeway near Heatherton by midday. It's late afternoon when I pull up beside the Albert Park Carousel. I'm not wearing my glasses, and my eyes are glassy from sleep deprivation. It's disgusting behaviour, putting so many people at risk behind the wheel, but I'm doing it anyway.

I'm mixed up and messed up and falling apart. I've done things I don't want to think about, things I can't outrun, things that are going to detonate in the media and go on public record. It's inevitable. Eventually I pull over on Inkerman Street in St Kilda and park. I get out my phone. I call the police and tell them they need to come and get me. *Don't worry about my name,* I tell the operator. *You'll very quickly find out who this is.*

The police find me in my car with an ice pipe on the seat and $1500 stashed in my jacket, in case I needed to score. I have 2 grams of ice with me, but I've thought to slip that down between my seat and the centre console, where nobody looks.

I'm thrown into the back of a divisional van for the first time in my life. I have to slide up through this little hatch in the back to get inside. It's a tiny space, and dark. I can't see anything. It becomes my own private sensory-deprivation tank. I marinate in my thoughts for all of three minutes, until they drive me into the St Kilda Police Station at 92 Chapel Street, where a secure roller door comes down, falling with a heavy metallic clatter, like a curtain closing on a bad performance.

no comment

It's 8:30pm on a Saturday night. You would think the streets of St Kilda would be busy enough to keep the cops occupied, but there are more than a dozen plain-clothed and uniformed officers here, all taking a look at me, as if they had heard in advance I was coming. I feel like an animal in a zoo enclosure – an attraction in some strange circus.

I'm taken into the interview room and I begin to speak openly about my gender issues and mental health. But then I can't be fucked. I think of the police out there on the station floor, having a giggle – and the ones who laughed as they counted my $1500. I decide they can all fuck off. I've answered a few questions – now I begin offering a belligerent 'no comment'.

They've taken my phone. *We need it for evidence,* they say. *You can give us your PIN now and get your phone back quickly. If you don't, it'll be months, or you might never get it back.* I give them my PIN.

The interview room is small, and I can see a two-way mirror in front of me. You can tell because it has these thin silver lines, and in the black parts between them you can make out moving shapes, outlines in the darkness. Somebody is out there. I will remember this later.

I get my fingerprints done. My lawyer tells me I've been refused bail and I'll be going to prison on remand. I start howling like an animal, but that's not quite right. It's more pathetic than that. It's wailing, then whimpering, like a child.

At some point I'm handcuffed and put in the back of a van and taken to the Melbourne Custody Centre below the courts in the city. I'm walked into a side room to be searched. You're supposed to get undressed in a corner of this room, behind a black line on the floor. Step over the line and you're on camera. I take off my wig first. Because I'm transgender, the rest of the search happens in two parts.

A female officer is here to search my top half. That means I get to leave my bottoms on, but take off my top, and my bra. I have my tits out and feel as degraded as can be.

Do you have any drugs on you? she asks.

I've been fucking searched already. No, I don't.

Well what the hell is this then?

I'd forgotten about the tiny remainder of a gram I'd stashed in a baggy inside my bra. If it had been found at St Kilda Police Station when I was first brought in, I would have been charged with possession. Being found with ice in the custody centre is far more serious – I'm charged with bringing contraband into a prison.

I put my top on and then a male officer comes in to search my bottom half. They take a photograph of my face with a Polaroid camera, which is uploaded onto the court system but also to the Law Enforcement Assistance Program. LEAP is the core crime database. It runs like MS-DOS from the 1980s, but it's effective. Any police officer on duty can now go into that program and see how my night has unfolded, which is what many of them do, checking out my wigless, strung-out mugshot. I look like a cross-dressing crack whore.

My top goes back on, skirt and knickers come off. It's humiliating. I bend over, grab my cock and balls and pull them forward, then pull my bum cheeks apart. Tears are streaming down my face now, and the crying takes on a different tone. I'm mewling like a baby.

I go back to my cell, shell-shocked, traumatised, making no eye contact whatsoever. On the way out of the room, a male guard asks me a question.

Who was the best you coached? He asks. *Archer or Carey?*

FUCK OFF!

I'm serious. Which one?

Cunt.

The realness hits home when they close the cell door. I wish I could just pass out and start again, but it's not like I'm drunk and will fall into some dark, fretful slumber. I've been firing my pipe for hours, topping up all day. I'm wired. I'll have to live in this fully alert moment for a long while yet, pacing back and forth in my own tiny square of captivity – a broken soul in a cage.

join in the chorus

I talk to my lawyer through a plexiglass screen, just like in the movies. He tells me the magistrate we've drawn loves publicity, so it's not worth asking for bail. Ask for bail and we'll need a big hearing, and media will come.

Your arrest is already everywhere, he says. *And worse, when you were being interviewed at St Kilda someone took a photo of you –*

I knew there was someone on the other side of the window.

– and it's been circulated, then published. The Polaroid taken of you here today has also been published. It's an absolute firestorm out there.

I wallow in self-pity. What will my kids think of me? What are my friends thinking? My colleagues? What does the world think of me?

I'm put into a van and taken to the Melbourne Assessment Prison. I've worked there for years with operations managers and supervisors, helping them climb the ranks. I used to wander in and out of this place with my white plastic pass. Now here I am, being dropped off as a prisoner.

When I first started working at the Department of Justice, there was a girl who started at the same time as me, who had been a prison officer and worked at the Melbourne Assessment Prison. She told me she used to always ask her dates a question.

What's your CRN? she would ask.

What's that?

Criminal record number.

I haven't got one of those.

Right answer.

But now I've got one. My CRN is 223348.

I get out of the van, still in my skirt and blouse, heels and wig. I'm taken into the supervisor's office to meet the general manager on duty. I don't know what I'm expecting. A dressing-down maybe. A disappointed reprimand. Then again, he's seen worse. He knows not to judge. He has a question and it completely disarms me – making me feel as though I'm safe for the first time in a long while. *First things first*, he says. *What would you like us to call you?*

I self-harmed less than a month ago, so I'm not taken into a regular holding cell. I'm taken upstairs to the psych ward. I've visited this place. I used to catch the tram down Collins Street to Spencer Street and then walk the six blocks north to attend meetings about prisoner wellbeing here. I know what to expect.

I'm given a smock that closes at the shoulders with Velcro. No underwear. There's a mattress on the floor. No pillows, but one stiff, scratchy piece of material, supposedly a blanket. There's a sink and a toilet but no toilet paper. You have to call to ask for toilet paper. This is because prisoners will often stuff wads of it into the sink drain and then run the water to flood their cell, so they can get out of there for a few moments. They have other tricks for getting momentary freedom. Bronzing, for instance. That's when you take a shit and wipe it all over yourself, or all over the walls. That gets you out, even if only for a clean.

Rock bottom comes when they shut the door on you in there, when you're no longer in transit, no longer trying to figure a way out, when you resign yourself to this being your destination.

There's a scene in *Saving Private Ryan* – I really like that movie – where a boy who's been shot just says over and over again that he wants his momma. That's how this feels, like dying with your eyes open.

I get a call from my son, who reassures me that he's building a team to help me. Anthony Stevens is pulling whatever strings he can through North Melbourne. We've been slowly reconnecting but this is above and beyond. Mark Brayshaw has mobilised the AFL Coaches Association – he's their CEO. Darren Crocker, Greg Ryan and Cade Brown are getting involved, too.

You don't understand what it's like out here, Dad, says Kane. *You're everywhere.*

Inside, I sleep for 18 hours a day and cry for the other six. I get my food through a little slot in the door. Brekkie is two of the smallest pieces of toast you've ever seen with butter and jam, a piece of fruit and a cold cup of tea. Lunch is the best – a fresh salad roll – and I come to look forward to that. Dinner is disgusting. Just slop on a tray. I close my eyes and eat it for energy.

Staff who I've met before try to keep me going, with little reassurances and the odd hot cup of English breakfast, but I'm no model visitor. I hit the buzzer to see the psychologist, and a female voice responds.

He came already, she says. *You didn't answer.*

I want to see him anyway! I'm no good!

You're in the right place. You're sick. Go to sleep.

Who the fuck are you? Do you fucking know who I am? I used to work here!

I have a small window that faces west. It's frosted so I can't see out, but I can tell when it's light outside or dark. There's one other way you can tell when night has fallen: the prisoners howl. One starts screaming and the others do, too.

danielle laidley

They aren't well, and I'm not either. The last three days inside are the hardest because I'm out of my fog and have piercing clarity about where I am and what's going on. I join in the screaming at night, just another crazed wolf howling at the moon. *Join in the chorus, and sing it one and all ...*

do what you're told

During my last few days inside the psych ward, I speak to Anthony Stevens. He calls me on the phone and he is my knight in shining armour. He garners support from the AFL Players Association and puts me in touch with a new lawyer, the high-profile scrapper Rob Stary. And he also plays a big part in connecting me with a man I've neither met nor heard of, named Jackson Oppy. Jackson, Anthony tells me, is willing to stand up in court and make me his responsibility. If the judge will allow it, I'll be bailed into Jackson's care at the Hader Clinic – an emergency admission drug and alcohol treatment facility that he runs in Geelong.

At first I recoil from this plan. It's Kane who breaks the detail of this news to me – my month-long stay in rehab, under supervision from a stranger – and it's also Kane who bears the brunt of my apprehension.

Who the fuck is this person? I yell. *I don't even know him. Get fucked!*

Kane has had enough at this point. He's helped me through so many dark times, agonizing over every intervention, looking on as his protector needs protecting. Understandably, he snaps.

Shut your mouth, you little bitch, he says. *You don't have a choice. You'll do what you're told.*

Fair enough. In court Jackson speaks for me, or at least on my behalf about what my immediate future will look like. I'm not there in person but connected by video link, and I can make out

293

the grainy, pixelated shape of a tall bald man, who I later learn was once himself a drug addict. Jackson was addicted to meth. During one of his many rock bottoms, he tearfully pretended to his mother that he was gay and needed $5000 to visit the man he loved overseas – $5000 which he promptly spent on his habit. Jackson makes clear to the judge that I'm about to begin a long journey, and he has the therapeutic facility to start me on that path.

References are tendered to the court as well.

Choco Williams writes of his shock and sadness, of my work as a proven, driven, innovative problem-solver and mentor, as someone who was proud and protective, who didn't drink or do drugs. *Something dramatically has changed in his life*, he writes. *My hope is for him to have the opportunity to restart his life and return back to the Dean I knew and loved. I will be here for him.*

Bluey McKenna writes of the first thing I said to him in the summer of 1987: *I'm going to help you become the best you can be – and in doing so it might cost me my place in the squad!* And then of my desire to develop others: *The man has constantly given and cared for so many over the thirty plus years I've known him. Now he needs us to stand by him and help him, like he has helped so many.*

Wayne Schwass describes me as his *loyal, protective and quietly caring friend* whom he admires. *The situation he now finds himself in, whilst upsetting and concerning, is not the person I have come to know and respect over the past 27 years.*

Dr Con Mitropoulos, my GP, and the North Melbourne club doctor when I played and coached there, reflects on me as someone who always put others first, who thrived under pressure and was never flustered. *Dean is a sensible, caring and well-meaning person who – despite his tough AFL persona – is a gentle soul, with an endearing personality.*

Denis Pagan refers back to my upbringing in the tough northern suburbs of Perth, and my fierce determination, and my at-times quiet, intense and withdrawn personality – and even *continually placing his body in front of a rampaging Tony Lockett* during the 1996 Grand Final. *He was the consummate team player and never caused a ripple of trouble.*

James Brayshaw talks about having played junior footy and cricket against me in Perth in the 1980s, where he found me an *intense, focused, driven and talented young person who looked you in the eye and held your gaze,* and as someone at North Melbourne who *shielded the vulnerable people underneath him from turmoil …* *This was something I admired very much.*

The barrister acting for me is Philip Dunn QC. He wears big glasses and has a mop of silver hair, and he seems to start each spiel by shuffling his papers on the desk. He reminds me of the Nutty Professor but he leads the police prosecutor on a merry dance. I'm not really coherent at this stage but that's fine, because Phil seems as eloquent a defender as I could wish for, like a character from an episode of *Ironside*. He talks about my needing help – not incarceration – and with all the information in hand the magistrate deems my support network strong enough to succeed. I'm bailed into the care of the tall, bald stranger.

The jail is surrounded by media so we get into Jackson's car, which is parked inside behind a locked roller door.

I'm wearing prison greens: tracksuit pants, white T-shirt, generic sneakers. I feel disgusting in male clothes, but my outfit from the night of the arrest is filthy and scrunched into a plastic bag I'm carrying, along with my wig. I crouch in the back seat, throw a jacket over my head, and we roll out of the complex to the snapping of what feels like 100 cameras.

We're headed to Geelong and thankfully lose most of the trailing photographers in transit. We pull into the McDonald's on the Western Ring Road, and as we edge into the drive-through the familiar snap and flash of a camera goes off, capturing an image of me that will run on the front page of the next day's newspaper. That's the price you pay, I guess, for needing a large McFeast meal with a No Sugar Coke.

two birds with one stone

This clinic was once a nursing home, and it has that same antiseptic feel. The sliding doors open and the reception could be that of any large suburban medical practice. I'm shown to my room with its single bed, chest of drawers, lamp and digital radio. A robe with empty hangers. A toilet and shower and basin.

You get given a day or so of grace to get your bearings – adjusting to relative silence is challenging. There are no phones and no media. Jackson will be my filter for all of that – for messages from family and friends, lawyers and police, *60 Minutes* and the *Herald Sun*.

I'm not really up for talking but I do need people and movement around me. Even as bad as I'm feeling I can't stay in this room by myself. I venture into the courtyard – a patch of grass with a few chairs and a smoking area. Two young girls with their own problems give me a hug. *You'll be alright.*

On my second night I'm standing there when a guy approaches. Let's call him Scotty, although that's not his name. He's a 5 foot 8 knockabout country guy in his 30s, reasonably fit with receding hair. I'm in leggings and a tight black long-sleeved shirt and leather jacket. He wants to know my story. Everyone does.

What's your poison? he asks. *How did you end up here?*

Scotty has only just been admitted, meaning he's been out in public all day and the week before that, consuming current affairs however he does – through the TV or the papers or the social media feeds on his phone. I draw a Winfield Blue from the packet, light the cigarette and exhale. *Have you been following the news?*

He stares at me silently, and then looks me up and down. *Nup. Really? Dean Laidley?*

I nod.

Mate, I'm a Kangaroos supporter and I FUCKING LOVE YOU.

He gives me an almighty hug, and after that I call him Kangaroo. We're allowed only two phone calls in rehab, and Kangaroo tells me he's going to use one of his shortly after our chat.

I'm ringin' my wife, he says, *and tellin' her to bring all my footy gear in 'ere!*

Every night the Narcotics Anonymous meeting ends in the same way, with an acknowledgement: *We are in a circle to symbolise that no addict needs to stand alone. The most important person in any meeting is the new person in that meeting.*

These people do not look like junkies, because that's too reductive. Because they are lawyers and teachers, garbos and accountants and physical therapists, and they give their stories to the group, and then we work together from the book.

Just for Today – Daily Meditations for Recovering Addicts is a set of instructions and suggestions for living daily life safely and sanely. They're simple ideas to digest but hard to implement.

Just for today … My thoughts will be on my recovery, living and enjoying life without drugs.

Just for today … I'll have faith in someone in NA who believes in me and wants to help in my recovery.

Just for today ... I will have a program, and I will try to follow it to the best of my ability.

Just for today ... I will try to get a better perspective of my life.

Just for today ... I will be unafraid, and my thoughts will be on my new associations, on people who are not using and have found a new way of life.

So long as I follow these guidelines I have nothing to fear, and because I am bailed into this place I have no choice but to buy in anyway. I'm a homebody and always have been. I used to hate going away for the weekend for a football game, and yet I know I'm going to be in here for 28 days. My only option is to dig in and work with my therapist and my group to peel back the layers of my life.

Immediately I find parallels between my drug use and my gender issues. The things that are raised in sessions – all these truths I need to confront – apply equally to both. I can't believe I haven't seen the similarities sooner. Doing the work feels like a string of epiphanies as again and again and again the underlying causes of my ice addiction match my gender dysphoria.

In my earliest memories, I felt like I didn't belong.

If I let others know me, I feared they would reject me.

The pain of alienation was hidden easiest with defiance.

The deeper my issues grew, the higher the wall I built.

When the world says it doesn't need me, I say I won't need the world either.

I know instantly that this is going to be life-changing for me, that I'm killing two birds with one stone, my addiction and my identity. My mind meanders to how strong I might feel when I emerge from this place. I ponder the possibility of a life lived without fear of rejection. I have daydreams about accepting myself and being accepted into the lives of others.

But I have nightmares, too.

One is about self-harm. Off to the side of the courtyard here is a covered pathway, sheltered by big wooden beams. A bench rests nearby, and in my dream I pull that bench under that covered pathway, and I tie my twisted sheet to those big wooden beams, and I wrap the other end of that twisted sheet around my neck. I jump from the bench and wake up with a jolt.

troubled strangers

My rehab routine is the same as everyone else's here. Wake up, clean room, make bed, have breakfast, take medication, all before 9:30am, when we have our first meeting. Then it's 'school' (group work) all day, with a few free hours in the afternoon. Dinner next, then a meeting at night, time to relax and then to bed.

It's not all work though, and not all grim either. There is plenty of light here, too, and it feels at times like a school camp. There's the harmless barter system that I master, for instance, trading out my daily coffee sachet – *I don't drink coffee* – for a can of No Sugar Coke, which I guzzle like a fiend.

I'm sitting on the couch watching TV one night when a new client turns to me and my new friends – *What about that football coach eh? Done for drugs and cross-dressing?* – and we're left stifling giggles, quietly chortling. Other times it's no use trying to contain the laughter – and it's not just gallows humour.

I'm watching a movie one night and go to make an ice cream. Someone from the couch wants one, too, and then another new client as well. I make three huge ice cream cones – big vanilla triple scoopers – but with one of them I get a long thin cocktail spoon and push it all the way down through the ice cream, making a thin vertical hole, like the vent in a volcano. I fill that vent with chilli sauce, then cover the top with more ice cream.

The new guy gets three quarters of the way through his lava cone without showing any reaction at all. *Dani,* he finally says – with complete sincerity – *this is the BEST ice cream I've ever tasted.* I'm rolling on the floor in stitches now, and it feels so damn good.

Some days after class, we go for a walk around the local footy oval and have a bit of kick to kick. I'm taking set shots at the goals and spear a drop punt flush through the middle. A guy running laps jogs past and the clients in the goal square can hear his reaction. *Whoa,* he declares. *She's got a bloody good leg on her!*

I end up staying 35 days instead of 28. I wasn't quite ready to leave, but now I am. The last night goodbyes are bittersweet. I wear a short glittery mini dress to mark the occasion.

People go around the room telling me the things I've done for the group, what I've contributed. They were once troubled strangers but I've been living with them for a month. How many people do you ever do that with in your adult life, while offering up the most personal parts of yourself?

They tell me how proud they are of me being me, accepting myself and accepting my struggles.

Keep working hard, they tell me. *One day your family will be proud of you again.*

i don't trust myself

The transition house sits on a quiet street in suburban Essendon. It's a squat red brick rectangle with a grassy central courtyard. I don't like it here. There's one other girl and a dozen men. There's no playful camaraderie. No sweet, teary hugs. No ice-cream jokes.

During the first week you're not allowed to leave the premises by yourself – you need a chaperone. It makes me feel as though I can't be trusted, and I don't need to be told that – I don't trust myself anyway.

It does make sense though. That becomes abundantly clear when I'm given freedom to move again. I can suddenly go anywhere I want. I have my phone back, too. I can talk and plan and circulate.

You essentially go from an environment of unyielding regimentation to one of complete freedom and autonomy. It's not unlike the terrifying plunge all footballers take upon retirement. They play a game that demands adherence to a schedule for training, games, meetings, rest. *Here's your uniform. Here's your diet plan. Here's your injury recovery program. Here's your match payment.* When all of that is lost, is it any wonder so many retired players feel adrift? Is it any surprise when they turn around and walk right back through those doors to take up coaching instead?

A worry for me is the location of this place. This house is in my neighbourhood. It's literally an eight-minute drive from here to my apartment in Moonee Ponds. I'm not worried about the temptation of going home before I've spent my allocated time here. I'm worried about the triggers in this particular patch of the city. I board a tram and go down Keilor Road to get dinner, and after three stops I pass an apartment block and a dirty feeling crawls through me: I used to score from there.

I've spent five weeks in Geelong and now six weeks in Essendon, but my recovery's not getting any easier to handle. My mindset is improving but it also feels like two steps forward, one step back.

Jackson is the only thing keeping me on track. His faith. His time. His mentoring. He keeps me alive. I'm up to step 4 of 12, taking an inventory of yourself. Every time I sit down to do it – to talk about the relationships I've had with others and myself, and the damage I've caused – I fall apart. And each time, Jackson puts me back together again.

Life is overwhelming. Or maybe just *my* life is overwhelming. I want to focus on my recovery but there's so much other shit I need to face. My criminal lawyer. My tax lawyer. My property lawyer. My civil lawyer. Twice I spend an entire week in bed in Essendon, moored and melancholy.

A friend picks up my car for me. More freedom, more decisions. Then I'm walking out of 7-Eleven one night and it hits me. *I wonder if that 2-gram bag is still wedged down between the driver's seat and the centre console?* I turn my phone light on, peer under the seat, and there it is. Fuck.

It's Thursday night. I don't use it that night – not because I'm trying to hold myself to a high standard, but because we have pee tests every Monday, Wednesday and Friday. I do my pee test the next day and I use the next night. I let myself down. I let everyone down. I've never seen myself as a drug addict until now, but now it's impossible to deny.

Jackson calls me on Saturday afternoon. He wants to see me at the transition house. I can see from the look on his face that he knows.

I need you to do a pee test now, he says, *and I need to see you do it.*

You know as well as I do that I don't need to do it.

Thank you for being honest, he says, sighing. *Go to your room. Pick up your stuff. You're going back to Geelong.*

get out of your own way

We drive to Anthony's house first, and I stay for four days. It's a quiet spot in Newtown across from Kardinia Park, not far from the clinic. We sit down around a table and I think a sympathetic pep talk is coming, but that's not what Jackson is interested in right now. Right now I feel his anger – his bitter disappointment radiates from his eyes. Then he cuts me down.

You're just a fucking drug addict, he spits. *Just a fucking predator, that's all you are.*

I go to say something and he cuts me off.

I didn't ask you to speak! he hisses. *You're a transactional friend. A transactional lover. You try to talk your way out of and through everything. Stop coaching!*

It's tough love. I recognise that. He knows he needs to hit me hard if he's going to shake me loose from myself, because he's seen this before in others. I'm too deep inside my own head. I'm not really navigating reality – I'm negotiating with it instead of joining in and finding my way.

Anthony says his piece, too, and it's mercifully brief but no less powerful.

If you ever do it again, he says, *you've lost me.*

Jackson softens a touch, too. His tone changes to fatigued exasperation.

You've just gotta get out of your own way, he pleads. *There's too much work to do. And too much at stake.*

only the work

Back at the clinic, I'm so angry. With myself. With this experience. I imagine the people I worked with last time, living their lives and making meaningful strides in their recovery – climbing ladders while I'm slipping down a red-bellied black snake.

I have to meet a whole new set of clients, and I'm not interested anymore. It's a different cohort this time. Lots of older women whose drinking has got out of control during Covid. I start to get hit on by some of the men and I can't deal with that. The other clients quickly find out I've come from a halfway house and have the dumbest questions. *Had a good time partying out there?* I want to scream at them, that I was trying to get better but I fucked up, and at any rate I was mostly in lockdown with the rest of Victoria. I hold my tongue though. I'm not going to focus on people this time, only the work.

I become manic about running laps of the rehab course. I'm fanatical about *Just for Today*, too, studying its messages, pulling them apart, questioning them and putting them back together again. The first time here they felt like revelations, like the words to some magic spell. The second time they look more like work – work that I'll do for the rest of my life. I don't like the sound of that idea but I believe it. It's more concrete and plausible. The first time, I thought I could surrender myself, learn the material, pass the test and move on. It doesn't work like that.

I pay more attention to the 12 steps, and a big part of that is surrendering yourself to a greater power. That scares a lot of people away – the use of the word God – but it's god as you understand her to be. It's your higher motivation – your reason. The first time, I settled on my grandmother, Olive May. But she passed away in 2015, at 93, and it's difficult talking and connecting with someone who's no longer present.

In my second stint, I settle on my name, Danielle May, and the questions it raises. *Why do you want to stay on this earth, Danielle May? What do you love most, Danielle May?* It's my children, of course.

I make a little book out of folded A4 paper sheets. It's called Danielle's Big Book, and in it I write sayings and exercises, and things I think might help guide me. Jackson sits with me after class, and helps explain all the concepts and ideas, and as I talk with him and write in my book, I realise that this person saves lives.

One of the most important pages in Danielle's Big Book is just a print-out of a chart for tracking your state of mind. You can find it online. It's called the Mood Meter.

It has an energy axis and a pleasantness axis. If you're feeling highly energised and highly pleasant, for instance, you might be cheerful, inspired or blissful. If you're feeling highly pleasant with low energy, however, you might simply feel tranquil, satisfied and carefree.

It's not good to have high energy and low pleasantness, of course, because that manifests as tense, panicked and troubled. But it's the very worst of all, naturally, to have low pleasantness with low energy. Then you feel disgusted, despondent, desolate.

That final one is the blue quadrant on the chart. It's the home of loneliness, depletion, alienation, and half-a-dozen other shitty emotions. I call it the kill zone. The point of the Mood Meter is to make a daily assessment of yourself, and evaluate the risk. It's a little like monitoring a bushfire: Watch and Act. If I'm feeling hopeless or morose or despairing, or any other emotion listed in the kill zone, I ask for help.

The work is wrenching but cleansing. It rips your soul apart and sticks it back together. Rehab is a little like football for me. Both nearly kill me. Both save me. I'll be allowed to leave soon, to go home while seeing Jackson three times a week. He becomes my sponsor. I'm tough enough to make it now, at least I think I am.

welfare check

I have this friend named Donna. Donna Leckie. DL. Just like me.

We go back a long way, to 1973, when we are both in grade 1 at Warriapendi Primary School. They make us sit together because we're left-handers and they want to change that. We resist together. Southpaws forever. I go to a different school for a few years when living with Nanna Olive, but I'm back with DL by grade 5.

We hit Balga High School together, too. She's the smart one, the head girl, dux of the school, state netball squad. I'm the one who misses a lot of school kicking a footy, wielding the willow, catching waves and pulling bongs. But we go out on and off, girlfriend and boyfriend. There's a very strong connection.

We drift eventually and lead our own lives, have our own careers and raise our own families. We're out of touch for three decades, really, until 2015, when I buy my villa in Bali and set up a Facebook page for renting it out. My other social media accounts are private, but this one is public, giving her a chance to reach out.

We begin to share our lives in spasmodic messages, which become frequent messages, which by 2017 become almost daily messages. We text, too, and before we know it we're flirting. Incessantly. She calls me a princess. I reply with high heel emojis, testing her to see if she suspects anything.

I slowly start to tell her things about my life, the bad things but not all the things, and certainly not the one big thing, not yet. Donna knows exactly when something is wrong. She can sense it from a brief reply or a single terse sentence. *Hey DL, this is the welfare check*, she writes. *What's going on?*

She's not a silly girl. She knows I'm in trouble. She gets me every time, and every time I spill my guts about my spiralling addiction. *That's it*, she says, *I'm coming over*. She does this often but I dissuade her often, and if she insists then I disappear. I ghost her until the threat of help is gone and I can go back to being miserable by myself.

I'm supposed to go west for Christmas in 2018, to spend the day with my mum and see Donna. I don't sleep the night before and arrive off my head, surprise Mum, then fall into a detoxing slumber. I make plans with Donna all week but I don't keep them. I know I can take her for granted. Kane calls to say he needs me in Melbourne, and I drop everything to fly home. I'm glad for the excuse to get back to the gear waiting in my apartment. I need a hit.

We meet in Bali in late 2019. I commit to visiting Donna, and I do. I walk into her villa after a night on ice, with half-a-dozen bottles of Black Jack (bourbon and cola) under my arm. I'm in a T-shirt, shorts and ponytail, and can't keep my eyes open. I'm a train wreck. Later I will find out that Donna wonders if she will ever see me again. She thinks I might be dead soon.

When everything goes to shit Donna tries to contact me – throughout my time in custody and rehab and transition. She wants to come to me in Victoria, even though under the Western Australian premier's staunch Covid-safe rules she won't be allowed back into Fortress Perth. She doesn't care. She offers money to help. She scrambles and strives while I'm trying to set myself right.

When I finally re-enter the world, I have hundreds upon hundreds of messages to get through. Many I simply have to ignore. But not those from Donna. I sit down one Wednesday night and write a long message of thanks for her support. And I finally tell her about my gender dysphoria.

I love you, always have, she replies. *I'll support you. I will not judge.*

disgraceful conduct

The public gaze is a funny thing. I've fallen in and out of that bright line of vision for almost four decades, and almost never on my terms. And now, after years spent wondering how or when or if I might present my real self to the world, that decision has been taken out of my hands. It's been done for me, in the most brutal fashion imaginable. And it's all there waiting for me as I resume my life in recovery.

There's the photo taken by the shadow on the other side of that two-way mirror in the St Kilda Police Station interview room.

The wigless Polaroid mugshot taken a day later during my strip search.

The details of my arrest from the LEAP database.

All of it has been shared with the world.

A WhatsApp group of coppers known as the SD1 Gentleman's Club is the first preferred method for disseminating this information. I'm able to read their exchanges – their banter – once my lawyers are involved. There's something about the rising gleeful tone of every line that gets to me, the way they go so quickly from 'I've seen the photos' to 'Full-blown ice head and tranny!'

It gets worse. The police confiscated my phone and asked for my PIN and I gave it, but now highly personal and private videos and photos are viewed and discussed by complete strangers with derision and sick delight.

Some of them know that I've been coaching local footy again, with Maribyrnong in the Essendon Football League. Kane is playing with the team. He's gotten himself fit for the first time in 10 years and earns five senior games as my centre half-forward – the hardest position on the ground. Watching my boy run and mark and kick and win – watching him playing a game for fun – might be my happiest memory in coaching.

'Still coaching a local team. Surely not ...' one officer notes. 'End of season trip would be interesting. Post match showers. Geez!!'

The photos break free of their initial group, spreading like wildfire – raging through Twitter feeds and Facebook groups and Instagram accounts and discussion boards, and then the mainstream media. I dominate the news cycle for weeks. My lawyers have a neat way of putting the storm in context for me. I become the most googled Australian public figure of 2020.

The officers see this developing, of course. Initially the speed with which the information moves becomes the subject of jokes: 'they'd have to sack every copper for forwarding it on too haha, I got bombarded last night with pics'.

Then this begins to worry them. Members of the initial crew begin asking one another if anyone has shared the images beyond their group. They're police officers, so they understand the power of a digital trail. They realise the gravity of the leak, and one by one they leave the SD1 Gentleman's Club WhatsApp group. By the next day, many of them are being interviewed at South Melbourne Police Station while their phones are forensically examined.

In time, 224 Victoria Police employees are cleared of any wrongdoing, but 39 officers and seven public servants face disciplinary action. They're charged with 'disgraceful conduct'. Compensation is coming. A civil case. But nothing will undo the damage done.

I live with it every day. I get anonymous, unspeakable messages of hate online. I leave my building and get papped by tabloid photographers. I walk down the street and a hoon leans out his car window and screams: *Show us ya balls, Laidley!*

you can hear a pin drop

I haven't clarified anything in the media. Not yet. To the public I'm still the dishevelled person in those leaked photos. I'm the cross-dressing drug addict ex-AFL player and coach who's gone off the rails.

My drug diversion case comes before the courts in late 2020. When the charge against you is minor, as mine was, you can ask for a diversion, which means a good behaviour bond, perhaps four months. If you behave then the charge gets struck off the record.

But that's not what's important about this hearing. Rob Stary, my lawyer, talks to me before the hearing about an idea he has – something that might change the narrative around my entire arrest and outing, if I'm willing to hear him out.

Dani, I'm going to do something here. You need to trust me, he says. *I'm going to turn the court on its head.*

He's going to tell everyone that I've been diagnosed with gender dysphoria and am in the midst of my transition. He's going to explain that I can be a useful vehicle in assisting the community to understand transgender issues, and that my experience can have utility. He's going to say what everyone has assumed but no one knows for sure.

He begins with a specific request to the magistrate, for something I've craved but never seized, a right that's always been mine, yet I've never taken up.

From now on, he tells them, I would like to be known as Dani Laidley.

From now on, my pronouns are 'she' and 'her'.

I'm not in the room at the time. I'm attending by audiolink. Nevertheless, you can hear a pin drop.

There's only one thing I want to change about this, and it's that I actually prefer 'Danielle'. Dani sticks.

welcome back

It's the beginning of the end of Melbourne's long Covid lockdown in November 2020 when a meeting I'm not expecting to happen – or at least not so soon – takes place. Mark 'Sticks' Brayshaw has engineered it. I'm going to speak to the AFL head honchos. I can't quite believe they're making time for me right now. They're incredibly busy and no doubt exhausted. AFL CEO Gillon McLachlan and his right-hand man, general manager of football operations Steve Hocking, are coming off the remarkable achievement of running a successful season despite all the hurdles the year threw up.

Sticks wants to make sure this meeting is a private affair, but Covid restrictions on numbers means it's still hard to organise such gatherings in homes or hotels or offices, so we consider an open-air meeting in Fawkner Park on Commercial Road, just down the street from the queer nightclubs I've frequented for so many years. I don't love the idea of being out in the open though. A photo of me is all that's required to make front-page news.

I'm still heading to the Melbourne branch of the Hader Clinic three times a week for drug testing, and it dawns on me that their office backs onto Fawkner Park. In fact they've got a private open-air courtyard. It's perfect.

I want this meeting to go well. I need it to go well. For so long I lived in fear of what the AFL world would think when they found out the secret I'd carried my whole life. Even though it's out in the open now, I'm still feeling the shame and embarrassment of letting down my brothers I played alongside and my boys that I coached. I was overcome with gratitude when I found out how much the AFL did for me when I was in rehab and I want to make a good impression.

Jackson buys six new outdoor chairs from Bunnings, and a new tablecloth, too. We get there early and sweep the place out. I've written a report for our guests and it's about my hopes and dreams – plans for what I might do to help. Diversity and inclusion are high on my list, having education and awareness programs within all workplaces and clubs, so that we might live without barriers. We've printed and bound the document, and place a copy in front of each seat.

There's no sign of the AFL heavyweights by 2pm, the scheduled time. By now I've moved into the preparation zone but Sticks and Jackson are starting to sweat bullets. Did we get the arrangements right?

Sticks makes a call. Steve is at the other end of Commercial Road. *My fault, hand up, sorry boys. I gave the wrong suburb.* When he arrives we chat about footy and the times I played against him when he was a dour back pocket for Geelong.

Sticks makes another call. I can see he's panicky. It sounds as though Gillon has mixed up his days, and today is club dividend pay day – a busy one in which the league hands millions of dollars to each club on a needs basis. That doesn't matter though – he'll make time for us. He's just down the road and on his way now.

When Gil arrives it's Covid elbow shakes all round and that's when it really hits me. This leader of a hugely successful organisation has actually dropped everything to come and meet the real me for the first time.

We get down to business. I give everyone a snapshot of my life: what's happening with my immediate family, the Laidley family history of addictive behaviours, my gender issues, what unfolded over the previous 18 months that led to my arrest. I'm getting better at my own potted history now. Gil interrupts only once to ask if I'm drug free. I say yes and continue, and by the end of my story I see only looks of dismay, surprise and care. *To be honest,* Gil says, *I don't how you are sitting there with what you have been through in your life.*

I let out a laugh, louder and more raw than I thought it would sound. Almost a yelp. *Thanks Gil,* I say, *but be assured I've only just made it – despite two attempts to take my own life.*

Gil goes on to talk about his own family, his ideals and the legacy he wants to leave the game, and how my cause could and should be part of that.

Dani, our game is for everyone, and you right now may be the most famous transgender woman in the country. Our game must be inclusive, and you could be that perfect example – you have a unique skill set, with unique experience.

A warm feeling rushes through my whole body.

Do you still like footy? he asks. Good question – it catches me off-guard.

Yes, I reply, and it's the truth. *Football is still my passion, but I've wrestled with it my whole life.*

When you're ready, Gil responds, *let's meet again and drill down into what you would like to do.*

I tell him I have put together some statistical evidence about trans people and that I feel with the right support I could use the AFL platform to make a difference. That I hope that people will respect what I've achieved in the first part of my life. That I believe if people will give me an ear, I could deliver the right messaging and education.

I hand him my report, and he smiles.

Dani, as long as I am CEO of this organisation, I will break down as many barriers as possible for you. Welcome back to the family.

After they've gone, the three of us sit, stunned, for a few minutes until Jackson breaks the silence. *Dani, do you realise what message this man has given you?*

Yes, I respond. *Yes, it's a little overwhelming but yes.*

But I don't, not really, until I've had a few days to reflect on the enormity of what just took place. And what I take away is that I have been given a great opportunity, as long as I continue to work on myself, and keep reconnecting with family, friends and colleagues.

This could be my medicine. My purpose. My work.

anywhere, anytime, anything

I'm heading south in an Uber, down towards DiMattina's restaurant in Lygon Street, Carlton, and I'm nervous. The city is lit up in the distance and usually that sparks me up – I sense the potential in all those places and people, and what they might bring my way – but other times it does the opposite. I feel dwarfed by all those faces and buildings, unable to meet whatever challenges the world has in store for me.

I'm about to meet a handful of the North Melbourne footballers I played with in the 1990s, in an upstairs dining room, to reconnect after all these years. I pass by the big Melbourne General Cemetery and shudder. I can't do this. I want to go home. Having butterflies is okay – I've always been able to harness those flutters, but sometimes it's impossible to get them all flying in the same direction.

I start recording a video on my phone, to shed some anxiety. I do this every now and then, taping my mindset as a kind of visual diary entry, something I might yet look back on. *I've lived in fear all my life*, I tell the screen. *I've done a lot of work on myself, and I'm now ready to meet some people I know well, who really don't know me that well at all – who definitely don't know my true self, but really should.*

I know it's different and a bit peculiar – this digital journaling of mine – but I find clarity in the telling, and in seeing myself on the screen, too. I'm me, sitting in this Uber, looking down on me in my iPhone, talking back up at me in the Uber, telling every version of me what I'm about to do and why everything is going to be fine. By the time I'm finished recording the driver pulls up in front of the restaurant. The hardest part is opening the door and standing on the street by myself, because that's the point of no return.

Mark Brayshaw has organised this meeting, too, with help from my old assistant Greg Ryan, and they're both there early to help greet and direct people and settle my nerves. I walk into the restaurant and then upstairs. Those steps take forever.

John Blakey is there. He was recruited to the Kangaroos at the same time as me. We were the mid-career veterans – the athletes and competitors tasked with raising a young group's standards. Matthew Larkin is there, too. Matty was captain the day I arrived at the club. They don't know whether to shake my hand or give me a hug, but I have a solution. One of the things I've started to do to break the ice when reconnecting with someone is wait for them to extend their hand for a handshake, and then whack it away and grab them in a hug instead.

Darren Crocker arrives next. Brett Allison, too. Glenn Archer comes, and Ian Fairley. Donald McDonald was my assistant coach and then footy manager, and he joins the party too. We have cheap red wine and pizza and pasta. They're as nervous as I am. I break the tension by getting a laugh. I go to the toilet but turn to them before leaving the room.

Don't you go looking at my arse, you boys, I say. *I may sit down to pee, but I've still got a mean left hook.*

I don't know where to start my story. It comes out as it comes out. I try to explain the person they saw back then and how that really wasn't me. I go through it all. The fact that this has been in me – a part of me, all of me – since childhood. The way I fought it and fought everyone else. *Kill or be killed.* The way I explored my subculture and found people I could trust, but how I was waylaid by drugs, and how through it all I remained entangled in this thing – footy – that gave me so much and took so fucking much, too. And I tell them how I fell and how I thought I would never stop falling, and how when I hit rock bottom I never thought I would stand again.

The room is silent, except for big, tough Glenn Archer, who's sitting next to me, sniffing through a few tears. He's emotional, this man I played with and then coached, this maniac on the field. *I can't believe what you've been through,* he says. *We're just so glad that you're happy, that you've gotten through.*

I only played one year with Matty Larkin, but he has my back. *All of us are here for you, anytime,* he says. *Anywhere, anytime, anything.*

Ian Fairley feels the same way. *We all go through our ups and downs in life, and I've been through mine. I'm here for you in yours – unconditionally.*

Darren Crocker, the Kangaroos new AFLW coach, is succinct. *I can't believe you're still with us. I'm just happy you're healthy and here.*

I did university study with Brett Allison, and he says more now than he ever did in any tutorial. *I love you for you. You might look a little different – you're still you.*

John Blakey is a man of few words. He doesn't know quite what to say, so he says nothing. But he says plenty throughout the night with his warm smiles and nods in all the right places.

I used to have massive fights with Donald McDonald when he was my footy boss, but he's here. I feel the need to grab him and share something. *When I was coaching North, what you did got me through and saved my life,* I say. *Your support meant everything. I feel indebted.*

A big part of my therapy is getting on my hands and knees by my bed each night, and praying to the greater power or just speaking into the air, and being thankful for what I have. Tonight I'm thankful for the love in that upstairs dining room, and the men supporting the woman I've become.

the whole story

The reunions and reconnections keep coming.

Wayne Schwass and I catch up for dinners and he's the same soulful brother as ever, only more polished now. His comprehension of mental health was once a deeply personal *felt* thing – something experienced and barely survived – but now he is also an advocate, a spokesperson, a leader in that fight. He has a new nickname for me, too – *Junkyard Bitch*. I kinda like it.

David King treats me with compassion and respect. The former fiery flanker now has a platform in the media and he uses it on my behalf, steering the public conversation that surrounds me. He lives half a kilometre from me, and we spend many Monday mornings at his house watching NFL. He invites me over to his place for Christmas dinner. Invites me to play poker with his mates. We're at an event at the Anglers Tavern in Moonee Ponds surrounded by hundreds of people, and he is attentive and caring. *Are you okay, Dani? Have you ordered food? I'll get you a drink. Let me introduce you to a few mates.*

I have different versions of these kinds of overtures and outings with so many of the guys I played with and coached. Boomer Harvey. Anthony Rock. Aaron Edwards. Brady Rawlings. Michael Firrito. Arriving in Victoria from Perth in late 1992, before the nationalisation of the AFL was fully realised, I had always felt a little like an outsider at Arden Street – like some interstate interloper – but that's gone now. We all bleed blue and white together.

Except those who bleed black and white. People I met at Collingwood reach out too. Paul Licuria and Chris Tarrant and Scott Cummings. Ben Johnson gets in touch, to share a message from all the boys. *Thank you for what you did for us. We were young and you showed us so much wisdom. You're a remarkable person.*

Soon after, Mark Brayshaw organises another get-together, this time with a group of guys I played football with at the West Coast Eagles – three decades ago – who all now live in Melbourne. I walk into the Sandringham home of Bluey McKenna and there's David O'Connell, Geoff Miles, Peter Melesso, Mark Zanotti and Alex Ishchenko. It's frosty but not in a bad way. The atmosphere is like that thin layer of ice on a puddle in winter – it's easy to crack and melts with a little sunlight.

I do my spiel again. The whole story. It gets a little easier each time. There's therapy in this. They shake their heads in disbelief, sigh, and offer the same incredulous stares. They're an inquisitive group, asking lots of questions. *How long have you been feeling like this? What was the anxiety like at its worst? You never, ever did drugs as a player – how on earth did you get into that?*

I talk, too, about something that has nagged me since my time at the Eagles – the way I've always felt subservient or unworthy somehow, having missed the club's biggest finals and that first flag. It's the stupidest thing, but not being selected in those sides made me feel unloved, or less loved anyway. I suppose that reaction isn't so dumb. It's the same rejection you feel as a kid when you're left out of any schoolyard game.

They're gobsmacked that I could have felt that way – that I could feel belittled by missing out. *You were well and truly part of that side*, they affirm. *You were the most unlucky person at the club.*

We've always looked on in awe at what you've achieved since then. Even more so now.

The calls keep coming, too. Paul Peos gets in touch. I spend hours on FaceTime with John Gastevand and we have lunch in Perth. Adam Simpson is busy coaching the Eagles now but organises a night at his home in Perth when I'm visiting there. I walk in and his youngest daughter strolls up to me.

Did you coach my dad?

Yes, I did coach your dad.

Did he lose you any games?

As a matter of fact he did!

We're all laughing, but this passing moment is precious to me. I haven't yet spent much time around children as myself, and this little girl comes up to me without blinking, without pause, without any double-takes or confusion. She sees what she sees. We're not born with prejudice, and clearly Adam hasn't instilled any in his daughter. He's always been a beautiful human. When he was being considered for the Eagles job, a headhunting firm called me for a reference. I was scheduled to speak to them for 10 minutes – we talked for an hour about his many strengths and qualities.

Adam has invited a motley crew. Peter Bell and Spider Burton are the brainiacs of the bunch, peppering me with a multitude of questions. David Hale is articulate and quiet, and stunned. Daniel Pratt, who was always the charmingly immature social butterfly – the joker in the deck – sits beside me and listens intently. His eyes are wide open, while Drew Petrie's mouth drops open and stays open. Then Daniel points out what they're all thinking: *I haven't heard you speak this much in your entire life!*

And he's right. I've spent years beating the shit out of myself because of what my mind told me. It's hard to get out of your head sometimes. You need people around you to draw you into another place. I think back to the gathering at Bluey McKenna's house, and his words at the end of the night. It brings me to tears every time.

We know your last 30 summers have been difficult, he said. *It's now up to us to make the next 30 happy and bright.*

I'm reconnecting with family and friends, too. There's Sean King – my best friend, my best man – and his wife, Anita. And the Kassis family, who have been part of my extended family for nearly 30 years. Through tears and laughter I discover the real strength of our friendship, and there's love. They love me for who I am.

Mum and Leif take a while to get their heads around their son now being their daughter, but they settle into it, with a few hiccups around pronouns.

Paul is candid. *You weren't a crash-hot brother*, he says. *You're already a much better sister.*

i'm all in

In the middle of 2021 the Western Australian border briefly opens, and I immediately think of Donna. We've been trying to connect, but Covid cancellations and delays and abandoned flights mean it hasn't happened yet. On Friday 9 July I book my flight west, and I'm in the air headed to Perth two days later. Donna picks me up at the airport and it's cinematic. I come down the escalators and through the automatic doors and we run to one another and hug. I hold on to her for so long.

We chat all the way home to her place in Scarborough, where we have a little party. We're the last ones standing when it's over, and we sit on her balcony looking out over the hills to the water and Rottnest Island beyond. She puts me up in a spare room, perhaps unsure whether I'm ready to be with her – to be some version of what we were in high school. But we both clarify that quickly.

All my chips are on the table, I say. *I'm all in.*

I was all in years ago, she says. *I love you before and after.*

She has a million questions and I answer them all. We talk all night.

She comes back to Melbourne with me for a two-week visit, then the borders shut and she's stuck in Victoria, but she doesn't mind. After a five-year online courtship, we now live together. Are we the odd couple? Perhaps. I don't eat mussels but I make Donna the best chilli mussels she's ever eaten. She makes me the comfort food I need – lasagne, or the perfect toastie. I instigate grand furniture reshuffles, and she instigates the household cleaning. (I chip in.) Date night is cooking together, blasting Lady Gaga on YouTube, and dancing like no one's watching.

We begin going out as a couple. Donna and Dani have dinner. Donna and Dani go dancing. Donna and Dani hit the Spring Racing Carnival, with a trip to Geelong for Ballan Cup Day.

Most of Donna's outfits are in Perth, so we go to Highpoint Shopping Centre to look for new dresses to wear to the races. We get spray tans. We get our hair and nails done. We get frocked up. We're in Geelong by noon.

A policeman takes a photo of me there and shares it with friends in yet another disparaging text, and it comes to light. The Independent Broad-based Anti-corruption Commission gets involved. I guess some people never learn.

Anthony is at the races, too. He organised our tickets in the members enclosure, behind glass, front-row seats, lunch and drinks. A perfect view, and out of view of prying eyes.

My new shoes keep slipping off my heel, and the double-sided tape on my dress is giving way, so I lose my cool a little. *Bloody hell, Donna, my shoes are slipping and my tits are showing,* I complain. *I want to go home.*

We stay though. Donna says her dad always took a quinella with 1 and 5 in each race, so that's what she does, and after lunch a quinella pays out $45. Anthony has something else in mind for a flutter, and he gives us a sweet sermon near the end of the day.

Girls, we are at table number 7, he says. *Danielle, you wore number 7, you coached North Melbourne for 7 years, the Ballan Cup is race 7, there are 7 horses in the race, and we are backing number 7.*

We go down to the concourse to watch the big race. I see a group of rowdy young men at the bottom of the stairs. They're hooting and hollering and taking the piss out of one another, and I begin to worry. I'm not yet used to these settings as myself. How are they going to treat me? Donna doesn't let me dwell on the answer – she just grabs my hand and leads me through, and I breathe a sigh of relief.

The gates burst open for the 1500-metre race. Halfway up the straight a brown horse in green silks named Turbeau takes the lead. With 200 left to travel, a six-year-old bay gelding from New Zealand, Kissinger, comes storming home, but not fast enough. Turbeau lunges at the line and takes it from Kissinger by a head. Number 7 wins!

After an amazing day, we all go out to dinner. Anthony and I settle in for a few drinks after the others go home. He calls the waiter over. *I want your best Scotch on the rocks and bourbon on the rocks, a round every seven and a half minutes.* I laugh loudly – that's the famous game plan from *The Wolf of Wall Street*.

After an hour or so we call it a night. As we're leaving, two men recognise Anthony and ask for a photo. I slip off to the side and keep walking.

One of the lads yells, *Hey darling, wait for your date!*

I turn around and call out, *Come on, Anthony darling!*

We are beside ourselves, laughing our heads off. If those boys only knew.

two tribes

Northern Melbourne is planning a press conference on Friday 19 November 2021. They've just used the number one draft pick on South Australian tyro Jason Horne-Francis. The physical redevelopment of the club is underway. The community programs in place are thriving. Yet this announcement is about the balance sheet.

The Kangaroos are out of debt. After posting a profit for the tenth year in a row, the club is in the black again for the first time in a long time – in 34 years to be precise. The last time they weren't in debt was 1987, the year I first played league football.

They want me to be part of the event, and I'm honoured to be asked, but it can't be about me. If my name is even put on the press release promoting the day, there is a real risk of distraction. I don't want to steal any focus from the footy club, so my attendance is kept under wraps – but in the background I'm quietly briefed on the day, who will be there, how it will flow and which questions emcee Tiffany Cherry will ask me.

I'm up until 3am the night prior. I can't sleep, so I'm doing my tanning, washing my hair, selecting outfits, reading those questions and coming up with answers, revising my dot points so I can speak off the cuff with clarity and concision. David King calls me and challenges me. *The press will take away one line – one truth – from you tomorrow*, he says. *What do you want that tagline to be?*

We discuss possibilities, like the club being financially strong but even richer in cultural capital. We talk about the Shinboner spirit. We settle on the potential power of bringing together the two tribes I'm representing now, the old and the new, the NMFC blue and white stripes, and the LGBTQIA+ rainbow.

Earlier in the year I went to my first transgender public event, where I met a lot of elderly trans people. I asked what life was like for them, before this era of blooming tolerance, and saw their pride and happiness and contentment – their gratification at being the generation who led the way. It struck me then that these smiling individuals with their prominent rainbow pins are so much like the past players you find at any football club, proudly wearing their club ties to events, finding enduring honour and dignity in their connection to something greater.

The only difference, of course, is that the latter tribe is lauded for what they have done – playing a popular sport – and the former tribe is vilified for being who they are – transgender men and women. I think to myself, if I can somehow explain what binds those two tribes together for me, then maybe I can sway a few more minds to see the similarities between our cultures, and in the struggles we've both faced.

I arrive just before the event starts and sneak in through a side door. The media sees me though, and they're like sharks to the burley. Cameras swivel and pivot my way. Reporters reach for their phones to call editors and producers. This should make me nervous but it doesn't. I laugh a little inside, actually, because I have no nerves here, because this place is my home. *What, all this fuss over little old me?*

I listen to the speeches of the current CEO, the wonderful Ben Amarfio, as well as former chairman and lionheart James

Brayshaw, and current chairman and former teammate Ben Buckley.

Then it's my turn. I talk about the rats that used to run across my desk when I was a coach. About the part-time work I did here as a player, painting the walls and mowing the grass. I talk about the decision to stay here at Arden Street in 2007, and I remember that this happened when the team was going well on the field, when I was coaching my most successful season, and that's when my little part in this continuum comes into focus, and I realise the genuine nature of my link within the chain of this club's very existence.

I chat to the coach who succeeded me, Brad Scott, about the pain we both know, of getting into preliminary finals and not quite making it over the line. I talk to the coach who succeeded him, David Noble, about how he's rebuilding the list and nurturing the countless green shoots he sees.

Since the collapse of my old life, I haven't yet given a single detailed interview to any media. All I've done is read and watch and listen to them grapple with my story, offering a little truth and a lot of bullshit. That's why the reporters are circling now, angling themselves into my path, getting ready to rush me.

But the people surrounding me – current captain Jack Ziebell, former captain Boomer Harvey, development coach Anthony Rocca, even my manager, Tony Box – they become a cluster of linebackers, blocking for me, protecting me, clearing my path indoors to morning tea, where so many people say so many nice things.

It's really great to have you back.

We love you.

You're going to do wonderful things.

It's nice to hear these affirmations, and feel all their faith.

Today I sit back and listen. Tomorrow, I'll tell my story.

don't look away

One of the first things I loved about playing senior football was listening to the war stories of the older players. The detail drew me into their world and I couldn't get enough of it. I saw how Mick Malthouse and Denis Pagan used stories to get us players to think and act in a certain way, to try different things. When I went to Carlton as an assistant coach, I was secretly thrilled one day when Chris Judd told Mick Malthouse why he always sat next to me on the bus. *I love listening to Tunnel's stories.*

Telling my whole story isn't easy but I know it's what I have to do in order to repair some of the damage I've done to myself and others. Eddie McGuire once offered me a piece of advice when I hit rock bottom: *When you're walking through hell, the most important thing is to keep walking.* I know if I share what it's been like to walk in my shoes for 55 years – all the blood and guts and shit and puke, the mistakes and the shame, the hugs and tears and fists in the air – it might lead to acceptance of others like me. It might help someone else to just keep walking.

For a long time I have had a picture of late-life contentment in my mind. I am sitting on a verandah somewhere – *my* verandah – quietly watching the sunset. It's human nature to imagine that soft landing. Rocking chairs. Blankets on knees. Cups of tea. I am surrounded by my son and daughters, and their partners, and my grandson, and future grandchildren, and my mum, and my brother, and my girlfriend, and all my friends. But I'm in no hurry to while away the days rocking on that verandah just yet. I'm patient, which is out of character for me. You see, I have finally found home, and it's inside me.

I know I am very much a work in progress. I'm still learning my new life. The flood of acceptance and curiosity and celebration and performance is sometimes like a sugar rush. My happiness is energetic, manic even, and then I can't find my handbrake, and I crash. I have days when I can't get out of bed. I am still learning the hardest of tasks: how to take care of myself.

I'm still learning practicalities, too and I'm working out when to make a stand on behalf of my own identity and that of my tribe.

Are pronouns the hill I will die on? Sometimes I'm not fussed – other times I am. How much does it matter when someone slips up and unintentionally refers to me as 'he'? If I get outraged by that every time, will my anger alienate the very people I want to reach? There's a whole vocabulary for this new universe that people are still grappling with. Does the average punter know what every letter in the LGBTQIA+ acronym stands for? Do they know what 'cis' means? Have they even heard that word before?

I'm at the supermarket buying ingredients for a stir-fry and a young lady says to me, *I really like your hair.* We start talking about wigs. *I don't want to be rude,* she says, *but what name do you go by now?* She acknowledges my past, but respectfully. It's a pleasant interaction. Then I go to pay for my things and the checkout chick says, *Thank you, sir.* I want to correct her, but how do I do that? Will I ever be able to do that?

Maybe I won't have to. The world is changing in wonderful ways. When I was young, if somebody said the wrong thing in your company, you let it slide. You didn't pull anyone up – you just tolerated whatever offence had been caused. It was a culture of silence. But kids today don't do that.

In grade six you don't just have school captains and athletic captains anymore, but social justice leaders, too. Caring has become a core value. This generation is being raised to defend the defenceless, and they won't tolerate those who bully or exclude. They march for climate change awareness. They wear pink pussy hats to political protests. They demand your attention and your kindness.

I won't demand anything, but I'll ask that people stop and listen, and give me an ear for a moment. Cis people have no idea how easy it is for trans women to tell the difference between someone who sees them as a woman, and someone who sees them as a man they have to remember to refer to as a woman.

I always know when a cis person is juggling that inner confusion but making a conscious effort to say the right thing. I hate that it's a struggle for them to see me as a woman but I appreciate that they're trying.

All I ask is that they don't look away – that they remain open to the possibility that one day they might see me as I see myself, as I am, as I was, and always will be.

I am Danielle May Laidley.

postscript

In May 2020, Danielle Laidley was arrested and charged with one count of stalking. In November 2020 she was placed on an adjourned undertaking of good behaviour for 18 months with no conviction recorded. She was in possession of 0.43 grams of methamphetamine at the time of her arrest and was placed on good behaviour diversion for three months for the drug charge.

In December 2020, three police officers were charged with unauthorised access of police information, unauthorised disclosure of police information without reasonable excuse and misconduct in public office. One charge of taking photos of Laidley's mugshots and distributing them was dropped by prosecutors.

By April 2022, the charges against all police officers had been dismissed on legal technicalities and the civil case against Victoria Police was settled.

The disciplinary board ordered eleven other police officers to pay Laidley between $500 and $3000 over the leaking of the custodial photographs.

At the time of writing, a lifetime diagnosis of depression is reported in 85 per cent of trans people, and 43 per cent of trans people have attempted suicide. In young trans people – 14 to 25 years old – the number who have self-harmed is 80 per cent, compared to around 11 per cent of adolescents in the general population.

acknowledgements

There are many people to thank for helping me to become the person I am today.

Mum and Leif and Paul: It's been quite a journey. Thank you for accepting me as your daughter and sister. Finally we are together as a family.

David Laidley: Dad, you're no longer here, but through discovering myself, I've learnt more about the man you were. Today I'm proud of you. I understand more about your struggles.

Sean King: You are my best friend, my best man and always part of Team Laidley. Thank you, and Anita and the kids, for being there for me.

The Kassis family: Peter, Christina, Tristan, Yvette, Josh and Monique, I thank you for being there in my darkest times, and now when the sun is starting to shine brightly.

Shani and Sean Martin: I feel blessed to call you family and my great friends. You'll never understand how much you mean to me.

David 'Bernie' and Nicole Quinlan: I have finally let you in. Thank you for your unreserved support without judgement; you just want the world to see me!

Anthony Stevens: You are my hero, the most special human being. I continue to learn from you every day. I am forever grateful but I will never be your date!

Wayne Schwass, David King, Ian Fairley and Darren Crocker: I am so very grateful for your unconditional support over the last two years, for your care and empathy and welfare checks.

Mark 'Sticks' Brayshaw: You are the voice of reason, my connector back to life. Eternal thanks to you and Debra.

Greg Ryan and Cade Brown: You two are the people I shared everything with over the last 20 years. Thank you for your loyalty, counsel and forever friendship

Tony Box and the TLA Worldwide family: Thank you for your guidance, care and empathy.

Jackson Oppy: I am humbled to call you my friend and am forever indebted to you and the Hader Clinic for saving my life.

My care team: Dr Con Mitropoulos, a true angel, Dr Rubina Rawal, Dr Ada Cheung, Dr Louise Du Chesne and others (you know who you are – what a team!).

Julian King and Rebecca White: I have had many great coaches and managers but you two stand head and shoulders above the rest. At the Department of Justice, you were my counsel, you both taught me so much, and your care, warmth and empathy are etched in my memory forever.

My legal team: Thank you for your tireless work, standing by my side over the last two years. Jeremy King and the team from Robinson Gill; Andrew Harris from Harris Carlson; Joseph Kelly from Kelly Workplace Lawyers; Jim McGarvie from Stary Norton Halphen and Robert Stary.

Eddie McGuire: Thank you for listening and for including me in the JAMTV family. Side by side, we keep walking.

Luke Tunnecliffe: What a journey we've been on, young man. I am so proud of you – your care for your family and friends is something to behold.

My football tribes: West Perth FC, West Coast Eagles FC and the North Melbourne FC. I am forever grateful for the opportunity to represent the colours of each club. There are too many people to mention and there's a risk I'd leave someone out. From the brothers I played alongside and the coaches I learnt from, to the sons I coached – thank you all for the parts you played in my story, and particularly those who reached out in my time of great pain, without judgement and without fear or favour.

The AFL, AFLPA and the whole AFL family: I thought football would eventually kill me because of the shame, embarrassment and fear I lived with for so long. Instead, I have been truly overwhelmed by the acceptance. Special mention to AFL CEO Gillon McLachlan, your support, empathy and inclusion in welcoming me back to the family has been truly remarkable. I am forever grateful.

Michael Malthouse: More than a coach, more than a boss. Your life lessons have taught me so much, thank you.

Jada: you are a wonderful young woman, one of a kind. You saw me at my worst, and I thank you for being there.

The transgender community: My new tribe, thank you for accepting me so graciously. Please remember I am here for us all, to educate, illustrate and represent our community in the wider society. A special mention to Alexia, Phil and Dee Scavo, Jay, Merrin and Gavin Wake for your unwavering love and support.

Craig Silvey: You are a remarkable author, and your generous guidance in the telling of my story has been brilliant. Most importantly, I am truly appreciative of your support and friendship, it means the world to me.

HarperCollins: Thank you for giving me the platform to tell my story. Our mantra was 'the best ideas must win' and indeed they have. Special thanks to Helen Littleton. What a team effort.

Andrea McNamara: Thank you for your wisdom and leading the experience of delivering a book I'm very proud of.

Konrad Marshall: You are an absolute magician. We spent untold hours together, we laughed, we cried, but we got there. Thank you Konrad, Nikki and Charlie for welcoming me and Donna into your family.

Joanne: We were just kids ourselves. We raised the three most amazing treasures and the five of us all grew up together – crazy, zany, loving and strong (someone even called us 'The Osbournes'!). Thank you for being the mother of my children and for the love you continue to show them.

Brooke: My treasured firstborn, I loved seeing you grow into a strong woman – a mother, wife and educator of young people. I couldn't ask for a better young man than Justin to walk the path of life with my daughter. Thank you both for bringing our now big 'little man' into this world. I miss you all.

Kane: My son, we have walked this path together before, and I thank you for your unconditional support; you've been the driver in getting me to where I am today. I am grateful for every minute I spend with you and Alicia. You are my greatest friends.

Molly Rose: My youngest daughter, larger than life, we always know when you're around. We laughed, 'Chonny', we cried, you were the yin to my yang for all those years we lived together. We were joined at the hip, and I am so unbelievably proud of the woman you are today.

The Leckies: Thank you for welcoming me into your family with open arms.

And finally, my girl, Donna Leckie. Grade 1, 1973 is an eternity ago, and there have been so many sliding doors throughout our lives before we finally walked through the same door at the same time. I am still here because of you, my shining light that glows so brightly. I want to walk the rest of this journey together, side by side, arm in arm. You love me for me, and I truly love you for you. We are the DLs.